Discovering H.P. Lovecraft,

Revised & Expanded

Edited by Darrell Schweitzer

To Alex

NPL is _____
sign this, so I'll have
to do. —

Darrell
Schweitzer

Philcon 2011

Novels

The White Isle
The Shattered Goddess
The Mask of the Sorcerer

Collections and Story-Cycles

We Are All Legends
Tom O'Bedlam's Night Out
Transients
Refugees from an Imaginary Country
Necromancies and Netherworlds (with Jason Van Hollander)
The Great World and the Small
Echoes of the Goddess (forthcoming)
Sekenre: the Book of the Sorcerer (forthcoming)
The Emperor of the Ancient Word (forthcoming)

Poetry and Light Verse

Groping Toward the Light
Non Compost Mentis
Poetica Dementia
Stop Me Before I Do It Again!
They Never Found the Head: Poems of Sentiment and Reflection

Non-Fiction

The Dream Quest of H.P. Lovecraft
Pathways to Elfland: The Writings of Lord Dunsany
Lord Dunsany: A Bibliography (with S.T. Joshi)
SF Voices (interviews)
SF Voices 1 (interviews)
SF Voices 5 (interviews)
Speaking of Horror (interviews)
Speaking of Science Fiction (interviews, forthcoming)
Windows of the Imagination
On Writing Science Fiction: The Editors Strike Back (with George
Scithers and John M. Ford)

As Editor

Discovering H.P. Lovecraft
Exploring Fantasy Worlds
The Ghosts of the Heaviside Layer by Lord Dunsany
Discovering Modern Horror Fiction (2 vols.)
Discovering Stephen King
Discovering Classic Horror Fiction
Discovering Classic Fantasy Fiction
Tales from the Spaceport Bar (with George Scithers)
Another Round at the Spaceport Bar (with George Scithers)

Discovering H.P. Lovecraft,
Revised & Expanded

Edited by Darrell Schweitzer

Wildside Press
Holicong, Pennsylvania

CONTENTS:

DEDICATION

For Robert Reginald,

with thanks and gratitude.

INTRODUCTION: LOVECRAFT FOREVER

by Darrell Schweitzer

They've tried to dismiss him in the past: Edmund Wilson, sneering in the pages of *The New Yorker* in the '40s ("Tales of the Marvelous and Ridiculous"), John Brunner in *Inside and Science Fiction Advertiser* in the '50s ("Rusty Chains"), Damon Knight in the otherwise classic *In Search of Wonder* (embarrassingly confusing August Derleth's pastiches of Lovecraft with the real thing), and many more. When any giant appears in literature, there will always be those who say no, that's not a giant after all. The test, of course, is time. Lovecraft's international reputation continues to grow. Books about him continue to appear. Generation after generation, he excites and intrigues new readers. He will not be dismissed.

After fifty years, Edmund Wilson seems mean-spirited and myopic. The terrible irony may one day be — and one sincerely hopes not, considering the merit of their other work — that one day John Brunner and Damon Knight, along with other Lovecraft detractors, will be remembered solely for what they said about Lovecraft, even as Lovecraft will surely keep August Derleth's name alive.

The verdict is now in: Lovecraft is the most important writer of supernatural horror fiction in English since Poe. While he hasn't (yet) generated as much secondary material as Poe, he probably is more widely read today, and more influential on new writers than Poe. His position in horror (or what he called "weird fiction") is rather like that of Robert Heinlein in science fiction: it is difficult to work in the field without responding to Lovecraft, even if only to reject him. If living literature may be seen as a kind of on-going debate or dialogue between many authors, Lovecraft has, in his own specialized area, made the opening statement. The rest is response. Even Joyce Carol Oates's acceptance speech for the Lifetime Achievement Award from the Horror Writers Association, defining her whole aesthetic in what she calls "the grotesque," was a direct and explicit answer to Lovecraft.

It is Lovecraft's vision that sustains him. He was indeed a visionary writer, on par with H.G. Wells or Olaf Stapledon, whose art encompassed the entire universe and meditated on mankind's (very small) place in the overall scheme of things. His radical innovation is — one might think anomalously for a virtually life-long "conservative" — one of *modernism*. Lovecraft rejected the old spiritual world which had driven the human imagination since the beginning of the species, and turned, instead, to the material universe revealed by science. Remember that in Lovecraft's time the universe was suddenly getting bigger in (literally) quantum leaps: Relativity was new; astronomers had determined that "spiral nebulae" were in fact galaxies beyond our own, unimaginably far away and receding; the planet Pluto was just discovered. A generation earlier, Darwinism had conclusively shaken people's formerly secure ideas of who they were and where they had come from. (And in Lovecraft's time, as today, there was still resistance to the uncomfortable truth. Lovecraft was doing much of his best work about the same time as the Scopes "Monkey Trial.")

Lovecraft, sensing vast changes in mankind's very conception of existence, was able to look ahead, imaginatively and emotionally, and consider the implications. This is why Lovecraft's stories seem vital when the masters of the traditional ghost story, no matter how technically skilled, come across as cozy and quaint. E.F. Benson and M.R. James are still entertaining, but Lovecraft is a serious writer, in the best sense of the term. He is not going away.

One bit of evidence that he isn't going away is that there is demand for a new edition of this book, which is over twenty years old. *Discovering H.P. Lovecraft* began life in 1976 as *Essays Lovecraftian*, published by T.K. Graphics, an amateur imprint just then in the process of going out of business. The 1976 edition was rushed, with virtually no proofreading, and many resultant horrors, not necessarily of the eldritch kind. The 1987 Starmont edition, the first under the present title, featured numerous corrections and updatings, and some changes in the actual contents, the most significant of which was the addition of S.T. Joshi's "Textual Problems in Lovecraft."

The material has aged well. Now, the Borgo Press edition has something of a retrospective quality about it. Here are significant articles about Lovecraft, spanning several decades. Fritz Leiber's "A Literary Copernicus" is one of the very first explorations of Lovecraft's "cosmic" outlook, and still one of the best. Yōzan Dirk Mosig's "Four Faces of the Outsider" was a landmark in the psychological criticism of Lovecraft, indicating a whole new direction that Lovecraft studies were beginning to take in the early 1970s, largely led by Mosig. At the same time, Richard Tierney's "The Derleth Mythos" threw off the shackles of Derlethism — a revolution in itself, probably not possible until Derleth's death in 1971. George Wetzel was one of the first important Lovecraft scholars, very active in the 1950s. His "Genesis of the Cthulhu Mythos" was, I suspect, reworked from earlier material.

And, of course, "Textual Problems in Lovecraft" marked a new turning point, the first time anyone had serious examined the transmission of Lovecraft's writing itself. The result of such inquiries was, ultimately, the new, corrected editions of Lovecraft's work, prepared by Joshi and published by Arkham House. But since most anthologizations and translations of the stories and, so far, *all* paperback editions are based on the old, defective texts, this article is more than a milestone long passed. It's a still valid warning: you may not be reading the real Lovecraft.

New to this edition is a major piece, "H.P.Lovecraft: the Books," by the late Lin Carter, reprinted from the Derleth-edited compilation, *The Shuttered Room* (1959), updated and annotated by the leading Lovecraftian scholars of the present day, S.T. Joshi, author of *H.P. Lovecraft: A Life,* and Robert M. Price, the editor of *Crypt of Cthulhu* magazine. With the help of Joshi and Price, Carter's listing of all the books and pseudo-books mentioned in Lovecraft and in the subsequent Cthulhu Mythos remains the best guide available anywhere.

The bibliographies and notes to this edition have, of course, been updated. A sequel is planned. Watch for *Discovering H.P. Lovecraft II,* probably under another title. The new volume will not be historical, but will concentrate on recent (even brand new) explorations of this endlessly fascinating writer.

— Darrell Schweitzer
Philadelphia, Pennsylvania

NOTES ON AN ENTITY

by Robert Bloch

It is difficult for me to comprehend that fifty years have passed since the death of Howard Phillips Lovecraft — and equally difficult for me to realize that I am now the youngest surviving member of what was once called "The Lovecraft Circle," comprised of friends and correspondents of HPL.

I was for four years of my life one of these correspondents and, I trust, counted by him as a friend, although I never had the pleasure of meeting the man face to face. That expectation was reserved for the summer of 1937, at which time August Derleth hoped to have Lovecraft as his house-guest in Sauk City, Wisconsin. Since HPL's longtime fellow-member of the amateur press organization, Maurice W. Moe, resided in Milwaukee, as did I, we both looked forward to a visit. But it was not to be: in March of that year, Lovecraft was dead.

As a fifteen-year-old fan, I'd entered into a continuing correspondence with the man I esteemed as the finest living writer of weird fiction. Within two years his encouragement and kindly critical advice had guided me to my own first sale, and at nineteen — the time of his death — I was solidly embarked on a permanent career as a writer.

My experience was not unique. Over the years many young fans and aspiring authors entered "The Lovecraft Circle" as appreciative readers, stayed on as charmed correspondents, and emerged as full-fledged fantasy fictioneers in their own right. And others, already appearing in print, found equal fascination in their contact with this remarkable intellect — and enriched their output thereby.

Like myself, they were profoundly influenced by the Lovecraft style, the Lovecraft concepts. The bulk of his output appeared in *Weird Tales* magazine, and during the dozen or so years during which his stories were printed there was no question as to who was the most popular writer for that period. His name was Seabury Quinn, and his stories about the "mercurial little detective, Jules de Grandin" almost invariably captured the cover-illustrations. But no one imitated, or was influenced by, the Seabury Quinn stories — and Lovecraft had a score of active acolytes in the fantasy field. Since his passing, the Lovecraft influence has spread; even today, in the works of younger writers the touch of HPLoquence is plainly discernible.

Let me put it less ponderously and more positively: no modern-day writer of fantasy and horror fiction has had more lasting influence on the field than H.P. Lovecraft.

Readers — and imitators — of Lovecraft's friend and contemporary, Robert E. Howard, may dispute this; unfortunately, while Howard's "sword-and-sorcery" sagas of Conan the Barbarian have been widely reprinted and widely copied, the fact remains that neither Howard's style nor his subject-matter were uniquely his own creation. What he borrowed from others, his followers have since borrowed from him.

But Lovecraft, with his Cthulhu Mythos, was an innovator.

Earlier writers, Robert W. Chambers among them, had written stories in which they hinted or referred to a malign pantheon secretly scourging Earth. But the sketchy and oblique references meant nothing, except to the extent that they prompted Lovecraft to invent and implement a full-fleshed mythology an cosmology of his own. He created a hideous, hidden history of mankind's past — and of the earth and universe prior to the emergence of man from primordial slime. And in so doing, he enriched the imagination of all fantasy writers — his contemporaries and those who came after.

Most of these contemporaries, like myself, have since broken away from Lovecraft style and largely abandoned the subject-matter inherent in the Mythos. I haven't written a "Lovecraftian" story, *per se,* in many years — though I suppose I could do so if I set myself to the task, as I once did whilst completing an unfinished tale by Edgar Allan Poe. (That "whilst," by the way, *is* pure Lovecraft.) However, I most generally prefer to do my own thing; a course of action which HPL strongly advocated to all his writing acquaintances.

HPL's work was not confined to the Cthulhu Mythos stories alone. He wrote science fiction, Dunsanian mood-pieces, and straight horror-stories. Each category had its own followers, amongst readers and writers alike; my own personal preference was for the out-and-out horror takes, or those in which the Mythos served merely as a background or explanatory device. "Pickman's Model," "The Shadow Over Innsmouth," and "The Whisperer in Darkness" are possibly my all-time favorites, although I am fond of the totally-different "The Silver Key" because it seems to mirror the Lovecraft I knew from his letters.

And to those of us fortunate in such knowledge, or the greater gift of personal acquaintance, Lovecraft the writer was always secondary in our esteem. It was Lovecraft the man whom we most appreciated and admired. I know I did. And today, half a century later, I still do.

The man who befriended a fifteen-year-old fan, who gave him a lifelong career, who set an example of fellowship and good-will, is the Lovecraft I choose to remember.

by Robert Bloch   5

Some years before his passing, HPL penned a brief autobiographical sketch which, with characteristic modesty and good humor, he entitled, "Some Notes on a Nonentity."

To me, Howard Phillips Lovecraft was an entity. A most important one. And I rejoice to see that his work — and his memory among readers and writers — endures.

[Robert Bloch died in 1994.]

A LITERARY COPERNICUS

by Fritz Leiber, Jr.

Howard Phillips Lovecraft was the Copernicus of the horror story. He shifted the focus of supernatural dread from man and his little world and his gods, to the stars and the black and unplumbed gulfs of intergalactic space. To do this effectively, he created a new kind of horror story and new methods for telling it.

During the Middle Ages and long afterwards, the object of man's supernatural fear was the Devil, together with the legions of the damned and the hosts of the dead, earthbound and anthropomorphic creatures all. Writers as diverse as Dante and Charles Maturin, author of *Melmoth the Wanderer,* were able to rouse terror in their readers by exploiting this fear.

With the rise of scientific materialism and the decline of at least naive belief in Christian theology, the Devil's dreadfulness quickly paled. Man's supernatural fear was left without a definite object. Writers seeking to awaken supernatural fear restlessly turned to other objects, some old, some new.

Horror of the dead proved to be a somewhat hardier feeling than dread of the Devil and the damned. This provided the necessary ground for the genre of the ghost story, ably exploited by Montague Rhodes James and others.

Arthur Machen briefly directed man's Supernatural dread toward Pan, the satyrs, and other strange races and divinities who symbolized for him the Darwinian-Freudian "beast" in man.

Earlier, Edgar Allan Poe had focused supernatural dread on the monstrous in man and nature. Abnormal mental and physiological states fascinated him, as did the awesome might of the elements, natural catastrophes, and the geographic unknown.

Algernon Blackwood sought an object for horror especially in the new cults of occultism and spiritualism, with their assertion of the preternatural power of thoughts and feelings.

Meanwhile, however, a new source of literary material had come into being: the terrifying vast and mysterious universe revealed by the swiftly developing sciences, in particular astronomy. A universe consisting of light-years and light-millennia of black emptiness. A universe containing billions of suns, many of them presumably attended by planets housing forms of life shockingly alien to man and, likely enough in some instances, infinitely more powerful. A universe shot through with invisible forces, hitherto unsuspected by man, such as the ultraviolet X-ray, the X-ray — and who can say how many more? In short, a universe in which the unknown had vastly greater scope than in the little crystal-sphered glove of Aristotle and Ptolemy. And yet a real universe, attested by scientifically weighed facts, no mere nightmare of mystics.

Writers such as H.G. Wells and Jules Verne found a potent source of literary inspiration in the simple presentation of man against the background of this new universe. From their efforts arose the genre of science fiction.

Howard Phillips Lovecraft was not the first author to see in this new universe a highly suitable object for man's supernatural fear. W.H. Hodgson, Poe, Fitz-James O'Brien, and Wells too had glimpses of that possibility and made use of it in a few of their tales. But the main and systematic achievement was Lovecraft's. When he completed the body of his writings, he had firmly attached the emotion of spectral dread to such concepts as outer space, the rim of the cosmos, alien beings, unsuspected dimensions, and the conceivable universes lying outside our own space-time continuum.

Lovecraft's achievement did not come overnight. The new concept of the horror story did not spring full-grown from his mind. In his earlier tales he experimented with the Dunsanian strain and also wrote a number of effective stories in the vein of Poe, such as "The Statement of Randolph Carter," "The Outsider," "Cool Air," and "The Hound." He shared Machen's horror of the human beast and expressed it in "The Lurking Fear," "The Rats in the Walls," "The Horror at Red Hook," and "Arthur Jermyn." Though even in these briefer tales we find broad hints of the new concept: vast life-forms from Earth's past in "Dagon" and a linkage of a human being's insanity with the appearance of a new star in "Beyond the Wall of Sleep." But with "The Call of Cthulhu" the line of development becomes clearly marked, as shown by the opening sentences: "The most merciful thing in the world, I think, is the inability of the human mind to correlate all its contents. We live on a placid island of ignorance in the midst of black seas of infinity, and it was not meant that we should voyage far. The sciences, each straining in its own direction, have hitherto harmed us little; but some day the piecing together of dissociated knowledge will open up such terrifying vistas of reality, and of our frightful position therein, that we shall either go mad from the revelation or flee from the deadly light into the peace and safety of a new dark age."

For a while Lovecraft tended to mix black magic and other traditional sources of dread with the horrors stemming purely from science's new universe. In "The Dunwich Horror" the other-dimensional creatures are thwarted by the proper incantations, while witchcraft and the new Einsteinian universe appear cheek-by-jowl in "Dreams in the Witch House." But when we arrive at "The Whisperer in Darkness," *At the Mountains of Madness,* and "The Shadow Out of Time," we find that the extra-terrestrial entities are quite enough in themselves to awaken all our supernatural dread, without any medieval trappings whatsoever. White magic and the sign of the cross are powerless against them and only the accidents of space and time — in short, sheer chance — save humanity.

In passing, it is to be noted that Lovecraft, like Poe, was fascinated by great natural catastrophes and new scientific discoveries and explorations, as is understandable in one who chose cosmic horror for his theme. It is likely that reports of such events engendered many of his stories. "The Whisperer in Darkness" begins with the Vermont floods of 1927 and one notes other possible linkages: reports of oceanic earthquakes and upheavals and "Dagon" and "The Call of Cthulhu"; the inundation of acres of woodland by a man-made reservoir and "The Colour Out of Space"; threat of demolition of some old warehouses on South Water Street, Providence, and the poem "Brick Row" which is dated December 7, 1929, and may have been the germ of Lovecraft's great sonnet cycle "Fungi From Yuggoth," written between December 27, 1929, and January 4, 1930; regional decay and degeneration and "The Lurking Fear" and "The Shadow Over Innsmouth"; ravages of German submarine warfare and "The Temple"; polar exploration and *At the Mountains of Madness*; discovery of the planet Pluto by C.W. Tombaugh in 1930 and "The Whisperer in Darkness," featuring that discovery and written in the same year.

It is a great pity that Lovecraft did not live to experience the unparalleled New England hurricane of 1938, when the downtown heart of his own Providence was invaded by the sea, to the accompaniment of terrific wind and downpour. What a story that would eventually have gotten out of him!

The universe of modern science engendered a profounder horror in Lovecraft's writings than that stemming solely from its tremendous distances and its highly probably alien and powerful non-human inhabitants. For the chief reason that man fears the universe revealed by materialistic science is that it is a purposeless, soulless place. To quote Lovecraft's "The Silver Key," man can hardly bear the realization that "the blind cosmos grinds aimlessly on from nothing to something and from something back to nothing again, neither heeding nor knowing the wishes or existence of the minds that flicker for a second now and then in the darkness."

In his personal life Lovecraft met the challenge of this hideous realization by taking refuge in traditionalism, in the cultivation of mankind's time-honored manners and myths, not because they are true, but because man's mind is habituated to them and therefore finds in them some comfort and support. Recognizing that the only meaning in the cosmos is that which man dreams into it, Lovecraft treasured beautiful human dreams, all age-worn things, and the untainted memories of childhood. This is set forth clearly in "The Silver Key," the story in which Lovecraft presents his personal philosophy of life.

In the main current of Lovecraft's supernatural tales, horror of the mechanistic universe gave shape to that impressive hierarchy of alien creatures and gods generally referred to as "the Cthulhu mythos," an assemblage of beings whose weird attributes reflect the universe's multitudinous environments and whose fantastic names are suggestive renderings of non-human words and sounds. They include the Elder Gods or Gods of Earth, the Other Gods or Ultimate Gods, and a variety of entities from distant times, planets, and dimensions.

Although they stem from that period in which Lovecraft mixed black magic in his takes and was attracted to Dunsanian pantheons, I believe it is a mistake to regard the beings of the Cthulhu Mythos as sophisticated equivalents of the entities, of Christian demonology, or to attempt to divide them into balancing Zoroastrian hierarchies of good and evil.

Most of the entities in the Cthulhu mythos are malevolent or, at best, cruelly indifferent to mankind. The perhaps benevolent Gods of Earth are never mentioned directly, except for Nodens, and gradually fade from the tales. In *The Dream-Quest of Unknown Kadath* they are pictured as relatively weak and feeble, symbols of the ultimate weakness of even mankind's traditions and dreams. It is likely that Lovecraft employed them only to explain why the more numerous malevolent entities had not long ago overrun mankind, and to provide a source of incantations whereby Earthlings could to some degree defend themselves, as in "The Dunwich Horror" and *The Case of Charles Dexter Ward.* In the later tales, as we have mentioned, Lovecraft permitted mankind no defense, except luck, against the unknown.

In contrast to the Elder Gods, the Other Gods are presented as powerful and terrible, yet also — strange paradox! — "... blind, voiceless, tenebrous, mindless ..." (*The Dream-Quest*).

Of the Other Gods, Azathoth is the supreme deity, occupying the top-most throne in the Cthulhu hierarchy, There is never any question of his being merely an alien entity from some distant planet or dimension, like Cthulhu or Yog-Sothoth. He is unquestionably "god," and also the greatest god. Yet when we ask what sort of god, we discover that he is the blind, idiot god, "... the mindless daemon-sultan ... ," "... the monstrous nuclear chaos. ..."

Such a pantheon and such a chief deity can symbolize only one thing: the purposeless, mindless, yet all-powerful universe of materialistic belief.

And Nyarlathotep, the crawling chaos, is his messenger — not mindless like his master, but evilly intelligent, pictured in *The Dream-Quest* in the form of a suave pharaoh. The Nyarlathotep legend is one of Lovecraft's most interesting creations. It appears both in the prose poem and in the sonnet of that name. In a time of widespread social upheaval and nervous tension, one looking like a pharaoh appears out of Egypt. He is worshipped by the fellahin, "wild beasts followed him and licked his hands." He visits many lands and gives lectures with queer pseudo-scientific demonstrations, obtaining a great following — rather like Cagliostro or some similar charlatan. A progressive disintegration of man's mind and world follows. There are purposeless panics and wanderings. Nature breaks loose. There are earthquakes, weedy cities are revealed by receding seas, an ultimate putrescence and disintegration sets in. Earth ends.

Just what does Nyarlathotep "mean"?

That is, what meanings can most suitably be read into him, granting that, by him, Lovecraft may not consciously have "meant" anything. One possibility is that the pharaoh-charlatan expresses the mockery of a universe man can never understand or master. Another is that he symbolizes the blatantly commercial, self-advertising, acquisitive world that Lovecraft loathed (Nyarlathotep always has that aura of the salesman, that brash contemptuousness). Yet a third possibility is that Nyarlathotep stands for man's self-destructive intellectuality, his awful ability to see the universe for what it is and thereby kill in himself all naive and beautiful dreams.

In this connection it is to be noted that Lovecraft, to his last month a tireless scholar and questioner, was the embodiment of the one noble feeling scientific materialism grants man: intellectual curiosity. He also expressed this passion in his supernatural tales. His protagonists are often drawn to the unknown as much as they dread it. Quaking at the horrors that may lurk there, they yet cannot resist the urge to peer beyond the rim of space. "The Whisperer in Darkness," perhaps his greatest story, is remarkable for the way in which the horror and fascination of the alien are equally maintained until almost the very end.

Lovecraft's matured method of telling a horror story was a natural consequence of the importance of the new universe of science in his writings, for it was the method of scientific realism, approaching in some of his last tales (*At the Mountains of Madness* and "The Shadow Out of Time") the precision, objectivity, and attention to detail of a report in a scientific journal. Most of his stories are purported documents and necessarily written in the first person. This device is common in weird literature, as witness Poe's "Ms. Found in a Bottle," Haggard's *She,* Stoker's *Dracula,* and many others, but few writers have taken it quite as seriously as did Lovecraft.

He set great store by the narrator having some vitally pressing motive for recounting his experiences, and was ingenious at devising such motives: justificatory confession in "The Thing on the Doorstep" and "The Statement of Randolph Carter"; warning, in "The Whisperer in Darkness" and *At the Mountains of Madness*; attempt by the narrator to clarify his own ideas and come to a decision, in "The Shadow Over Innsmouth";

scholarly summing up a weird series of events, in *The Case of Charles Dexter Ward* and "The Haunter of the Dark."

The scientifically realistic element in Lovecraft's style was a thing of slow growth in a writer early inclined to a sonorous and poetic prose with an almost Byzantine use of adjectives. The transition was never wholly completed, and like all advances, it was attended by losses and limitations. Disappointingly to some readers, who may also experience impatience at the growing length of the stories (inevitable in scientific reports), there is notably less witchery of words in, say, "The Shadow Out of Time" than in "The Dunwich Horror," though the former story has greater unity and technical perfection.

And Lovecraft's own restricted and scholarly life hardly fitted him to be an all-over realist. He always observed a gentlemanly reserve in his writings and depicted best those types of characters which he understood and respected, such as scholars, New England farmers and townsmen, and sincere and lonely artists; while showing less sympathy (consider "He") and penetration in the presentation of business men, intellectuals, factory workers, "toughs," and other admittedly brash, uninhibited, and often crude denizens of our modern cities.

There were three important elements in Lovecraft's style which he was able to use effectively in both his earlier poetic period and later, more objective style.

The first is the device of *confirmation* rather than revelation. (I am indebted to Henry Kuttner for this neat phrase.) In other words, the story-ending does not come as a surprise but as a final, long-anticipated "convincer." The reader knows, and is supposed to know, what is coming, but this only prepares and adds to his shivers when the narrator supplies the last and incontrovertible piece of evidence. In *The Case of Charles Dexter Ward* the reader knows from almost the first page that Ward has been supplanted by Joseph Curwen, yet the narrator does not state this unequivocally until the last sentence of the book. This does not mean that Lovecraft never wrote the revelatory type of story, with its surprise ending. On the contrary, he used it in "The Lurking Fear" and handled it most effectively in "The Outsider." But he did come more and more to favor the less startling but sometimes more impressive confirmatory type.

So closely related to his use of confirmation as to be only another aspect of it, is Lovecraft's employment of the terminal climax — that is, the story in which the high point and the final sentence coincide. Who can forget the supreme chill of: "But by God, Eliot, *it was a photograph from life*," or *"It was his twin brother, but it looked more like the father than he did,"* or "They were, instead, the letters of our familiar alphabet, spelling out the words of the English language in my own handwriting," or ". . . the face and hands of Henry Wentworth Akeley?" Use of the terminal climax made it necessary for Lovecraft to develop a special type of story-telling, in which the explanatory and return-to-equilibrium material is all deftly inserted before the finish and while the tension is still mounting. It also necessitated a very careful structure, with everything building from the first word to the last.

Lovecraft reinforced this structure with what may be called *orchestrated prose* — sentences that are repeated with a constant addition of more potent adjectives, adverbs, and phrases, just as in a symphony a melody introduced by a single woodwind is at last thundered by the whole orchestra. "The Statement of Randolph Carter" provides one of the simplest examples. In it, in order, the following phrases occur concerning the moon: ". . . waning crescent moon . . . wan, waning crescent moon . . . pallid, peering crescent moon . . . accursed waning moon . . ." Subtler and more complex examples can be found in the longer stories.

Not only sentences, but whole sections, are sometimes repeated, with a growing cloud of atmosphere and detail. The story may first be briefly sketched, then told in part with some reservations, then related more fully as the narrator finally conquers his disinclination or repugnance toward stating the exact details of the horror he experienced.

All these stylistic elements naturally worked to make Lovecraft's stories longer and longer, with a growing complexity in the sources of horror. In "Dreams in the Witch House" the sources of horror are multiple: ". . . Fever — wild dreams — somnambulism — illusions of sounds — a pull toward a point in the sky — and now a suspicion of insane sleepwalking . . ." while in *At the Mountains of Madness* there is a transition whereby the feared entities become the fearing; the author shows us horrors and then pulls back the curtain a little farther, letting us glimpse the horrors of which even the horrors are afraid!

An urge to increase the length and complexity of tales is not uncommon among the writers of horror stories. It can be compared to the drug addict's craving for larger and larger doses — and this comparison is not fanciful, since the chief purpose of the supernatural tale is to arouse the single feeling of spectral terror in the reader rather than to delineate character or comment on life. Devotees of this genre of literature are at times able to take doses which might exhaust or sicken the average person. Each reader must decide for himself just how long a story he can stand without his sense of terror flagging. For me, all of Lovecraft, including the lengthy *At the Mountains of Madness,* can be read with ever-mounting excitement.

For it must be kept in mind that no matter how greatly Lovecraft increased the length, scope, complexity, and power of his tales, he never once lost control or gave way to the impulse to write wildly and pile one blood-curdling incident on another without the proper preparation and attention to mood. Rather, he tended to write with greater restraint, to perfect the internal coherence and logic of his stories, and often to provide alternate everyday explanations for the supernatural terrors he invoked, letting the reader infer the horror rather than see it face to face, so that most of his stories fulfill the conditions set down by the narrator of "The

Whisperer in Darkness": "Bear in mind closely that I did not see any actual visual horror at the end . . . I cannot prove even now whether I was right or wrong in my hideous inference," or by the narrator of "The Shadow Out of Time": "There is reason to hope that my experience was wholly or partly an hallucination — for which, indeed, abundant causes existed."

Strangely paralleling the development of Lovecraft's scientific realism was an apparently conflicting trend: the development of an imaginary background for his stories, including New England cities such as Arkham and Innsmouth, institutions such as Miskatonic University in Arkham, semi-secret and monstrous cults, and a growing library of "forbidden" books, such as the *Necronomicon,* containing monstrous secrets about the present, future, and past of earth and the universe.

Any writer, even a thoroughgoing realist, may invent the names of persons and places, either to avoid libel or because his creations are hybrid ones, combining the qualities of many persons or places. Some of Lovecraft's inventions are of a most serious sort altogether, definitely distorting the "real" world that forms the background for many of his later supernatural tales. Not only are the *Necronomicon,* the *Unaussprechlichen Kulten* of von Junzt and other volumes presumed to have a real existence (in a few copies and under lock and key, rather closely guarded secrets), but the astounding and somewhat theosophical tale they have to tell of non-human civilizations in earth's past and of the frightful denizens of other planets and dimensions, is taken seriously by the scholars and scientists who people Lovecraft's stories. These individuals are in all other ways very realistically-minded indeed, but having glimpsed the forbidden knowledge, they are generally more susceptible to cosmic terror than ordinary people. Sober and staid realists, they yet know that they live on the brink of a horrid and ravening abyss unsuspected by ordinary folk. This knowledge does not come to them solely as the result of the weird experiences in which the stories involve them, but is part of their intellectual background.

These "awakened" scholars are chiefly on the faculty of imaginary Miskatonic University. Indeed, the fabulous history of that institution, insofar as it can be traced from Lovecraft's stories, throws an interesting light on the development of this trend in his writing.

In June 1882 a peculiar meteor fell near Arkham. Three professors from Miskatonic came to investigate and found it composed of an evanescent substance defying analysis. Despite this experience, they were highly skeptical when later on they heard of eerie changes occurring on the farm where the meteor fell and, contemptuous of what they considered folk superstitions, they stayed away during the year-long period in which a hideous decay gradually wiped out the farm and its inhabitants. In other words, they behaved as professors are conventionally supposed to behave, intolerant of ghostly events and occult theories — and certainly showing no signs of having read the *Necronomicon,* if there was a copy at Miskatonic at that date, with any sympathy. It is significant that the story in which these events occur, "The Color Out of Space," is praised by Edmund Wilson, a generally adverse critic.

But in the course of the next twenty-five years, perhaps as an insidious result of the strange meteor fall, a change took place in Miskatonic University and in the intellectual equipment of at least some of its faculty members. For when the child prodigy Edward Pickman Derby entered Miskatonic he was able to gain access for a time to the copy of the *Necronomicon* in the library; and Nathaniel Wingate Peaslee, the political economist, during his five-year amnesia which began May 14, 1908, made indecipherable marginal notes in the same volume. Still later, a stranger who was picked up near-dead in Kingsport harbor on Christmas (in 1920, I think) was allowed to view the dread book in St. Mary's Hospital at Arkham.

During the 'twenties there was a wild, decadent set among the students (Miskatonic's lost generation, apparently), who were of dubious morality and were reputed to practice black magic. And in 1925 the *Necronomicon* was consulted yet again, this time by the uncouth and precocious giant Wilbur Whately. He sought to borrow it, but Henry Armitage, the librarian, wisely refused.

In 1927 (the year they were surveying for a new reservoir for Arkham) the talented young mathematician Walter Gilman also obtained temporary access to the volume. He came to a hideous end in a haunted rooming house, but not before he had presented to Miskatonic a queer, spiky image formed of unknown elements and later placed on display in the Miskatonic museum, which also boasted some strangely alloyed and fantastically piscine gold jewelry from Innsmouth.

In the late 'twenties Asenath Waite, fascinating daughter of a reputed Innsmouth sorcerer, took a course in medieval metaphysics at Miskatonic, and we can be sure she did not lose the opportunity of prying into even more dubious branches of knowledge.

On the whole, the late 'twenties were a period particularly productive of spectral occurrences in and around Arkham; in particular the year 1928; which can in this connected be termed "The Great Year," and in even greater particular September 1928, which may be titled "The Great Month."

We can presume that the unfortunate Gilman perished that year and that Asenath Waite was one of the student body, but those assumptions are only a beginning. Consultation of the *Journal of the American Psychological Society* shows N.W. Peaslee than began to publish a series of articles describing his strange dreams of earth's non-human past. And on May sixth Albert N. Wilmarth, an instructor in literature, received a disquieting letter from the Vermont scholar Henry A. Akeley about extra-terrestrial creatures lurking in his native woodlands. In August Wilbur Whateley died horrifyingly while attempting to burglarize the

Miskatonic library and steal the *Necronomicon*. On September ninth Wilbur's twin brother, who took after his non-human father to an even greater extent, broke loose near Dunwich, Massachusetts.

On September twelfth, Wilmarth, lured by a forged letter, set out to visit Akeley in Vermont. On the same day Dr. Armirage learned of the eruption of Wilbur's twin brother.

That night Wilmarth fled in horror from Akeley's farm. On the fourteenth Armitage set out for Dunwich with two of his colleagues, and next day managed to destroy the Dunwich horror.

It is startling indeed to think of two such tremendous sequences of supernatural events reaching their crisis at almost precisely the same time. One likes to think of the frantic Armitage passing the apprehensive Wilmarth as the latter hurried to catch his train. (The most obvious explanation is that Lovecraft prepared a rather elaborate chronology for "The Dunwich Horror," written in 1928, and then made use of the same chart in laying out the plot of "The Whisperer in Darkness," written in 1930 with no other tales intervening.)

After the excitement of The Great Month, almost any events seem anticlimatic. However, one should mention the Miskatonic Antarctic Expedition of 1930–31; the discovery of the secrets of the Witch-House in March 1931, with further accessions to the museum; and the Australian expedition of 1935. Both expeditions included Professor William Dyer of the geology department, who also knew something of Wilmarth's dreadful experience and who can perhaps therefore lay claim to having been involved in more preternatural events than anyone else on the faculty.

One can only speculate as to why Lovecraft created and made such intensive use of Miskatonic University and the *Necronomicon*. Certainly the Miskatonic faculty constitutes a kind of Lovecraftian utopia of highly intelligent, aesthetically sensitive, yet tradition-minded scholars.

As for the *Necronomicon,* it appears that Lovecraft used it as a back door or postern gate to realms of wonder and myth, the main approaches to which had been blocked off by his acceptance of the new universe of materialistic science. It permitted him to maintain in his stories at least occasional sections of the poetic, resonant, and colorful prose which he loved, but which hardly suited his later, scientifically realistic style. It provided him with a cloud of sinister atmosphere which would otherwise have had to be built afresh with each story. It pictured vividly his Copernican conception of the vastness, strangeness, and infinite eerie possibilities of the new universe of science. And finally, it was the key to a more frightening, yet more fascinating "real" world than the blind and purposeless cosmos in which he had to live his life.

THE FOUR FACES OF THE OUTSIDER

by Yōzan Dirk W. Mosig

H.P. Lovecraft did not write to entertain, nor did he tailor his impressive fiction with the paying market in mind. Instead, he relied on his work as a revisionist or ghost-writer, and on the meager proceedings of the rapidly vanishing Phillips estate, for the small but regular income which allowed him to lead a frugal existence. When Lovecraft turned his encyclopedic mind to the careful craftsmanship of one of his memorable tales, he did so to attain a measure of artistic self-expression. As becomes obvious from even a superficial reading of his published letters, he did not care if his work found an appreciative public. A perfectionist, he was never satisfied, even with his greatest masterpieces. Nevertheless, he never abandoned completely his attempts at creative self-expression — at communication. His works posses remarkable depth, and it is up to us to attempt to understand the message of the gentleman from Providence.

"The Outsider" is undoubtedly one of the finest tales to come out of Lovecraft's pen. It is also one of the most profoundly meaningful and symbolic, albeit often baffling and enigmatic for the critic. Working under the assumption that there is no such thing as "correct" interpretation, the present study attempts to investigate the "message" in Lovecraft's powerful story from four different viewpoints. "The Outsider" lends itself quite readily to a psychoanalytic interpretation, but it also becomes meaningful when viewed from a more metaphysical frame of reference. Its autobiographical overtones have been discussed by many, while it is also possible to translate this narrative in terms of Lovecraft's philosophical Weltanschauung. Finally, there is also the traditional interpretation within the context provided by other Lovecraftian tales (such as "Pickman's Model," *The Dream-Quest of Unknown Kadath,* etc.) identifying the outsider as a human child kidnapped by ghouls and growing up in their subterranean abode. An unusual variant of this type of interpretation was offered by David Brown (in *Nyctalops* 8) who suggests that the outsider's identity is Richard Upton Pickman, antihero of "Pickman's Model," who is changing into a ghoul. But even if Lovecraft's Mephistophelic characterization of the ultimate artist were indeed the true fictional identity of the outsider, this would tell us little about the meaning, the implications, the message that Lovecraft is trying to communicate in his paroxysm of ecstatic self-expression.

In the following pages we will attempt to present the main outlines of the four interpretations mentioned above. No claim is made as to the validity or exhaustiveness of any of these different appreciations of the same tale. Naturally, alternative explanations are also possible, and may be equally valid. Nevertheless, in our conclusion we will attempt to evaluate the four suggested views on their merits, that is, their ability to account for available data on Lovecraft, his works, and his views.

Finally the personal preference of the author will be stated, a view necessitated by his personal bias and perhaps not arrived at in complete objectivity.

1. The Autobiographic Interpretation:
H.P. Lovecraft: Outsider

Taken as an autobiographic statement, the tale begins as a relation of Lovecraft's unhappy childhood, full of "fear and sadness." The anxiety and depression of the child, deprived of a paternal figure at the age of three, controlled by an over-protective mother, and rejected by his peers because of the unique interests generated by his precocious genius, are easily understood.

Lovecraft spent countless of the "lone hours" of his childhood in the "vast and dismal chambers" of his grandfather's library, whose "maddening rows of antique books" provided the main source of entertainment in his solitude. From such books he "learned all that (he) knew," without the urging or guidance of any teacher.

Such was the lot of this "dazed" twentieth century Poe, this genius destined to meet a "barren" existence, full of disappointments and unfulfilled expectations which would leave him "broken" and eternally dissatisfied with even his most brilliant creations.

And yet, as shown by the letters in which he referred to this period as the happiest of his life, Lovecraft was "strangely content" (proof of the relativity of all things) and clung desperately to the "sere memories" of his childhood, when his mind threatened to sink into the pits of melancholy and despair that moved him to repeatedly consider and defend the idea of suicide, even though he was only thirty-one years old when this tale was written.

In a continuous stream of morbid childhood memories, Lovecraft continues to describe the dampness of his abode and the peculiar odor of the gigantic library room, always producing an atmosphere of "brooding and fear" and shadows . . . to the extent that the child had to light candles for relief. Perhaps we can even trace Lovecraft's preference for the nocturnal hours to this unique early development.

He refers to his thirst for acceptance, his desire to belong, his need for warmth, affection, and friendship, and compares his goal to the "black inaccessible tower" that reaches into the "unknown outer sky," the heaven of social acceptance, but which "cannot be ascended save by a well nigh impossible climb. . . ."

The period of isolation and solitude is perceived by the child's mind as countless years slowly and agonizingly grinding by, and no memory is kept of the adults that cared for him, particularly of the father he hardly knew. . . . In his neurotic mother he only could see a distorted, shriveled image of himself.

As a child, Lovecraft naturally considered himself as akin to other children, whose youthful pictures he saw in the books — at least until his mother told him that he was utterly hideous, ugly, and different from all other children . . . and that other youngsters would probably be repelled and horrified by his mere appearance. Sarah Phillips Lovecraft, who died a diagnosed psychotic the same year "The Outsider" was written (1921), deeply resented her husband's general paresis, a hatred that was displaced to the child, only to produce deep guilt feelings and anxiety to the troubled woman. The reaction formation which followed her inability to cope with her neurotic and moral anxiety resulted in the compulsive overprotection that characterized her relationship with the child. But her deep hostility toward her son occasionally broke through her defense mechanism, as when she succeeded in making him feel ugly and distorted (a feeling that he was never able to completely overcome) — all the while rationalizing that she was doing this for the child's own good, keeping him close to her, under her "protection," and away from other children and the rest of the world that might try to hurt him. The added imminence of financial disintegration was the final stress she could not endure, the straw that broke the remaining thread of sanity in a wretched woman who was to spend her last years in the insane asylum. And her son was not by her death bed when she was stricken by her final illness. . . .

In his abysmal solitude, the child would often lie, outside, under the "dark, mute trees," and "dream for hours about what (he) read in the books," picturing himself among the "gay crowds" that must exist in the "sunny world" beyond his "infinitely old and infinitely horrible" prison-home. He tried to escape, but as he moved away from the house, his anxiety and his insecurity became unendurable, the air became "filled with brooding fear," and he ran swiftly back in defeat. So, through what to him appeared to be endless twilights, he "waited and dreamed, not knowing what (he) waited for." Finally, his longing for light, for happiness and acceptance, "grew so frantic, that (he) resolved to scale the tower," fall thought he might, in his desperate attempt to reach out and attain his impossible dream. Life was not worth living any longer "without ever beholding light," without joining the illusive world of gaiety, of belongingness, of love.

The decision to reach out to others was not an easy one, and is represented in the story as the perilous, slow, and arduous ascent of the tower, with frantic hope mixed with mounting anxiety and incertitude.

But finally, coming out of his shell, he emerged from his precocious seclusion.

The realization that his peers were not equally encumbered by a crippling psychological environment, is for him a grotesquely unbelievable shock. This act of the will, this emergence from his psychological prison, has not elevated him to dizzying heights but simply placed him on a level ground, natural to everyone else. But determined to make the most out of his position, he proceeds with a "frantic craving" in his quest for acceptance and love. Ultimately he arrives at the castle of lights, the goal of his childhood dreams.

His innocent heart is filled with delight as he observes the inviting "open window, gorgeously ablaze with light, and sending forth sound of the gayest revelry." But as he gathers sufficient courage and attempts the actual social contact his inner nature demanded, he does so only to step from his "single bright moment of hope to (his) blackest convulsion of despair and realization." He experienced the psychological blow of social rejection and isolation.

To his anxious and subjective mind it did not appear as if his peers' reaction was due to his different interests, in part , the consequence of his superior intellect, which made him prefer the acting of historical roles to the childish games of others. . . . (One who knew him in childhood later referred to him as "crazy as a bedbug.") No, he perceived himself as shunned because of the actual revulsion and nausea caused by his hideous ugliness. Mother had been right! He was a loathsome monster! Seeing his image in the mirror of the mind, the psychological eye perceived only a distorted abnormality, that had "by its simple appearance" turned a group of playing children into "a horde of delirious fugitives. . . ."

This cataclysmic collapse of his self-concept brought him "avalanche of soul-annihilating memory," he could understand now "all that had been. . . ." He knew now why he had not been allowed to come in contact and play with other children, why his mother always needed to protect him and keep him away from others, he knew the truth about his hideous deformity. . . . How could he know that in reality he was a rather handsome child with a monstrous mother in the throes of growing personality disintegration. . . ? This traumatic experience had far-reaching and long-lasting effects, and the dreamer from Providence never completely overcame his feelings of ugliness and social inadequacy. For the rest of his life he was more or less a recluse, going out at night and preferring to deal with his friends through correspondence. It is true that in his latter years, particularly the last decade, he was able to compensate for this handicap to a great extent, perhaps due in part to his brief marriage and his New York "exile," which contributed to make him more fully human. But "The Outsider" was written before he was exposed to the healing effect of those influences.

Returning to the text of the story, we notice that the experience of such completely negative self-concept produced a tremendous burst of anxiety in his young but lacerated mind, and that "in the supreme horror of that second" he repressed his excruciating self-awareness as well as the traumatic event leading to it . . . he "forgot what had horrified" him. He tried to retreat once more to the consolation of his mother, to the relative security of his home — but the door was closed: things would never be the same again.

He rationalized, saying that he was not sorry for his alienation, and turned for companionship and inspiration to the inner world of fantasies and dreams, riding with the "mocking and friendly ghouls" — the "night gaunts" of his dreams — in the catacombs of his own imagination. In his extreme introversion, he realized that "light was not for (him), nor any gaiety," save that produced by his own fantastic creations. And in his "new wilderness and freedom," his independence from others, he "almost welcomed the bitterness of alienage," realizing always that he "was an outsider, a stranger in this century and among those who are still men," among those still able to find happiness through interpersonal relations. Rejected by his peers, oppressed by his mother, and misunderstood by all, he renounced society and the twentieth century. Finding security and esthetic pleasure only in the past, he often reminisced the "happiness" of his childhood in his latter years, and turned to the eighteenth century for beauty and inspiration. As August Derleth, his first biographer, noted, he remained an outsider all his life, and his spirit flourished in his rightful and beloved eighteenth century. His unique genius and imagination allowed his mind to fly at prodigious heights well beyond the reach or conception of common men, but like all mortals, his life was the product of an accidental combination of heredity and environment that could not have resulted in a different outcome.

"The Outsider" is a powerful and touching statement about the early years of the "gentleman from Angell Street."

2. An Analytical Interpretation:
Allegory of the Psyche

"The Outsider" almost appears to have been written in order to fit the analytical theory of Carl Gustav Jung. Even though interpretations using Freudian psychoanalysis or Adlerian individual psychology, among others, are also possible, Lovecraft's tale acquires unusual psychological significance when viewed as an allegorical voyage through the Jungian conception of the unfolding human psyche and its fundamental conflicts. Even though Lovecraft's letters show that he was well aware of Jung's theory, the question of whether this story is a case of conscious artistry or a manifestation of the author's own unconscious and dynamic psyche, is not settled.

The subterranean castle in the tale stands for the Collective Unconscious, the unfathomable psychic ocean common to all men, and containing "rows upon rows" of "antique books" or archetypes. The archetypes, or primordial images, are the psychic representations of the primordial experiences of the species throughout eons of evolution: they are the depository of the ancestral wisdom of the human psyche. (For the reader unfamiliar with Jung's analytical theory, J. Jacobi's *The Psychology of C.G. Jung,* Yale University Press, New Haven, 1962, would provide an ideal introduction.)

As a child is conceived and later born, his psyche is composed of global, undifferentiated contents. These contents are dependent on the genetic factors which determine the unique development of his brain. During the first months, even years, of life, the unconscious contents become gradually differentiated through the process of individuation, into the psychic structural constructs characterizing the normally functioning adult psyche. It is to this slow and gradual process of psyche development that the outsider, the archetypal prototype of the ego, is referring, when mention is made of the "years" passed in the castle, although he "cannot measure the time."

"I know not where I was born, save that the castle was infinitely old and infinitely horrible." The budding ego emerges slowly and gradually from the depths of the unfathomable Collective Unconscious. The contents of the unconscious are infinitely old (the hereditary predispositions and instincts accumulated through literally millions of years of organic evolution), and infinitely horrible, at least as perceived from the point of view of the conscious ego (the narrator) because of their primitive, savage, undifferentiated, and archaic nature. These unconscious elements "silently wave twisted branches far aloft," manifesting themselves distortedly in dreams and nightmares, striving to assert themselves and acquire a charge of libidinal energy.

"There was an accursed smell everywhere, as of the piled-up corpses of dead generations," the countless generations of ancestors, transcending the family, going back beyond this origins of the tribe, the nation, the race, and even the species, to our subhuman and animal ancestry, and even to the primordial slime where life first originated. . . . The experiences of countless generations exposed to similar types of conflicts or situations, with individual survival on the balance, have resulted in the natural selection of those reactions or predispositions with adaptive, or survival, value. Or, more specifically, those combinations of genetic alleles making such adaptive reactions more probable, tend to increase in frequency within the gene-pool of the species, until becoming universal. From the piled-up corpses of dead generations we have inherited ancestral tendencies, such as fear of snakes and fear of the dark. The presence of such fears in primitive man would increase the probability of his surviving to reproductive age (escaping the predators of the night and the poisonous bite of snakes), while those members of the tribe unable to experience or develop such fears seldom lived to pass on their genetic flaw . . . and even though in modern times such fears, as well as many other unconscious tendencies and predispositions, have ceased to have significant adaptive value, they form part of our inseparable heritage.

"It was never light" in the unconscious castle, because neither consciousness nor reason can exist in the depths of the primordial, archetypal jungle. There was one "black tower," a symbol for the process of individuation, which reached above the unconscious forest, into the "unknown outer sky," the one" point of contact of the global, undifferentiated, unconscious psyche, with the real and objective world. This is the tower that the emerging archetypal ego must ascend, at all costs, to behold the light, to reach consciousness.

The outsider's only memory of a living thing is that of "something mockingly like (himself), but distorted, shriveled, and decaying, like the castle." This is a reference to either the other archetypal processes in the unconscious (such as the archetypal persona), or, more likely, specifically to the budding archetypal nucleus which will later lead to the development of the foul and loathsome Shadow, the ego's inescapable "dark brother". . . .

"Bones and skeletons strewed the stone crypts *deep below the foundations,*" symbolizing the axial archetypal systems at the very bottom of the Collective Unconscious, in the deepest layers whose contents can never be made conscious. These skeletal systems, these genetically coded ancestral potentialities, lie dormant until experience activates them. A skeleton cannot move without muscles, and an archetype cannot manifest itself unless the organism experiences stimuli corresponding to an archetypal model of reaction. But for the archetypal ego, these "bones and skeletons" appear as "natural everyday events."

The outsider has learned all (he) knows from the "mouldy texts" of archetypal lore, without the urging or guidance of a teacher, that is, impelled by innate instinctual forces and archetypal memories.

Note that "there were no mirrors in the castle," because there can be no opposites, no mirror images, in the unconscious, before the individuation of the contents of consciousness. The principle of opposition in the human psyche always applies to a conscious vs. an unconscious system (i.e., ego vs. shadow, persona vs. soul image, introversion vs. extroversion, feeling vs. thinking, sensation vs. intuition), but there can never be opposition between two unconscious constructs or functions: there are no mirrors within the castle. . . .

"Through endless twilights," the archetypal ego "dreams," expressing itself in fantasy images and symbols of the unconscious, until the time for individuation is ripe. Then, with a frantic longing for light, or psychic consciousness, the outsider ascends the "black tower," and reaches the realm of the Personal Unconscious, the crypt lying above the subterranean castle of the Collective Unconscious, at the border of consciousness. This crypt contains countless oblong boxes, which are to become the depository of forgotten-and repressed material during the lifetime of the individual.

At last, the stone trapdoor, the portal to consciousness, is found and forced open, as well as the final barrier, the iron grating, through which shines "the radiant full moon." In the symbolic language of the psyche, according to analytical theory, the moon stands for a manifestation of the mother archetype as well as for the mother complex, when it appears in dreams. (The mother complex consists of experiences and other material repressed out of the conscious sphere, and encapsulated by the unconscious, which cluster around the powerful nuclear element providing by the Great Earth Mother archetype — the "magna mater" — derived from ancestral experiences with mothers throughout the ages.) Fittingly enough, the outsider states that the moon, the mother archetype, has previously appeared only "in dreams and in vague visions," in ancestral "memories."

The stumbling that follows the veiling of the moon, or mother symbol, by a cloud, represents the extreme dependency of the emerging consciousness of the growing infant on the interaction with the maternal psyche. And as the moon comes out again, the view from the borderline of consciousness is clear again, though "stupefying." The emergence of the conscious ego is not the end but only the beginning of the psychic quest, because the goal of personality development is not the emergence of the ego, but the realization of the Self. . . .

The following wanderings of the outsider represent the odyssey of the human psyche toward the fabled castle of lights, the Self. The outsider's progress is not fortuitous, as a kind of "latent memory" guides him, since the transcendent function of self-realization is also an archetypal process. It is significant here to notice that the outsider sometimes follows "the visible road," or the way dictated by reason and experience, but sometimes leaves it "to thread across meadows where only the occasional ruins" bespeak "the ancient presence of a forgotten road," or, in other words, pursues his goal following the path indicated by the unconscious wisdom of the archetypes, a path which may appear at times as illogical or irrational, but is nevertheless psychically necessary. The tendency to strive for self-realization is innate, encoded in the genetic combinations carrying the "latent memories" or archetypes from our ancestral past.

In this quest, the outsider has become the "wandering hero," the traditional symbol of man's voyage toward Selfhood, of the ego's longing for the ultimate expansion of consciousness. Finally, he reaches his destination, the "ivied castle" whose windows are "gorgeously ablaze with light." The castle of lights stands for the Self, the unification of consciousness and the unconscious, the realization of the total psyche. This is, according to Jung, the purpose of human existence, even though complete equalization, complete self-realization, is not possible, because the lack of gradient implies total entropy — the flow of libido coming to a standstill — and this cannot occur save in death, the goal of all life. (One reason why total entropy never occurs during the individual's striving for wholeness, is that the psyche is only a partially closed energy system, with energy loss due to work, and energy gain through food).

The outsider peers through a window of the ivied castle and finds there a merry company, the contents of consciousness, rationality, sanity . . . but as he enters in an attempt to join or integrate with the rest, consciousness reacts not only to him and his feeble persona, but to the inevitable and escapable Shadow that always accompanies him (and every human being), the unconscious and inseparable opposite of the ego which in one instant shatters the illusion of rationality and the hopes of self-realization.

The final horror comes in the moment of truth, when the ego perceives its own Shadow, its unconscious opposite reflected in that fateful mirror. The outsider sees the atavistic nightmare that always lurks at the threshold of rationality, and which Lovecraft so skillfully described as "the compound of all that is unclean, uncanny, unwelcome, abnormal, and detestable," all that the ego abhors, rejects, and represses because of rational, esthetic, or ethical reasons: his "dark brother" who becomes blacker, denser, and more powerful the more it has been alienated from consciousness. It is "the ghoulish shade of decay, antiquity and dissolution," the conglomerate of all the ego perceives as ultimate evil, clustered around the archaic, undifferentiated Shadow archetype. "It was the awful baring of that which the merciful earth should always hide," of that which (from the point of view of the shocked and horrified ego) should have always remained underground, buried in the unconscious. With deep loathing, the outsider notices that the apparition presents "a leering, abhorrent travesty on the human shape," being the distorted, unconscious parody of the conscious ego.

Then, as the outstretched fingers of the outsider touch those of his unconscious and nightmarish mirror image, an instant of ego-shadow fusion occurs, that goes beyond mere recognition or understanding. This is the closest the outsider ever comes to self-realization and psychic wholeness. . . . For the cataclysmic revelation of the Shadow within himself, the understanding that he and the monstrous abomination standing before him are one, instantly shatters sanity as he experiences (and is unable to cope with) the most traumatic experience of human existence.

In that instant "there crashed upon (his) mind a single and fleeting avalanche of soul-annihilating memory." As consciousness and unconsciousness touch, fuse for an instant, "all that had been" becomes evident, all is understood in a moment of terrible insight. But the flood of anxiety is unendurable, awareness of the truth is too painful, and a desperate repression occurs. With this regressive flow of energy or libido, the outsider "forgets" what has horrified him. "The burst of black memory vanished in a chaos of echoing images," that is, in the chaos of opposing systems within the psyche. The price of unification, of Selfhood, is too high, and it is better to live in ignorance than to accept the awful reality of man's atavistic and unconscious nature. This utter failure leaves the outsider "dazed, disappointed, barren, broken". . . . Lovecraft, the pessimistic realist, is telling us that self-realization is an impossible dream.

The outsider escapes from the now empty and desolate castle, in a dream under the ever present moonlight. An attempt to return to the subterranean castle, to regress to the claustraum, to find total oblivion in a reversal of the individuation process, fails. The ego cannot escape from the world of consciousness and reality: the stone trap-door is immovable.

His "new freedom" is provided only by insanity, and the outsider, unable to recover from his "soul-annihilating" experience, rides now with the "mocking and friendly ghouls," his archetypal fantasies and complexes (or perhaps his fellow inmates in the insane asylum). But in his bitterness he almost welcomes the new freedom of schizophrenia, the new wildness of breaking away from reality — of being "an outsider among those who are still men," who are still sane and have not yet felt the icy fingers of terror and the holocaust of ego-disintegration in the ultimate confrontation with the Shadow.

Lovecraft, familiar with Jungian theory, was well aware that few, if any ever achieve any significant approximation to Jung's idealized ego-expansion and self-realization. In his conviction that "the most merciful thing in the world is the inability of the human mind the correlate all its contents," the dreamer from Providence has painted a gloomy and devastating picture of man's destiny: not a glorious psychic integration, but the ever imminent collapse of the ephemeral illusion of rationality.

3. An Antimetaphysical Interpretation: The Absurdity of Post-Mortem Destiny

H.P. Lovecraft, a rationalist, a logical positivist with absolutely no belief in the supernatural, used his celebrated tale "The Outsider" as medium to convey, in disguised form, his sardonic contempt for the incongruity of metaphysical beliefs and dogmata such as life after death, immortality, and resurrection. With the searing irony of the materialistic philosopher, he unleashed this piece of macabre sarcasm on the vain hopes and illusions of a gullible world.

The subterranean castle is simultaneously Lovecraft's cynical conception of heaven and of the kingdom of Dis on the pattern of Dante's Inferno, while the outsider is a corpse that has been dead and buried for countless years. Some uncanny psychic residue allows this "carrion thing," this unnatural denizen of the tomb, to become an animated corpse and continue his unthinkable existence in the underground vaults of the cemetery. Lovecraft has granted, for the sake of argument, man's survival after death, and is ready to carry this notion to its absurd implications.

The living corpse exists in the "subterranean castle," sole survivor among the "piled-up corpses of dead generations," while his deteriorated brain retains only vague memories of the past. The "mouldy books," containing the traditional beliefs of his ancestors, convey to him hopes and dreams of light, of happiness, of rebirth, of future glory. . . . Lying in his underground crypt-vault-castle, and "unable to measure the time," he dreams of rejoining the world of the living, the world of light and of gay figures he sees in the books and which always evoke half-memories of his mundane past. He dreamed and waited, "not knowing what he waited for." Finally, his longing for light "grew so frantic," that he decided to climb the single "black tower" leading "to the unknown outer sky." With tremendous effort, the rotting and inconceivable monster manages to scale this sole avenue of escape, and achieves his unholy resurrection as he emerges from the crypt. He finds himself standing in the midst of the graveyard where his body was laid to rest in the unmeasurable past, something for him "abysmally unexpected" and producing the "most demoniacal of all shocks," since he had fancied himself the inhabitant of a castle and not a denizen of the underworld. . . . Lovecraft, to show us that the metaphysical dream is sheer insanity has allowed life to linger in this disintegrating corpse, and now has resurrected it, returning it to the world of the living.

The grisly creature, still nursing a frantic craving for light, for companionship, for happiness, and even for the mythical glory of heaven, runs swiftly and eagerly under the moonlight, guided by remote recollections from his distant past. He recognizes landmarks and buildings, rivers and bridges, but he finds them all changed, altered, aged, and crumbling, an indication of the long time elapsed since the grim reaper put an end to his natural life. (Incidentally, this is an idea that was later elaborated by Lovecraft's friend and fellow author, Clark Ashton Smith, in "Xeethra.")

This decaying, pitiful parody of living men ultimately arrives at his destination, the "venerable ivied castle" where he once lived or reigned, noting here also the ravages of time. The castle was "maddeningly familiar, yet full of perplexing strangeness . . . the moat was filled in, and . . . some of the well-known towers were demolished." But, without attempting to understand the implications of the changes that time has brought to the places he knew in the far past, he is attracted "with interest and delight" by "the open windows," through which he observes an "oddly dressed company," "making merry and speaking brightly to one another." He sees in all this "gorgeous light and revelry" the fulfillment of his hopes, the glory he had only dated dream of before.

In his brightest "moment of hope" he decides to enter the castle of life and steps through one of the low windows to join the gay party . . . only to sink into his blackest moment of despair. At the sight of the putrefying corpse creeping in through the window, "there descended upon the whole company" a panic "fear of hideous intensity," that Lovecraft paints in vivid and unforgettable colors. Everyone fled madly, stampeding desperately from the unthinkable apparition that now stood there, "alone and dazed," in the throes of melancholic anguish, unable to comprehend the reason for this sudden manifestation of delirious terror. He clings to the tenuous hope that the horrified mass reaction was due to something "that might be lurking near" him. . . .

When he sees that fateful reflection in the mirror of reality, he does not perceive the nightmarish image as his own, since in his dreams he had always conceived himself as "akin to the youthful figures" in his books . . .

by Yōzan Dirk W. Mosig   27 and now is confronted with the "putrid, dripping eidolon of unwholesome revelation," with a "carrion thing" that "the merciful earth should always hide." With horror, he detects in "its eaten-away and bone-revealing outlines a leering, abhorrent travesty on the human shape."

As he stumbles, he touches "the rotting outstretched paw of the monster" but feels only "the cold and unyielding surface of polished glass." In that mind-shattering instant he realizes the truth, he remembers the past, he recognizes the "altered edifice" where he now stands, and worst of all, he becomes agonizingly aware of his own condition. Overwhelmed by this nightmarish revelation of ultimate horror, this cruel mockery of all his dreams and hopes, the outsider sinks to the most abysmal depths of despair. But in that moment of supreme anguish, his tortured mind dissociates his painful awareness, and he experiences the merciful oblivion of amnesia.

In his mordant yet morbid humor, Lovecraft shows us now this tragic and pitiful parody of immortal man running blindly and frantically back, attempting to return to the graveyard, to the earth where he belongs — only to find the slab to the subterranean vault immovable. He experiences no regret, since he can only abhor the prospect of continued and meaningless existence in the crypt. Now he rides with the "friendly ghouls," the necrophagous scavengers who become his sole companions in a final gruesome and grotesque mockery of man's impossible dreams.

The outsider finds not the glory of Heaven, nor even the torments of Hell, but only the "unnamed feasts of Nitokris beneath the Great Pyramid. . . ." Man's ultimate fate, man's final destiny, is not the glory of supernatural existence, but the feast of the maggots.

With "The Outsider" Lovecraft achieved an equally effective, yet vastly different statement on the absurdity of immortality, as Aldous Huxley's *After Many a Summer Dies the Swan*. To cease to exist is certainly preferable to the kind of unholy survival found in the outsider, and to conceive of any other kind of personal survival in a mechanistic and purposeless cosmos was a vastly more absurd proposition for the thinker from Providence.

4. A Philosophical Interpretation:
Man's Position in a Mechanistic Universe

That H.P. Lovecraft was a first rate thinker and philosopher is shown by such brilliant essays as "Materialism and Idealism: A Reflection" and "The Materialist Today," as well as by the numerous and profound philosophical speculations found in his extensive correspondence. His works of literature, such as "The Outsider," cannot be appreciated or interpreted independently of his serious convictions. If Lovecraft was trying to communicate a deep message to mankind, it is here, in his philosophical works, that we shall find the key to the deepest and most significant meaning of all his unique fiction.

Lovecraft was a mechanistic materialist, influenced by Haeckel, but ˹

going far beyond the nineteenth century rationalist. He was an ardent believer and supporter of science and scientific method. A conservative in matters of art and morality, he showed himself to be an extreme modernist in his intellectual outlook. He was convinced of the validity of Darwin's theory of evolution, and to a much lesser extent, of the modern discoveries of psychoanalysis. His deepest scientific interest was in the area of astronomy, an interest which he maintained until the end of his short life.

Although he greatly appreciated the esthetic beauty of the myths and traditional beliefs of the past, he fully accepted the implications of the information available to his probing scientific intellect, and abandoned all traces of religious and superstitious beliefs at an early age. He conceived the cosmos as entirely purposeless and mechanistic, and man's position therein as a mere insignificant accident lasting an instant in eternity.

Lovecraft had the unique ability of being able to achieve complete intellectual objectivity. He was capable of detaching his consciousness, of achieving a frame of mind of "cosmic outsidedness" and becoming a dispassionate observer of man and the universe. He was able to conceptualize a cosmos where our entire universe was reduced to a grain of sand, a mere atom in infinity, and at the same time to observe the amusing behavior of his fellow men with the same objectivity with which we might study the antics of ants, rats, or monkeys. His incisive mind was quick to spot the inconsistencies and incongruities of human hypocrisy, and he condemned the blindness of the fanatic theist together with the unjustified hopes of the idealistic atheist.

Lovecraft's view of life was essentially pessimistic. He felt that most people are basically unhappy, and that a life of suffering is not preferable to the oblivion of death. Seriously contemplating suicide, he decided against it on the grounds that the esthetic pleasure he derived from the study of eighteenth century art slightly tipped the scales in favor of life. He considered the quest for truth, for new knowledge, the sole possible justification for the existence of the human species, and his eternal question was "What is reality?"

For Lovecraft, man, as well as the cosmos, has no purpose, no final goal. A rock, a man, a planet, and the entire universe, all are equally meaningless, and equally valuable in a purposeless cosmos. Life did not exist a moment ago, and will have ceased a moment hence, and the memory of man will be eternally forgotten.

But man must live by the relative values imparted by culture and tradition, and from these he derives an illusion of security and stability. These values and traditions Lovecraft accepted as long as they did not contradict what his cold, rational intellect knew to be true. He opposed the blind iconoclastic fury of those all too willing to tear down what they could never replace.

Nevertheless, Lovecraft was intellectually too perceptive to become a philosophic missionary. With unparalleled objectivity, he was able to realize that a complete awareness of reality is not necessarily the best for all men, and that for many an illusion is preferable to the truth. Man exists for the merest instant, and anything making life less punishing and more endurable has relative value.

Lovecraft had little faith in man's ability to cope with reality, and in his brilliant letters and fiction predicted what we now call "future shock." With deep regret he prophesied man's retreat into insanity or the superstitions of a new dark age when faced with the new discoveries of science pointing toward the abysmal insignificance of man. The introductory paragraph of "The Call of Cthulhu" provides an excellent summary of Lovecraft's views, and also supplies us with the essential key for the interpretation of "The Outsider" within the framework of his mechanistic philosophy:

> "The most merciful thing in the world is the inability of the human mind to correlate all its contents. We live on a placid island of ignorance in the midst of black seas of infinity, and it was not meant that we should voyage far. The sciences, each straining in its own direction, have hitherto harmed us little; but some day the piecing together of dissociated knowledge will open up such terrifying vistas of reality, and of our frightful position therein, that we shall either go mad from the revelation or flee from the deadly light into the peace and safety of a new dark age."

Lovecraft has been often misunderstood in this paragraph as opposing scientific progress. Nothing could have been further removed from his intention. He simply stated what he perceived as the inevitable and deplorable consequence of man's inability to cope with the new horizons opened by science, while still regarding knowledge as the ultimate good. That his pessimistic prophecy was justified becomes evident when we witness the growing interest in, or rather, retreat to, the occult, astrology, magic, religion, witchcraft, and superstition, the countless new cults emerging everywhere, the fads of pseudo-mysticism, the drug-culture. . . . All the frantic attempts at regaining some of the lost security destroyed by Galileo, and Darwin, and Freud, and Einstein, and Skinner, and countless others. . . .

It is this ultimate conflict of man facing the cosmos and reacting with horror to the realization of his impotent insignificance, that constitutes the theme of "The Outsider."

The subterranean castle is the womb, where embryonic man is being shaped by his inherited potential and genetic characteristics. He experiences the pains of birth trauma after the arduous travel up the vaginal tower. Man is filled with dreams and expectations, with illusions about his own destiny. He strives for happiness, freedom, dignity, knowledge. . . . The cherished traditions of the past tell him that he is the lord of creation, the center of the Universe. He sees himself as the ultimate

THE FOUR FACES OF THE OUTSIDER

product of evolution, the culmination of all life. In his quest for knowledge and perfection, he hopes to find an answer to all questions in science, and sees in this castle of truth, the key to ultimate happiness.

But when the narrator reaches his destination and enters the bastion of reality, he finds not happiness, security, and fulfillment, but only the bare, cruel, merciless truth. As he correlates the body of dissociated knowledge, he achieves instant comprehension of reality. He knows "all that had been." A terrifying vista of reality has been opened for him, and of his "frightful position" therein. In the mirror he sees reflected, not the lord of creation, but the loathsome, abominable vermin polluting a grain of sand in a purposeless universe. He recognizes himself as a meaningless atom of corruption, an ephemeral infection in the accident of Life. No destiny, no purpose, no dignity, no meaning. . . .

Unable to cope with this "soul-annihilating" revelation, "in the supreme horror of that second" man forgets the truth and runs frantically back to the hopes and superstitions of the past, but finding the stone trapdoor closed, collapses into the "new freedom" of insanity. He can never be the same again. He is an outsider. He knows.

This ultimate conflict, the final confrontation of man with reality is a recurrent theme in Lovecraft's fiction. The outcome reflects Lovecraft's pessimistic view of human nature and perfectibility. Lovecraft, as a thinker, was a realist, and painted reality as he saw it in the powerful strokes of his incomparable fiction. He wrote with the realism of Richard Upton Pickman, Lovecraft's uncanny self-portrait in "Pickman's Model." "The Outsider" provides a vivid representation of man's pathetic helplessness in the cosmos.

Discussion and Evaluation

The autobiographic interpretation is quite appealing, because it seems to fit well with known facts of Lovecraft's life. To suggest that all the similarities between settings and incidents in "The Outsider," and events or places in the life of the Providence author are mere coincidences, would be nothing short of preposterous. Nevertheless, although biographical data may have provided some of the "form" or setting in this excellent tale, it does not necessarily follow that the meaning of the story is to be read as an expression of Lovecraft's hypothetically frustrated gregariousness. Frank Belknap Long, Lovecraft's intimate and long-time friend, for example, disagrees emphatically with the notion that Lovecraft had a "social inferiority complex," and insists that he "never made the slightest attempt to reach out for liking and understanding" (*Nyctalops* 8). "The Outsider" may not be Lovecraft's cry of social anguish after all.

The analytical interpretation is also attractive, and there appear to be too many similarities between Jungian theory and Lovecraft's chiller for this to be dismissed as coincidence.

H.P. Lovecraft, as a craftsman of consummate skill, was a perfectionist, always searching for the *mot just,* and constantly revising his tales before arriving at their final form. He also constantly incorporated bits of factual knowledge stored in his encyclopedic mind into the fabric of his fiction, giving them an added element of believability, so essential in achieving the temporary "suspension of disbelief" in the reader. Since Lovecraft's published letters gave ample evidence of his familiarity with both Freudian and Jungian psychoanalysis, it is plausible that he may have intentionally incorporated into many of his takes some of the universal symbols that Jung was so fond of interpreting as verifications of his theory of dreams.

There is some specific evidence in Lovecraft's fiction and poetry that he intended a psychological meaning for at least some of his works. For example, "The White Ship" described a voyage through the psyche, and *The Dream-Quest of Unknown Kadath* takes place entirely in the dream-world of the narrator. And out of his poetry, consider the following lines from "Aletheia Phrikodes":

> "Things vague, unseen, unfashion'd, and unnam'd
> Jostled each other in the seething void
> That gap'd, chaotic, downward to a sea
> Of speechless horror, foul with writhing thoughts."

Nevertheless, our analytic interpretation is quite vulnerable to the accusation of subjectivism — too many assumptions are made which cannot be empirically verified. And besides, even if a psychological interpretation is adequate, why this particular one? Why not a Freudian explanation based on Lovecraft's hypothetically repressed "sex instinct" (note the phallic symbolism of the "black tower"), or perhaps on a pathological manifestation of a deep-rooted "death instinct" (notice his perception of himself in the mirror as an already decaying corpse), or perhaps the monstrous image in the mirror represents the instincts of the Id perceived in a paroxysm of neurotic anxiety? Or perhaps the Adlerian "will to power" will supply a better answer; the "striving for superiority" that compensates for the outsider's abysmal inferiority complex may be what is meant by the ascent of the tower, while the castle of lights is the "directive fiction," the goal of his "life-style". . . . Or is the question perhaps "how can you make words mean so many different things . . . ?"

The main defect of all the possible psychoanalytic interpretations, is that the theories on which they are based are themselves built on hypothetical constructs of doubtful validity. Such theories are usually judged merely by their usefulness in the clinical setting, and not in terms of any absolute parameter of truth or falsehood.

And the interpretations can hardly be more valid than the theories they are based on. . . . For this reason, although this type of explanation is very attractive, and although Jung's analytical theory may appear to fit the story better than other similar theories, such interpretations must be taken with a grain of salt. The anti-metaphysical interpretation is the most shallow and superficial of the four presented in this study. Although interesting and perhaps amusing, and in spite of being compatible with Lovecraft's personal beliefs, it simply does not fit with his personality, always characterized by those who knew him well as one of tolerance and kind understanding. Lovecraft just did not possess the morbid and caustic humor implied by this interpretation. And, besides, the kind of survival shown in the tale does not correspond to traditional metaphysical notions. When engaging in this type of polemic, Lovecraft could do much better, as we can see in some of his letters to M. Moe and others, as well as in his essay "The Materialist Today." This interpretation is perhaps the least valid of the four presented.

The philosophical interpretation is another matter altogether. It fits well with Lovecraft's *Weltanschauung* and with the context provided by his other writings. Lovecraft, a scientist at heart, never tired of defending his views in letters to his friends, but being also a keen observer of human nature, did not expect others to share his convictions. He was a visionary able to foresee the general rejection of materialistic and iconoclastic science by those in which it produced too much dissonance. The interpretation of "The Outsider" within the framework of his cosmic-minded mechanistic materialism is probably the most valid of the four versions.

Even though Lovecraft has achieved what appears to be a permanent place in world literature with his powerful dramatic fiction, he has been generally neglected in the past as a significant thinker, perhaps due to the fact that most of his works appeared initially in pulp magazines and amateur publications. Now that his selected letters have been published in five volumes, and some of his essays are becoming more readily available, recognition will come, even if belatedly, to this great "thinker from Providence." It is the present author's conviction, after having carefully studied Lovecraft's letters, essays, and fiction, that he has had no peer as a materialistic philosopher, and that his realistic Weltanschauung is becoming more relevant today than ever before, now that the scientific analysis of behavior seems to have made the final statement in favor of determinism. . . .

Postscript

After finishing the foregoing article, I realized that I had neglected to consider an alternative explanation of "The Outsider" which is consonant with both Lovecraft's philosophical outlook and available biographical data, and which may yet turn to be the best interpretation of all. Perhaps the reason it escaped me at first is because it is so obvious.

Here, then is the *fifth face* of "The Outsider:"

5. The Outsider
A Critique of Progress.

The underground castle stands for the Past, the level ground is the Present, while the castle of lights is the Future. Man emerges from the past with high dreams and hopes for the future, but encounters only abysmal disillusionment. In the past there was safety and security, and the frightful revelations of the future are too much to bear. Man experiences "future shock" and runs blindly back in a frantic attempt to return to the tranquillity and stability of the past. But the buried past cannot be regained: the stone slab is immovable. The past is dead, and now alienated Man must continue a meaningless existence in an ever changing present, from which the only escape is the regression of insanity. . . .

This interpretation is really a twist of the "philosophical" explanation in the previous pages.. Of course, many other alternative elucidations are also possible, and the reader will have to decide which is most satisfactory.

THE FIRST LEWIS THEOBALD

by R. Boerem

Many people knew of H.P. Lovecraft as "Lewis Theobald, jun.," the name he signed to many poems, articles, at least one revision, and to innumerable letters, whose readers knew him as "Grampa Theobald." But as Lovecraft knew, there had actually been a person by that name and, as Lovecraft probably intended, there was more than a name in common between the two.

Lewis Theobald (pronounced TIB-ald) was born in 1688 at Sitting-bourne, Kent, near the lands of Lewis Watson, first Earl Rockingham, for whom he was named. Still young when his father (an attorney) died, Theobald had the good fortune to have Lord Rockingham take an interest in his education. He accompanied Rockingham's son in a remarkably fine liberal education at a private school and proved to be precocious in his own way, taking advantage of his studies to become such an exceptional classical scholar that, however bold his future enemies, they hesitated to attack him in this field.

Theobald took a career in law which, though probably never aban-doned, was second to his interest in ancient and modern literature, particularly drama. By the age of twenty, he had published a book of (horribly written) Pindaric odes, had a play performed at Drury Lane, and had moved to London where, like other young hopefuls, he managed a living by doing hackwork — biographies, prologues, poems, essays, most of which tended to be respectable pieces with modest success but little distinction. In 1713, he entered a contract to translate Plato's *Phaedo*, the next two years following with published translations of Sophocles and Aristophanes. During this time he wrote a periodical, *The Censor* (pat-terned after *The Spectator* and began an association with the theater owner-producer-manager, John Rich, which was to give Theobald much experience in the stage. He helped in the preparation of operas and pantomimes, supplied as much as a third of Rich's repertory verse, and was involved in the composition of a number of plays. His strong interest in literature continued unabated, however, in his labors over a complete translation of Aeschylus and in a study of Shakespeare which resulted in an imitative poem, *The Cave of Poverty* (1715) and a fairly successful adaptation of *Richard II*. It was Pope's edition of Shakespeare, published in 1725, which was to provoke a reaction from Theobald greatly affecting his future life and reputation.

In the publishing practices of the early eighteenth century, a famous poet would often be asked to edit the works of a previous poet that the fame of both would aid in the sale of the edition. Usually, the "editing" was little more than correcting textual errors by assumption and rewriting passages to the taste of the time. Alexander Pope, asked to edit Shakespeare for the usual reason, accepted the task with neither the method nor the ability to do so effectively. Theobald, on the other hand, was knowledgeable of the advances in textual criticism achieved by the classical scholar, Richard Bentley, who had combined a wide comprehension of languages with a careful, logical comparison of texts to produce more accurate and more understandable editions of the classic authors. Furthermore, Theobald had a familiarity with Shakespeare exceptional for the period, as well as experience with the stage, neither or which had Pope.

The year after Pope's edition, Theobald demonstrated his knowledge by publishing *Shakespeare Restored,* a volume correcting the large number of errors resulting from the utter carelessness of Pope's editing, a style of editing, we should remember, common at that time. There is no reason to believe that Theobald had any enmity toward Pope, but Pope reacted with characteristic vindictiveness by leading an attack upon Theobald's works and reputation culminating with Theobald being condemned as the King Dunce of the first *Dunciad* (1728). Though he had answered the relatively vicious attacks with explanations and charges of his own, the appearance of the *Dunciad* led Theobald to decide to let his own edition of Shakespeare vindicate him.

1730 brought Eusden's death and a vacancy in the poet-laureateship which had been a sinecure for bad poets for several years. Theobald sought the doubtful honor because he was never financially secure and the guaranteed income would allow him to devote himself more to his scholarly studies. The post, however, went to Colly Cibber and this affable but incompetent scribbler later replaced Theobald as the King Dunce of the *Dunciad* (1743). After a number of delays, Theobald's edition of Shakespeare was published in 1734, demonstrating his reputation as a scholar by attracting many publishers (Pope's own, Jacob Tonson, outbidding the rest) and an impressive list of subscribers. Theobald's Shakespeare went through at least nine editions during the eighteenth century and later editors adopted his methods.

When Theobald died in 1744, he had a fairly sound reputation as a scholar, but the image of the Dunce clung to him nevertheless. Pope, the leading poet of the age (ironically born and buried the same year as Theobald), was so thorough in his derogation of Theobald that the same editors (Samuel Johnson among them) who used Theobald's method and scholarship continued to think of him as Pope's dull pedant. It was not until the mid-nineteenth century that his accomplishments were recognized. Then, the false image surrounding Theobald was first exposed in Professor T.R. Lounsbury's *The First Editors of Shakespeare* (1906), and he was fully vindicated in R.G. Jones's *Lewis Theobald* (1919). Today, Theobald's accomplishments as a textual critic are finally respected as such.

Lovecraft's use of Theobald's name leads to an interesting comparison of the two. Both lost their fathers at an early age, and both earned a living doing other than what they would have preferred: Theobald as a lawyer, Lovecraft as a ghost writer. Both supplemented their incomes by writing successfully in a medium of lesser distinction. Theobald probably made most from writing "pantomimes" (eighteenth-century verbal burlesques unrelated to classic mime) considered as vulgar a form as they were popular. Lovecraft published ninety percent of his fiction in a pulp magazine, *Weird Tales*. Both wrote a great deal of material for ephemeral publications and Theobald, though not so much as Lovecraft, was also involved in revision work.

It is questionable whether Lovecraft knew of these comparisons when he chose the name as a pseudonym. The more detailed biographical information as researched by Lounsbury appeared in a rather specialized volume, and Jones's comprehensive book was published at least three years after Lovecraft adopted the name. The subtitle to Lounsbury's book indicates that his subjects were Theobald and Pope, and perhaps the sight of the full title would have drawn Lovecraft to investigate further. But there is no evidence and the matter will probably have to rest as is.

But there is little question that Lovecraft must have first met Theobald in Pope's *Dunciad,* and that this would have given him sufficient note of Theobald's image. Lovecraft states that he had made a "close study" of the poem (*Something About Cats,* p. 254) which he calls one of his "prime favourites" *(Selected Letters,* I, 72). In either of the two versions of the poem, Lovecraft could have read Pope's note that Theobald was "the Author of some forgotten Plays, Translations, and other pieces," and in the first version Theobald is described as the King Dunce sitting supperless and studiously amidst a hoard of books (I, 109–11).

Given Lovecraft's eighteenth century predilections, it is understandable that some of his pseudonyms would have been chosen from this period. Lewis Theobald lived during the Augustan era of English life and letters so admired by Lovecraft. But he had the added qualification, perhaps, of being reputed to be a dull writer.

When Lovecraft signed the name "Edward Softly" to several of his poems, he knowingly used the name of the tasteless poet (in Addison's *Tattler 163*) who compensated for a lack of poetic genius by devoting himself to outdated standards. By using this name, Lovecraft was identifying some of the faults he knew to be in his own poetry. Similarly, there may have been some self-criticism in his choosing to become Theobald,

by R. Boerem   37 junior, the twentieth-century writer of forgotten works. The use of such deflating pseudonyms as "Humphrey Littlewit," "Edward Softly," and "Lewis Theobald" permitted Lovecraft to demonstrate, perhaps, a lack of pretense about his work.

The description of Theobald as supperless, studious, and sitting amidst books certainly must have struck a note of familiarity to a man who ate irregularly, possessed wide erudition, and had a study full of books (of the photograph of Lovecraft's study in *Marginalia*). That Lovecraft may have taken Pope's description of Theobald to be a caricature of himself may account for Lovecraft's continuing identification with Theobald.

Thus, Lewis Theobald had three characteristics which would seem to have made his name attractive as a Lovecraftian pseudonym: he was a man of letters in the early eighteenth century; he was described as unsuccessful and dull; he was pictured in an image that Lovecraft could relate, however humorously, to his own. Though most of his friends and readers probably never recognized it, Lovecraft had adopted the name of the "first" Lewis Theobald.

STORY-WRITING: A Letter

from H.P. Lovecraft

66 College St.,
Providence, R.I.,
Oct. 4, 1935

Dear Mr. Perry:

I found your card of Sept. 5 awaiting me upon my return from an absence of 3-1/2 months — & such was the engulfing pressure of piled-up work that I have not until now been able to acknowledge it. Your wish to cite my methods of story-writing in the *Fantasy* article gives me a very flattered feeling, & I trust the ensuing remarks may not arrive too late to be of any use.

In a way, it is impossible for me to give a detailed account of how I write a story — from the moment of conception till it is sent out to gain one of Wright's rejection slips — since I've scarcely ever used the same method for any two stories. It all depends on the individual circumstances.

The one thing I never do is sit down & seize a pen with the deliberate intention of writing a story. Nothing but hack work ever comes of that. The only stories I write are those whose central ideas, pictures, & moods occur to me spontaneously — beforehand — & virtually demand formulation and expression.

These ideas, pictures, & moods come from every possible source — dreams, reading, daily occurrences, odd visual glimpses, or origins so remote & fragmentary that I cannot place them. Naturally, they come in different stages of development — sometimes a bare incident, effect, concept, or shade of feeling which requires a whole fabric of deliberate story-construction to support it, & sometimes a sequence of incidents which forms a goodly part of the final story. . . . One story I wholly dreamed, "The Statement of Randolph Carter" being a literal recording of what sleep brought me one night in December 1919.

If there is any one method which I follow, I suppose it is to be found by taking an average of my lines of procedure in all cases where I have done a great deal of deliberate construction. For example — behind "The

Whisperer in Darkness" were two initial impelling concepts: the idea of a man in a lonely farmhouse besieged by "outside" horrors, & the general impression of weirdness in the Vermont landscape, gained during a fortnight's visit near Brattleboro in 1928. Upon these notions I had to build a story — & in doing that I followed a course which may or may not be typical. Here, then, is a rough idea of what I did in that case — & what I do more or less in similar cases.

First, a coherent story — or a rough approximation of one — must be thought out. This is a mental process, before pen & paper are approached. It is not often necessary to fill in details, or even to carry the plot forward to a definite end. The point is to think up some sort of definite series of developments which shall give the initial concept or concepts a plausible reason for existing, & make it or them appear to be that logical, inevitable outgrowth of some vital & convincing background. This "plot" or series of steps need not be a permanent one. Perhaps it will lose all its salient points during later manipulation — other & better ways of accounting for the central idea being discovered. But it is a useful starting point — something to work with & build upon. When it has attained some definite shape in one's head, the time has come to turn to writing materials.

Yet even the second — or first recorded — stage is not that of actual storywriting. Instead, one had better begin with a synopsis of the given plot — listing all developments *in order of their supposed actual occurrence,* not the order in which they will finally reach the reader. This is to provide a logical working background for the writer, so that he can envisage his plot as something which has really happened, & decide at leisure on what narrative devices to adopt in preparing a dramatic, suspense-filled version for the reader. In writing such a synopsis I try to describe everything with enough fullness to cover all vital points & motivate all the incidents planned. Details, comments, & estimates of the *consequences* of certain points are often desirable. The result is rather like an official report of some chain of happenings — each event set prosaically in precise order of occurrence. Often the previously-planned plot will suffer great changes in the course of this recording.

Then comes the next stage — deciding *how to tell* the story already thought out. This begins mentally — by thinking of various effective ways to arrange certain unfoldings and revelations. We speculate on what to tell first & what to save for later presentation in order to preserve suspense or provoke interest. We analyse the dramatic value of putting this thing before that thing, or vice versa, & try to see what selection of details & order of narration best conduce to that rising tide of development & final burst of revealing completion which we call "climax." Having roughly made our decisions regarding a tentative arrangement, we proceed to write these down in the form of a *second synopsis* — a synopsis or "scenario" of events *in order of their narration to the reader,* with ample fullness & detail, & ultimate climax. I never hesitate to change the original synopsis to fit some newly devised developments if such a devising can increase the dramatic force or general effectiveness of the future story. Incidents should be interpolated or deleted at will — the writer never being bound by his original conception, even though the ultimate result be a tale wholly different from that first planned. The wise author lets additions & alterations be made whenever such are suggested by anything in the formulating process.

The time has now come *to write the story* in the approximate language the reader is to see. The first draught should be written rapidly, fluently, & not too critically, following the second synopsis. I always change incidents and plot whenever the developing process seems to suggest such change — never being bound by any previous design. If the development suddenly reveals new opportunities for dramatic effect or vivid story-telling, I add whatever I think advantageous — going back & reconciling early points to the new plan. I insert or delete whole sections when I deem it necessary or desirable — trying different beginnings & endings till the best is found. But I always take infinite pains to make sure that all references throughout the story are thoroughly reconciled with the final design. Then — in completing the rough draught — I seek to remove all possible superfluities — words, sentences, paragraphs, or whole episodes or elements — observing the usual precautions about the reconciliation of all references. So open-minded do I keep during this stage of writing, that several of my tales (such as "The Picture in the House," "The Dunwich Horror," & "The Shadow Over Innsmouth") end in a manner totally unforeseen when I began them.

Now comes the *revision* — a tedious, painstaking process. One must go over the entire job, paying attention to vocabulary, syntax, rhythm of prose, proportioning of parts, niceties of tone, grace & convincingness of *transitions* (scene to scene, slow & detailed action to rapid and sketchy time-covering action and vice versa . . .), effectiveness of beginning, ending, dramatic suspense & interest, plausibility & atmosphere, & various other elements. That finishes the story — & the rest is merely the preparation of a neatly typed version . . . the most horrible part of all for me. I detest the typewriter, & could not possibly compose a story on one. The mechanical limitations of the machine are death to good style anyway — it is harder to transpose words and make the necessary complex interlineations when bound to keys and rollers, while delicate prose rhythms are defeated by the irrelevant regular rhythms of line-endings & roller-turnings. Nothing was ever composed on a typewriter which could not have been composed better with pen or pencil.

Well — as I have said, this list of composition steps is merely an average or idealized one. In practice, one seldom follows every step literally. Often one or more of the things supposed to be done on paper can better be done in one's head — so that many tales (such as my "Music of Erich Zann" or "Dagon") never had any kind of written synopsis.

Nor should the given method be followed even mentally in some cases. Sometimes I have found it useful to begin writing a story without either a synopsis or even a bare idea of how it shall be developed & ended. This is when I feel a need of recording & exploiting some especially powerful or suggestive mood or picture to the full — as in "The Strange High House in the Mist." In such a procedure the beginning thus produced may be regarded as a problem to be motivated & explained. Of course, in developing this motivation & explanation it may be well to alter — or even transform, transpose beyond recognition, or altogether eliminate — the beginning first produced. Once in a while, when a writer has a marked style with rhythms & cadences closely linked with imaginative associations, it is possible for him to begin *weaving a mood* with characteristic paragraphs & letting this mood dictate much of the tale. This is what I did with "The White Ship" — though it must be moved that the result was not very successful.

I try always to keep a supply of story-ideas on hand — recording all bizarre notions, moods, dreams, images, concepts, etc., (& keeping all press clippings involving such) for future use. I do not despair if they seem to have no logical development. Each one may be worked over gradually — surrounded with notes & synopses, & finally built into a coherent explanatory structure capable of fictional use. I never hurry, nor seek to emulate the commercial writers who boast of their wordage per day or week. The best stories sometimes grow very slowly — over long periods, & with intervals in their formulation. *Too long* intervals, though, are to be discouraged; insomuch as they often alienate the writer from the mood and tempo of his task.

Random notes: In a tale involving complex philosophical or scientific principles, I try to have all explanations *hinted* at the outset, when the thesis is first put forward (as in Machen's "White People"), thus leaving the narrative & climactic sections unencumbered.

I am always willing to spend as much time & care on the formulation of a synopsis as on the writing of the actual tale — *for its synopsis is the real heart of the story*. The real creative work of fiction-writing is originating & shaping a story in synopsis form.

In order to ensure an adequate climax it is in rare cases advisable to prepare one in considerable detail *first,* & then construct a main synopsis explaining it. I followed this plan in "The Tree," "The Hound," & other minor pieces. With one it works less satisfactorily than with others.

I always endeavor to read & analyze the best weird writers — Poe, Machen, Blackwood, James, Dunsany, de la Mare, Benson, Wakefield, Ewers, & the like — seeking to understand their methods & recognize the specific laws of emotional modulation behind their potent effects. Such study gradually increases one's own grasp of his materials, & strengthens his powers of expression. By the same token, I strive to avoid all close attention to the prose & methods of pulp hack writers — things which insidiously corrupt & cheapen a serious style. I would advise all serious literary aspirants to cultivate a sort of defensive semi-blindness in skimming cheap magazine fiction — development an ability to sift out incidents & follow a plot without closely paying attention to the language. And most plots of this sort had better be followed very lightly & emulated not at all. In a year's output of pulp magazines there are scarcely a dozen stories seriously conceived & artistically written to an extent justifying remembrance, preservation, or imitation. The genuine writer must forget editors & possible audiences, resign himself to very infrequent sales, & labour only to, express himself & satisfy his own inward standards of fiction. Commercialism & decent literature have no meeting-point except by accident.

And so it goes. I don't know whether any of this meandering will be of use to you, but it's the best I can provide amidst my present rush of work. Use it as you like, & let me know if there are any other points which you'd like to have covered. Hope my rotten handwriting isn't giving you too much trouble — ought to type this, but I simply haven't the energy to spare. If you wish to make any extended quotations, you might want to send the final Ms. to me — leaving blank spaces for the words you cannot decipher. I'll then go over the text, supplying the absent words & straightening out all the difficulties as best I can. But perhaps this arrives so late that you will not be able to use it at all.

No — I have no accepted stories awaiting publication in *WT* or any other professional sheet. *WT* has gone detective, & for a long time Wright has been hostile toward my Mss. He says my stories are *too long* — & then proceeds to accept some interminable serial by one of his regular hacks! There's no use trying to land anything with an editor who frankly caters to illiterates. I haven't submitted any Ms. to Wright for two years . . . although stories which I have "ghost-written" for various clients have occasionally appeared. If you'd care to see any of my recent work, I'll lend you Mss. Most of it is probably destined to remain in manuscript form!

With best wishes for your coming series, & apologies for this late response to your card, I remain

Yrs most cordially & sincerely,

H.P. Lovecraft

CHARACTER GULLIBILITY IN WEIRD FICTION

or, Isn't Yuggoth Somewhere in Upstate New York?

by Darrell Schweitzer

How many times have you, a seasoned fantasy reader, encountered a tale which runs something like this? Theobald Q. Protagonist, a scholarly recluse from Rhode Island, discovers to his great dismay that reclusing isn't as lucrative a business as he had though it to be, and, in order to stave off total bankruptcy, he accepts a mysterious offer from the governing council of the remote village of Hokum, Massachusetts, whereby he is to occupy a deserted and disreputable farmhouse on the edge of town. Nothing else is required of him, and to induce him further, the council will *pay* him twenty-five dollars a month for his efforts. As he gets off the train in Hokum he meets a degenerate-looking old man who says, "Sonny, ye're dad-blamed foolish. Nobody thet ain't out of his gourd would stay in *that house,* not after what happened back in the winter of '28." The old man then shuffles off, resisting all entreaties to tell more.

This doesn't discourage Theobald, however, for he knows a bargain when he sees one. He remains nonplused when he finds that the unpaved road leading up to his new abode is blocked with a crudely-lettered sign reading, "Beware of Monster." Likewise, when he walks along this road and encounters a strange hunchback with a *cloven head* he merely makes a mental note to donate something to the March of Dimes next year.

He has only dwelt in the farmhouse one night when he hears horrible animal screams coming from the barn. Grabbing a flashlight, he runs out to investigate and is shocked to discover the bodies of twelve cows, their spines all tied into neat sailor knots. This is even more remarkable because Theobald Q. doesn't own any cows, but still he dismisses it as the work of vandals and returns to bed.

The next night he hears eerie chanting and looks out the window to see a couple hundred hooded figures holding some sort of orgiastic ceremony in his back yard, This, he decides, is too much. He tries to call the cops, but the line is dead. A quick investigation reveals that the telephone cable has not been cut; it has been *gnawed.* So Theobald makes a note to summon a repairman in the morning and retires, after first spending some time perusing the ancient and moldering tomes with which these houses always seem to be equipped. He is disturbed by what he has read. Something decidedly strange is going on, he concludes.

The next morning he discovers the entire house is enveloped in a pulsating mass of green slime which seems to be mumbling, "Yog Sothoth . . . dada . . . googoo . . . dada . . . Yog Sothoth. . . ." Yog Sothoth is the name of a legendary creature he read about in one of the books. However, more immediate things are to be dealt with, such as the slime, about which he can only remark, "Why can't those d——d Ku Kluxers learn not to put yeast in the lime-flavored jello? And who said they could have a picnic on my property anyway?" But, not wishing to offend the local people before he gets to know them better, he merely endeavors to extricate himself from the mess, which he still believes to be lime-flavored jello. He gets a spoon and tries to eat his way out. It tastes funny. Suddenly the spoon, and his right arm, dissolve. "You taste funny," the green slime gibbers. And the hero meets his unmentionable doom.

I would guess that by the time the veteran reader is a third of the way through this epic, he will have gotten the impression that its hero is remarkably *thick*. By the time the reader gets halfway through he's on the verge of screaming, "The monsters did it, you dolt! *They* tied up the cows like pretzels!" And by the time the protagonist reads the *Necronomicon* (a book which, despite its rarity, always seems to turn up) and he still doesn't grasp what's going on, the reader must be ready to give up in disgust.

Yet there is nothing wrong with the character's disbelief. I would say that there is a lot *right* with it. Probably the only unlikely thing in the whole story is the matter of the spoon. I don't think an unspeakable being from some vast alien cosmos would be sufficiently susceptible to our natural laws to be eaten that way. Otherwise, it all works. What the jaded reader and especially the lazy writer, who wants to hurry up so he can get to the delicious (and obligatory) Doom Scene, fail to realize is that the characters in a story are supposed to be living in the "real" world. Also, they probably don't read fantasy fiction, and thus they can't predict the outcome of a situation like this so easily. When it becomes obvious that the monster did it and the hero is a dummy, stop and think for a minute: In the real world there are no such things as monsters. If inexplicable events happened and someone were to proclaim, "Aha! the purple toad men of Valusia are responsible!" *before* having exhausted every possible natural explanation, no matter how remote, the person making such claims would be promptly escorted to the booby hatch, leaving the Valusian toad men to do whatever they pleased.

H.P. Lovecraft was one of the few people to realize that the weird story has to be crafted with a certain amount of subtlety, and that the characters therein must be realistic. In fantasy, a realistic character often seems stupid. HPL's "Dreams in the Witch House" has often been unjustly criticized for the imbecility of its protagonist. The critic has probably read the story either in a fantasy magazine or a collection of Lovecraft stories, so in context he knows that the improbably elements in these stories always turn out to be real. Walter Gilman, on the other hand, is supposed to be living in the "real" world where things like Brown Jenkin are beyond the range of normal experience. Gilman *knows* that they are impossible. The human mind is a stubborn thing, and when it is convinced of something, it isn't always dissuaded by mere proof. I find Gilman's attempt to rationalize the whole thing off as a dream perfectly believable, even when he finds himself with physical evidence to the contrary. He does what any normal, sane person would do.

This then is the major drawback of most horror fiction, the conflict between what the reader knows and what the characters can believably know. Unless all heroes are occult detectives, we cannot expect them to readily accept the fact that the laws of existence have been violated. In too many modern Cthulhu Mythos stories the heroes accept everything far too soon, almost without resistance (so much for the shattering of minds), as if they have already read all the other Mythos stories written and are aware of the rules.

There is a fine line that must be maintained here. Even Lovecraft failed a couple of times, by attempting to carry this supernatural-story device into science fiction. *At the Mountains of Madness* is a fine example of how it can go wrong. The novella is about extra-terrestrial beings, and this isn't exactly an inconceivable concept. The possibility was being considered even when Lovecraft wrote. It is exciting, yes, but not exactly the sort of thing to violate all knowledge and reason. Therefore, once the characters have discovered an alien city and perfectly preserved specimens of its inhabitants, it isn't much of a mental leap to accept the fact that the creatures are still alive, especially when the specimens start disappearing, dogs are found mutilated, etc. In this case Danforth and company really *are* dense. It is true that characters in science fiction stories can't be expected to read science fiction, but then again we're not dealing with the *unknowable,* because the whole purpose of the SF story is to make unlikely things understandable.

Fortunately there is little difficulty of this sort in modern/line science fiction. The only case of an incomprehensible phenomenon in recent years has been Stanislaw Lem's *Solaris,* but even there the characters behave believably and arrive at sensible conclusions. Probably the reason for this is that few modern SF writers have any background in weird/horror fiction, and the matter just never occurred to them. Science fiction is about the knowable; weird fiction is about the unknowable. Even Lovecraft ran into trouble when he treated one as the other. But today's would-be Lovecrafts must learn not to make their characters accept too much too soon, in a manner similar to the detective who seems to be in telepathic contact with the criminal. In either case you don't get very much suspense.

SOME THOUGHTS ON LOVECRAFT

by Arthur Jean Cox

1.

"Lovecraft was not a good writer." This blunt judgment by Edmund Wilson in his *New Yorker* essay, "Tales of the Marvelous and the Ridiculous," has lodged itself, like an inextricable and uncomfortable foreign object, in the body of Lovecraftian discussion. "One of Lovecraft's worst faults," says Wilson, "is his incessant effort to work up the expectations of the reader by sprinkling his stories" with certain adjectives, of which he gives a long-enough list but to which we might nevertheless add two more, "eldritch" and "unutterable." He goes on to say, "Surely one of the primary rules for writing an effective tale of horror is never to use any of these words. . . . I happened to read a horror story by Mérimée, "La Vénus d'Ile," just after I had been investigating Lovecraft, and was relieved to find it narrated — though it was almost as fantastic as Lovecraft — with the prosaic objectivity of an anecdote of travel."[1] *

All this is true, but it is not enough. Any criticism of Lovecraft, after making these observations, should go on to note that his stories are, for the most part, carefully written, and that their objectionable qualities — the over-loaded and too-insistent adjectives, the ludicrous touches which don't quite make us laugh, the italicized last sentences — are not so much lapses as intentional literary devices. Lovecraft is not nodding when he writes them. Rather, he is deliberately employing the jargon and stilted mannerisms of a kind of writing so specialized as to be almost his personal creation, his task and pleasure being the extension and elaboration of a few conventions (that is, phrases, characters, settings, and ideas repeated from story to story) into a self-conscious *genre* or tradition. He means these words, such as Wilson particularized, these phrases and ideas, to be loved and relished for their own sakes. Judged seriously, they must be considered faults of taste; but Lovecraft did not mean for them to be judged seriously — an observation which we make not from motives of

---

* Superscript numbers refer to notes that have been placed at the end of this chapter.

charity but in the interests of accuracy. The element of *play* is very prominent in any Lovecraft story, much more so than in any similar narrative by Mérimée (or by Poe, whom Wilson almost mentions); and it is to this element that his many admirers and friends have most happily responded, some of them taking up its most elaborate manifestation, the "Cthulhu Mythos," and adding their own fancies and conceits.

Perhaps that is why, judging by the testimony of my own nerves, there is little real horror in any of Lovecraft's fiction (apart from a moment here and there, such as in "The Color Out of Space"). Horror is constantly touched upon but it is conventionalized and sentimentalized. If we make the expected comparison with Kafka, we cannot help but see that Kafka is disturbing where Lovecraft is not — "The Metamorphosis" causes anxiety, and nothing in Lovecraft ever does that. In fact, it is when we think of Kafka that we recognize that Lovecraft's work is somehow comforting and cozy. He is (to let the thought take another step) an ideal writer for those who dread terror, metaphysical and moral terror; for he evokes fear but playfully renders it harmless. If his stories were truly horrifying, it is probable that they wouldn't be very popular — at least, not with many who are now his most ardent admirers.

<h2 style="text-align:center">2.</h2>

Why do certain of Lovecraft's phrases *almost* make us laugh? It is because they are incongruous with the rest of the writing, especially in the shorter pieces. They don't matter much in a story like "Pickman's Model," where the submerged humor lies closer to the surface, but "Cool Air," for instance, would have been more effectively developed with such expressions omitted. "Fled screaming and mad-eyed" — that raises an embarrassed smile, because the circumstantiality with which the story is otherwise told creates a prosaic realism not in keeping with the hollow solemnity of the phrase. Why don't we actually laugh? Because the incongruity is not great enough: we have been forewarned by various hints. What these little shocks and jars mean is that the stories are marred by the author's wish to graft them onto a literary tradition narrower than that to which they might freely belong.

This disadvantage does not weigh so heavily on some of the longer stories, such as those of the Cthulhu Mythos, which are his most popular productions and form the main grounds of his reputation. In "The Call of Cthulhu," for instance, the writing is of a piece with the whole conception. The expressions and touches embody the same spirit as the general story-line and atmosphere, and the resultant lack of any embarrassment or inhibition — in other words, of any internal retardation in the writing — makes possible, in the climatic scene, its peculiar tone of abstract exultation. The emergence of Cthulhu from his slimy lair, "ravening for delight," is a triumph of excess.[2]

However, in some of the later and still longer works, such as "The Whisperer in Darkness," "The Shadow Out of Time," and *At the Moun-*

tains of Madness — this last being, I think, his masterpiece — the Cthulhu mythology, far from justifying and liberating the style and story-- movement, becomes itself obstructive. The buzzing cry of *"Iä! Shub- Niggurath! The Black Goat of the Woods with a Thousand Young!"* is completely irrelevant to "The Whisperer in Darkness." It is an interjec- tion, whose only function is to connect the story with those of the Cthulhu series. The natural development of the later fiction would seem to be away from this pantheon of ungainly gods and in the direction of something recognizable as science fiction. The author, anyway, must have been keenly conscious that these later stories are most effective precisely where they are unambiguously naturalistic: and we might speculate, as Fritz Leiber once speculated,[3] that Lovecraft by this time would have liked to give up the Cthulhu tradition, or at least to adapt it to new purposes. There is more than one hint of this, such as the reference in "The Whisperer in Darkness," to "that nuclear chaos beyond angled space which the *Necronomicon* had mercifully cloaked under the name of Azathoth,"[4] suggesting that he was tempted by the possibility of translat- ing the Cthulhu lexicon into a quasi-scientific vocabulary. But I think he would have found it very hard to give up the mythology he had created, or to seriously alter it. It would have seemed an act of disloyalty, perhaps to the past and certainly to that circle of friends who had so elaborately and admiringly followed his example. This may be one of the reasons why he wrote so little during the last two or three years of his life.

3.

If we glance in the direction of the general dramatic character of the stories, what do we see? We see a desire for a protective enclosure (an enclave of any sort: a well of houses, a New England town, a familiar rustic countryside) troubled by a fear that the enclosure will be disturbed by something from the outside. This is particularly so of the longer stories, but we see it in at least one of the shorter, "The Music of Erich Zann." In most of the shorter tales, though, the valence is reversed: the enclosure is small, confining, oppressive, and there is a longing for the freedom outside, as "In the Vault," "The Outsider," "The Picture in the House," and such variations as "Pickman's Model" (with its fear of subways and cellars) and "Cool Air." Roughly, in the longer stories the horror consists of a familiar and comfortably home-like world, usually the Arkham country, penetrated by awesome forces from Outside — forces made terrible by their destructiveness and horrible by their association with family and race degeneracy and with madness.

But it will be noted that the settings of these longer stories are not unqualifiedly loved. This is partly because, in their vulnerability, they are "shadowed," and partly because there is not enough to them — that is, the environment is insufficiently supportive. The New England country- side and towns have beauty but are pathetically subject to decay. They have a past and therefore a prideful antiquarian and historical interest,

by Arthur Jean Cox   49 but no future. There is some comfort in them but no encouragement. They are not enough . . . but what else is there? The only presented alternative is the forces from the Outside. These forces, though ostensibly fearful, are nevertheless attractive. When the supposed Henry Akeley, in "The Whisperer in Darkness," writes exultingly of his old conversion to sympathy with the visitors from Yuggoth, the narrator comments, " . . . I felt myself touched by the contagion of the morbid barrier-breaking. To shake off the maddening and weary limitations of time and space and natural law . . . surely such a thing was worth the risk of one's life, soul and sanity!"[5] Surely . . . but, still, the temptation is resisted. The forces from Outside, with their "utter annihilation in the chaos that transcends form and force and symmetry" (p. 262) are absolutely destructive of everything. The lavish particularity of the story is perhaps not only a necessary complement of this abstractness but also an anxious clinging to the skirts of actuality.

The natural tendency of any growing body of literary work (to lay down one of my basic critical assumptions) is in the direction of the working out of the basic contraries of the fiction, which, if it is ever successfully done at all, is usually done by way of a transcendence: that is, the characteristic opposites in the writer's work are finally seen as parts of a larger unity. It is curious to consider what this working out might have been like in the present case, if there had been more of the stories. I think we see in "The Shadow Out of Time" one of the latest of the stories and surely one of the best, a foreshadowing of how this resolution might have been worked. Here, there is no inside or Outside — except in the sense in which the narrator uses the latter work when, remarking that "there is nothing whatever of the mad or sinister in my heredity and early life,"[6] he insists that the shadow which fell so suddenly upon him came "from *outside* sources" (the emphasis of course being his). For the first time, the other world — that other world which has so threateningly lurked in the offing previous stories; the world of the Great Race in the present instance — is metaphysically identical with this one: it is discovered to be continuous with this one and just as solid. In other words, the Alien has been admitted and the world hasn't fallen to pieces. And for the first time there is a future; though, unfortunately, not an open future but one as congealed and fated as the past.

4.

We might now risk some connecting of the literary character, the dramatic character, of the stories with the personal character of the man whose named is signed to them.

Our first guess would be that he conservatively sought a resigned security as a precaution against the pressure of some inward wildness, which he thought would destroy his world if it should ever slip through unguardedly — possibly thinking that it was a premonitory hint of that madness which had infected his parents, when, poor fellow, it was most likely nothing more than a natural desire for release from some internal constraint.

More fully and accurately, the situation looks like this: something has blocked up the prospect. There is no future, no possibility of open and unlimited development. So the man allows himself only modest ambitions, the writer falls back upon regionalism and a slight literary mode. But his animal spirits are too great for such a restrictive way of life — look again at those photographs of the bouncing baby Lovecraft and his parents, which seem to me among the saddest family pictures ever published — and so a "wildness" constantly threatens the domestication, a wildness which is of course identified by the more deliberate self with whatever it is that has darkened the prospect. So even the resignation is not safe. It is pressured by energies that are feared because they are dangerous and which are yet attractive because they promise release from the self-imprisonment: they are partly submitted to and welcomed. The curious result is a writer who is both resigned and fatalistic (most writers, and most men, being merely one or the other). Life, viewed from such a position, cannot be completely serious and yet it is grim; which, we may observe, is an ideal philosophy for a writer of melodrama, but hardly a happy one for a man.

But these remarks must be qualified by our observations above on "The Shadow Out of Time," which suggest how close Lovecraft had come to accepting the "forces from outside" as his own and to recognizing that they would not destroy his world if he allowed them expression.

NOTES:

[1] *Classics and Commercials: A Literary Chronicle of the Forties* (New York: Farrar, Straus, 1950), p. 288–89.

[2] I make a few remarks, from a different standpoint, on this story in "The Call of Nature: A Note on 'The Call of Cthulhu' by Howard Phillips Lovecraft" in *Science Fiction Review* no. 40 (October, 1970), p. 35.

[3] In a letter in *Fantasy Commentator*, I (Summer, 1945), p. 163.

[4] *The Dunwich Horror and Others* (Sauk City, Wis.: Arkham House, 1963), p. 262.

[5] *Ibid.*, p. 248–49.

[6] *Ibid.*, p. 371.

THE DERLETH MYTHOS

by Richard L. Tierney

The "Cthulhu Mythos" is largely the invention of, not H.P. Lovecraft, but August Derleth.

Lovecraft, of course, did the groundwork. He invented most of the gods, demons, and servitors — and, above all, he provided the spooky, Gothic atmosphere necessary to the genre. Yet it seems to me that it was Derleth who established the concept of a "Mythos" to comprehend all the Lovecraftian concepts.

Lovecraft himself seems never to have entertained such a concept. His outlook on the supernatural and the cosmos seems to have been basically dynamic — it was constantly developing throughout his life. Derleth's attitude on the other hand was large static; he appreciated Lovecraft's concepts but cared more for systematizing them. His efforts were interesting but less than successful from an aesthetic point of view. This is not to say that Derleth was unaesthetic but merely that, in my opinion, his basic outlook was non-Lovecraftian and his attempt to carry on the Lovecraft tradition left out something vital.

Derleth probably coined the term "Cthulhu Mythos." If he did not, he certainly developed the attitude that goes with that term. Consider the basic premises of the "Mythos": a cosmic cluster of "good guys" (Elder Gods) protecting the human race from the "bad guys" (Ancient Old Ones) who are striving to do us (humanity) in! Derleth maintains that this is all a parallel of the "Christian Mythos," with its bad against good, and with humanity the focal point of it all. Evil Ancient Ones are striving to take our planet from us, but angelic Elder Gods always intervene in time to save us.

I grant Derleth the right to his view of the cosmos, but the sad thing is that he has made all too many believe that his view is that of Lovecraft also. This is simply not true. Lovecraft's picture of the universe and Derleth's are completely dissimilar.

Derleth seems determined to link the Cthulhu pantheon with Christianity and the medieval tradition by making it a struggle between "good" and "evil" from an anthropocentric point of view. Too, the concept of "elemental forces" in the Mythos seems to be Derleth's own — borrowed from the ancient theory that all things known to us are compounded from four elements: fire, water, earth and air. Derleth runs into many contradictions here. For instance, he makes Cthulhu and his minions *water* beings, whereas "The Call of Cthulhu" has them coming down from space and building their cities on land; only later are their cities submerged by geological upheavals, and this is a catastrophe which immobilizes the Cthulhu spawn. Hastur is portrayed as an "air elemental," while at the same time Derleth implies that he lives on the bottom of the Lake of Hali. Yog Sothoth and Nyarlathotep, probably the two most purely cosmic of all Lovecraftian entities, are squeezed into the "earth" category; while, finally, he invents the fire elemental, Cthugha, to round out his menagerie of elementals. (Lovecraft invented no beings that could be construed as "fire elementals"). Cthugha comes from the star Fomalhaut — presumably because Lovecraft once mentioned that star in one of his sonnets.

Elementals aside, the whole basic concept of Derleth's "good-versus-evil" Mythos seems as non-Lovecraftian as anything conceivable. Lovecraft actually regarded the cosmos as basically indifferent to anthropocentric outlooks such as good and evil. The "shocker" in his best tales is usually the line in which the narrator is forced to recognize that there are vast and powerful forces and entities basically indifferent to man, because of their overwhelming superiority to him.

Most writers continuing the "Cthulhu Mythos" in fiction or documenting it in scholarly articles are merely perpetuating the misconceptions begun by Derleth. I feel Lovecraft reached his highest imaginative peak in the two novels, "The Shadow Out of Time" and *At the Mountains of Madness*. In both these tales, Lovecraft turned the whole universe into a haunted house, so to speak, linking the findings of modern science to the flavor of Gothic horror. In so doing, he created a type of "creepy" story that twentieth century man could continue to believe in even after the traditional trappings of cemeteries, crumbling castles, haunted mansions, etc. began to acquire the flavor or clichés. But Lovecraft's followers have never pursued this line of development. Without exception they all leave Man and his values at the center, in the Derleth tradition, and most of them even continue to use the non-HPL devices of "Elder Gods," "elementals," etc. while writing endless variations on the basic Lovecraftian themes dealing with Dunwich and Innsmouth.

To sum up, The Cthulhu Mythos as it now stands is at least as much Derleth's invention as it is HPL's. The line of Lovecraft's development remains open — no one has really taken up as yet where he left off — and it leads toward the cosmic. Yet if one wants to get to the heart of what Lovecraft felt about the cosmos, one must sidestep Derleth and his followers.

by Richard L. Tierney

GENESIS OF THE CTHULHU MYTHOS

by George Wetzel

In "Autobiography: Some Notes on a Nonentity," Lovecraft said, "About 1919 the discovery of Lord Dunsany — from whom I got the idea of the artificial pantheon and myth-background represented by 'Cthulhu,' 'Yog-Sothoth,' 'Yuggoth,' etc. — gave a vast impetus to my weird writing. . . ."

One cannot dispute that statement of the creator of the "Cthulhu Mythos" as to where the *idea* of creating them came from. But aside from the idea from Dunsany, plus emulating Dunsany's concocting exotic names by combining the phonemes of different languages, Lovecraft's Mythos owes more to Greek mythology. Lovecraft never admitted such, but the proof can be readily seen by showing said Grecian influences in his prose and poetry.

That Grecian influences run through most of his work appears startling because such instances have never before been collected and pointed out. I will further assert that beyond the suggesting of an artificial pantheon from Dunsany, the Dunsanian influence is not strong or as basic as later Lovecraft students affirm, save perhaps in a very few stories (such as "The Quest of Iranon," "The Doom That Came to Sarnath," etc.).

The Greek mythology colored the Cthulhu Mythos sometimes in subtle form (the use of Greek mythic concepts) and other times openly.

The starting-place of my theory is best begun with the data of Lovecraft's juvenile years' interest in Greek mythology.

In Lovecraft's "The Brief Autobiography of an Inconsequential Scribbler" (1919) he incorporates some lines from his poem "The Poem of Ulysses" (1897), with its plain-to-see interest in Greek literature.

In his "Idealism and Materialism," (1919) he mentions that at the age of six he first read the legends of Greece; and "That until the age of eight was a rapt devotee of the old gods, building altars to Pan and Apollo . . ." etc. During this interval he stated he believed "that the ancient (Greek) gods were true," and added that he believed he saw with his own eyes dryads, fauns, and satyrs. Of course he admitted later he saw them only in the eye of the imaginations. But the point he was making in this article was that he had as much fervor in his belief in the existence of pagan gods as a Christian for his God.

This idea was more elaborately developed in his "A Confession of Unfaith" (1922). Herein he reiterated his discovery of Hellenic myths at the age of six and adds that they were in Hawthorne's *Tanglewood Tales* and *Wonder Book*. (This latter fact strengthens another contention of mine in an earlier article that Hawthorne was one of the influences upon Lovecraft along certain lines.) Soon afterwards he read Bullfinch's *Age of Fable*.

In this same article he mentions that "The most poignant sensations of my existence are those of 1896 when I discovered the Hellenic world. . . ."

There is the evidence of Lovecraftian poetry in which the Grecian influence exists: poems like "Hellas" (1918), "Astrophobos" (1918), "To Greece" (1917), "Damon and Delia" (1918), "Monos: An Ode" (1918), "To Selene" (1919), "Myrrha and Strephon" (1919), and many, many others.

Though the above list is only a partial one of HPL's Greek-influenced poetry, it still leads to the premise that he had a "Greek period" in his creative output where poetry was concerned.

In 1920 appeared his collaboration "Poetry and the Gods," plus two other collaborations, "The Crawling Chaos" (1921) and "The Green Meadow" (1921), all of which are fantasies using the Greek mythos. There are other HPL stories containing such but for the present the above three collaborated stories are best discussed first and separately for good reasons which will shortly become apparent.

"Poetry and the Gods" (which story was not mentioned in the Laney-Evans biblio of HPL and hence was unknown to them and Derleth) was discovered by myself some time ago. Upon reading it I was immediately struck by two things. First, that it contained several germ ideas that formed parts of later Lovecraftian stories; second, that it suggested Grecian myth influences that underlaid the Cthulhu Mythos and originated the basic data of the present essay.

The germ idea of later HPL stories will be considered first.

In this story occurs this: ". . . tonight she felt the immeasurable gulf that separated her soul from all her prosaic surroundings . . . was it some greater and less explicable misplacement in Time and Space whereby she had been born too late, too early, or too far away from the haunts of her spirit ever to harmonize with the unbeautiful things of contemporary reality?"

That quoted passage has several significant ideas in it for the HPL student. First, there is the escapistic thought — which I designate the "ex oblivione" theme because of its continuous recurrence in HPL's prose and poetry and will form the topic on another future essay — the escapistic thought which in the present story is connected with a longing to return to the Golden Age of Greek mythology. This evidences again HPL's preoccupation with Grecian myth.

Then there is adumbrated HPL's "dislocation in time-and-space" theme which he used to good effect in the later "Shadow Out of Time" (1934), "He" (1925), "Dreams in the Witch House" (1932), and "The White Ship" (1919) — this last prior to it.

The "dislocation" takes place in "Poetry and the Gods" but not with the force in most of the above stories. The main character visits the Greek gods in Greece and travels backwards in time to the Golden Age, bodily it appears, even though her perception of them is through the dream state of mind. This latter condition is a curiosity and might help explain some seeming paradoxes in a few places in the Cthulhu Mythos of later stories.

Another passage of significance: "In thy yearning hast thou divined what no mortal, saving only a few whom the world reject, remembereth: *that the gods were never dead,* but only sleeping their sleep and dreaming the dreams of gods in lotus-filled Hesperian gardens beyond the golden sunset. And now draweth nigh the time of their awakening, when coldness and ugliness shall perish, and Zeus sit once more on Olympus. . . ."

Quite a few more significant sentences follow upon the heels of that last sentence, in the same paragraph, which contain more noteworthy ideas and adumbrate other later ideas in the Mythos; but for the present only the above quoted passage will be discussed.

The Greek gods in "Poetry and the Gods" were but sleeping. wrote Lovecraft; and in "The Call of Cthulhu" (1926) the chant of the Cthulhu cult followers read "In his house at R'lyeh dead Cthulhu waits dreaming." With Cthulhu in R'lyeh were the Great Old Ones, the other gods in the Mythos, who likewise were bound there under a spell and who, like the Greek gods of HPL's story, waited a time when they would be released from their thralldom at which time the world would become wild and evil.

The Cthulhu story has more antecedents in this story of Greek gods in which later HPL wrote: "This night shalt thou know . . . those dreams which the gods have through ages sent to earth to show that they are not dead. For poets are the dreamers, and in each and every age someone hath sung unknowing the message. . . ."

In "The Call of Cthulhu" ". . . the Great Old Ones spoke to the sensitive (of mankind) . . . by molding their dreams. . . ."

There are some hints of Nyarlathotep in this Greek story; that is, the function he performs as a messenger of the gods and as a herald of the earth's end are portrayed in both the prose-poem (1926) and the poem (1931) of his name.

In the Greek story there is very definitely a similar catastrophe spoken of and a similar herald of sorts whose dreams are filled with the Olympian gods' message.

There are additional minor similarities but the foregoing should suffice to make my "legal brief." The interesting point is that many later ideas in the Cthulhu Mythos came from the early "Poetry and the Gods." Mere lifting of ideas from one to the other does not dismiss the case. From everything thus far studied and essayed about of Lovecraft's stories by myself, I have found he invariably tied a number of past, unconnected stories together (see my discovery of the ghoul-changeling theme) and made them a part of the Mythos. "The Call of Cthulhu" did this for several past stories, as did "Pickman's Model" and, similarly, HPL's part of "The Challenge from Beyond" did for a number of past stories relating to his "avatar" or "psychic possession" recurrent theme.

With "Poetry and the Gods" the process seems to have been in an early rather than a later story. I do not necessarily mean a number of his are of quasi-Greek mythos. But I do mean his usual action of explaining unrelated former stories by a more elaborately informative later story happened in "Poetry and the Gods" to have occurred *preceding* later stories, and explained a certain Grecian cast not readily observable.

In "The Hound" (1922) appeared the *Necronomicon* for the first time. That book's title is Greek, further proof of the underlying Greek influences in the Cthulhu Mythos. The translation of the title into English (which Lovecraft never gave *anywhere,* not even in his separately written "History and Chronology of the *Necronomicon"*) is "Book of the Names of the Dead." This transliteration suggests — and permit the digression — some possible relationship to the Egyptian "Book of the Dead" which is composed of the funeral papyri placed in Egyptian tombs to aid the soul in its journey to their other-world (Duat) and in giving the proper answers to the judges there.

Lovecraft, in his "History of the *Necronomicon,"* states that the author of that book had visited, among other places, "The subterranean secrets of Memphis" (in Egypt), thus strengthening some relation to Egyptian ideas in the conception of the *Necronomicon.* What Lovecraft meant this book to be is not quite clear. That it was not a magic book to conjure up dreams seems certain to me, but rather a descriptive geography of the curiously commingled dream world and other-world of the dead of his Mythos. By consulting it an incautious reader could learn the whereabouts of gateways giving access to this dream and otherworld of the dead. Harley Warren, in "The Statement of Randolph Carter," carried to an unknown doom beneath a graveyard a book that was without doubt a copy of it, and met the guardians of such a gate there.

But where is the Greek influence in this concept of a dream and otherworld of the dead? First, consider this from *The Dream-Quest of Unknown Kadath,* that King Kuranes "could not go back to these things in the waking world because his body was dead." The soul of a dead man dwelt in this dream-world, thus it must be in some fashion also the afterworld of the dead. And, consider this from that same novel when the main character ascends to the crag of the ghouls and realized "that he was probably nearer the waking world than at any other time since . . ." The ghouls inhabited the nameless regions below the graveyards according to "Pickman's Model," "The Outsider," and "The Statement of Randolph Carter."

That through such regions gateways to this dream-world were found might be further proved by the lines in Lovecraft's poem "Nemesis" (1918): "Through the ghoul-guarded gateways of slumber."

In Greek mythology Sleep and Death were twin gods, and on Grecian sepulchral monuments they were carved together. Lovecraft apparently found no paradox in his commingled dream and afterworld of the dead in his Mythos, having absorbed (in my opinion) the idea from Greek mythology.

Occasional gateways to it were located contiguous to physical regions of the dead — graveyards' subsurfaces — and so that a soul of a dead man might exist in this dream-world, making also a sort of afterworld.

In *The Manual of Classical Literature* by J.J. Eschenburg (1839), page 416, "The residence of departed souls was termed by the Greeks, Hades. It is important to bear in mind this fact in reading the passage of the New Testament, where this word occurs. The term, although sometimes rendered *grave* and sometimes *hell,* properly signifies the world of the departed, and includes both the place of happiness and the place of misery."

That describes rather well Lovecraft's dream-world and certain gateways to it from under graveyards besides gateways existing in different locales.

Another quote helps. *Outlines of Primitive Beliefs* by Charles Keary (1882), page 267: "The prehistoric grave mounds witness in a curious way to the prevalent notion that the grave mouth was the gate by which ghosts returned to 'walk' the earth. To prevent these apparitions men of prehistoric days had recourse to a strange practical method of exorcism. They strewed the ground at the graves's mouth with sharp stones and broken pieces of pottery, as if they thought a ghost might have his feet cut, and by fear of that be prevented from returning to his old haunts. . . . The grave becoming in this belief *ipso facto* the entrance to Hades, burial was necessary for admittance into the other world."

Continuing the thread of the above, there is Lovecraft's article "A Descent to Avernus" (1929) in which he describes his guided tour through the Endless Caverns of Virginia.

Well, to start with, Avernus is a very real place, a cave which Virgil represented as the entrance of the infernal regions. Throughout European mythic belief all very deep caves and abysses lead to Hades.

Keary wrote in his book, page 269, "But no living man ventures to the bottom of this dark valley (Hades), or if he do go he shall scarcely return. The secrets of that place are well kept. And great was of old the fear of the infernal deities, lest men should pry into their prison house. Wherefore Hades cried aloud when Poseidon was shaking the earth, lest that god should rend it asunder and disclose his mansion to the day — 'mansions dolorous fearful which the gods themselves loathe.' "

The atmosphere in "A Descent to Avernus" reads like a fragment of a Lovecraft story and may well have been such. Fearful entities or demons lived underground in stories in the Mythos, but Lovecraft more often just dwelt on nameless dread or horror of the physical underground, as in the just mentioned article. This dread formed the theme of "Mother Earth" from "A Cycle of Verse" (1919), and recurred in other works of his. The Greek god Chthonius, the god of the underground, supplies a descriptive adjective from his name, with which to label this recurrent idea of the dreadful subterranean in the Mythos, which I call "Chthonic horror."

This Chthonic horror theme is present in "A Descent." The liking of the Endless Caverns to some Avernian passage into Hades is the Greek influence again. In this same essay he speaks of lower depths beneath these Endless Caverns, which depths he describes as "awesome deeps of Tartarean-knighted horror"; Tartarus is a bit of Greek mythic geography. In Eschenburg's *Manual of Classical Literature,* page 416, it is stated: "These regions below the earth were considered as the residence of departed souls, where after death they received rewards or punishments according to their conduct upon earth. The place of reward was called Elysium; that of punishment, *Tartarus.*" Thus again other proof of the undercurrent of Greek mythic ideas in the Mythos.

This Greek belief of an Elysium and a Tartarus both underground seems the same as Lovecraft's dream world, which was entered not only in dream, or a drowned fane ("The Temple"), or abyss ("The Nameless City") but also through underground passages inhabited by diverse entities but in the main by ghouls. His dream world was both a place of pastoral beauty and "sinisterra" of evil and horrible demons and presences (similar, at once is seen, to the Greek Elysium and Tartarus which are also contiguous).

There is a trilogy of quasi-Greek stories that Lovecraft wrote; the first one, "Poetry and the Gods," has been amply discussed. Before considering their Grecian passages, their bibliographic data should be looked at, for reasons that will soon become apparent.

(1) "Poetry and the Gods" (printed 1920), by Anna Helen Crofts and Henry Paget-Lowe.

(2) "The Crawling Chaos" (printed in the *United Amateur* in 1920, according to the Laney-Evans "HPL Biblio"; printed in *The United Cooperative,* 1921, according to copyright in *Beyond the Wall of Sleep* written by Winifred V. Jackson [pseud. — Elizabeth Neville Berkeley] and H.P. Lovecraft [pseud. — Lewis Theobald, Jr.])

(3) "The Green Meadow," in *Vagrant,* in 1927, by Winifred V. Jackson (pseud. — E.N. Berkeley) and Lovecraft (pseud. — L. Theobald, Jr.).

The first question that pops into my mind is: Is Anna Helen Crofts a second alias of Winifred Jackson? Lovecraft used a second alias also on that first of the quasi-Greek mythic trilogy. It is also to be observed that the first and second stories appeared in the same year — 1920 — which just might lend some belief to my theory that Miss Jackson collaborated on the entire trilogy.

Possibly some facts of their two known collaborations might be found in the biography Lovecraft wrote, "Winifred Jackson" in *United Amateur*

XX–4, March 1921. I have not had the opportunity of perusing said biography so cannot answer authoritatively.

Nyarlathotep is not mentioned in "The Crawling Chaos," but that there is some distinct connection between that god and this story is unavoidable since Lovecraft, in *The Dream-Quest of Unknown Kadath* (1926), calls Nyarlathotep "the crawling chaos."

In the prose-poem "Nyarlathotep" (printed in the *National Amateur*, July, 1926) that god was again referred to as "the crawling chaos." It would appear that quasi-Greek mythic tale preceded these two 1926 works and would bolster my theory as to a Grecian genesis of the god. However, in all thoroughness, I'd best mention that in a chronological list of HPL's works I find I have listed the prose-poem "Nyarlathotep" under "1920, Nov.," which could cause some slight revisions in premise.

Unfortunately, as some of my original bibliographical notes are gone, I cannot check this. One Dave Hammond, to whom I sent in good faith a compilation of HPL's work — based on existing and the same lost notes — could answer this question; never having published this biblio, he still retains it. This is all said lest later on the "1920, Nov." and the magazine where published turn up and I be accused of grave error based on using a date of a *reprint* and not original appearance.

However, tentatively assuming the 1926 date to be first printing, it proves this: That the story "The Crawling Chaos," containing as title a variant appellation of Nyarlathotep and preceding the prose-poem in time of writing, embodies the embryo or adumbration of that god, who finally crystallized in 1926 (later).

The end of the world is depicted in "The Crawling Chaos" with nearly the same incidents of the same disaster as shown in "Poetry and the Gods." Like classic mythologies and various religions, the Cthulhu Mythos has its own Ragnarok. In "Poetry and the Gods" a Golden Age is ushered in after it; but in "The Crawling Chaos" and "Nyarlathotep" (both the poem and the prose-poem) only complete oblivion succeeds that ending of the world, and is one of the contradictions in the Mythos.

Only the gods escape this Ragnarok (in "Chaos") in domains called Teloe, Cytharion of the Seven Suns, and in Arinurian streams, all beyond the Milky Way. The supernal being who delivers this revelation to the narrator was like a "Faun or demigod," the only openly Grecian touch. Nevertheless, I consider this story one of the quasi-Greek mythic trilogy.

The third story, "The Green Meadow," is of a strange Ms. in Greek paleography. The narrator, who is obviously a Greek of 2 B.C. according to the paleography, told of his terrible delvings into the papyri of Democritus (a philosopher of Greece, who died in 357 B.C.). Germane to the present topic, and worthy of notice, is the disclosure of the same narrator of having translated some disquieting knowledge out of an Egyptian book "which was in turn taken from a papyrus of ancient Meroe." This initiates speculations as to any possible relationship to the *Necronomicon*.

Foundation for that speculation exists in the lines following the just-quoted passage, in the story, that further elaborate on the Egyptian book: "lines telling of very antique things and forms of life in the days when our earth was exceeding young. Of things which thought and moved and were alive, yet which gods and men would not consider alive."

The writer of the *Necronomicon* is said to have visited Egypt in the history that Lovecraft wrote of that book. Maybe Lovecraft meant to eventually show that most fearful contents of the *Necronomicon* were discovered in that Egyptian book spoken of in "The Crawling Chaos"; the transliterated meaning of the *Necronomicon* supports an Egyptian source of its contents.

Parenthetically, I will say that, though the *Necronomicon* is *named* first in "The Hound" (1922) (and not, by the way, in "The Festival" (1923) as Derleth says on p. 74–75 of his *HPL: A Memoir*), it is described slightly in "The Statement of Randolph Carter" (1919) and its antecedent sources are indicated in "The Green Meadow" (1927).

Fritz Leiber, Jr., in his essay, "A Literary Copernicus" (*Acolyte,* Fall 1944) made the very keen appraisal: "Most of the entities in the Cthulhu Mythos are malevolent, or, at best, *cruelly indifferent to mankind.*"

The underlining is mine. Leiber's observation evidences another Grecian influence in the Mythos. The Greek philosopher Epicurus taught that the Greek gods lived in a state of passionless tranquility and gave no attention to sublunary affairs, which they considered beneath their notice or else were entirely unconscious of human affairs. This is practically the identical attitude of most of the deities in the Cthulhu Mythos according to Fritz Leiber.

A provoking sidelight is that Epicurus' philosophy was based in part on that of Democritus (of whom later Lovecraft spoke in "The Green Meadow" as having written papyri of terrifying knowledge).

Another datum showing Lovecraft's fascination for Grecian things occurs in this passage from "H.P. Lovecraft as His Wife Remembers Him" by Sonia Davis (in *The Providence Journal,* Aug. 22, 1948):

> At least once on each visit we would have our dinner at a Greek restaurant which H.P. favored for its tiled walls depicting scenes from Greek classics. He loved to talk to me of ancient Greece and Rome. . . .

Lovecraft's story "Hypnos" (1922) has for its title the name of one of the lesser gods of sleep in Greek mythology. Within the story itself the narrator's companion, who is turned into a marble statue, appears to be Greek. What meaning there is behind the word "Hypnos," as used in the story, is yet obscure, but that some Grecian meaning lurks somewhere is certain.

Completely Grecian was Lovecraft's story "The Tree" (1920). One of the two main characters, Kalos, was thought to model his statues on fauns and dryads he was supposed to have conversed with in wooded areas. The tree that sprung from the tomb of Kalos after his death, bore resemblance

by George Wetzel   **61**

to a man, and caused the final destruction of a rival's statue. The metempsychosis of the dead Kalos into a tree is the explanation of this chain of supernatural events. The Grecian dryad as the metempsychosis' end result from a human being is hinted at here also.

"The Moon Bog" (1921) relates of a survival of the Greek moon-goddess in Ireland. Ritual music of flutes and drums in this story foreshadow similar ritual music that surrounds Azathoth in the Mythos.

For the present all the foregoing will suffice to substantiate my premise of the formative influence of Greek and quasi-Greek mythic concepts exerted on the Cthulhu Mythos and various stories. The Greek period in Lovecraft's prose overlapped his Greek period in his poetry. The poetry of Grecian origin ran roughly from 1917 to 1923, the prose from 1920 to 1922 with *The Dream-Quest of Unknown Kadath* (1927), though isolated from that period, still an outstanding example of assimilated Greek ideas.

LOVECRAFT'S LADIES

by Ben P. Indick

One of the commonplace stereotypes about H.P. Lovecraft is that he had very little interest in women. His marriage itself, to Sonia Greene, is dismissed as some sort of aberration. L. Sprague de Camp, in his biography, remarks on "a lack of women in his stories."[1] * Indeed, Lovecraft himself writes: "There is no such thing as 'love' in any unified, permanent, or important sense."[2] In a letter to Frank Belknap Long, he states: "(women) are by Nature literal, prosaic and commonplace, given to dull realistick Details and practical Things, and incapable of vigorous artistick Creation and genuine, first-hand appreciation."[3] In letters referring to the young woman he was soon to marry, he is distinctly unsentimental and unromantic, referring to her by such terms as "Mme. Green" or "SH" or "SHG," and such praise as he may bestow on her is for her good practical and business ability and quick intelligence.

Nevertheless, a hasty count of feminine names in a 1974 index of his stories and their characters[4] produces at least several dozen. Quite obviously, de Camp's statement, as well as popular supposition, is incorrect. True, none of his narrator-protagonists is feminine, and sexual discussion or even romantic warmth are absent; however, he was hardly ignorant of women, and in his serious as well as in some of his lighter-hearted works, women are important characters. A number of these feminine names are merely parts of the genealogies which are so important in his fiction, befitting his antiquarian interest, and establishing a realistic depth in the families in which will so often appear a degenerate or alien strain. Most often, the subsidiary female characters are humorless but busy homemakers, which is in itself hardly atypical of the life of the wife and mother of the seventeenth through nineteenth centuries.

Perhaps his most completely realized female character is the driven Asenath in "The Thing on the Doorstep." Asenath was the daughter of Ephraim Waite, sired by him in his old age, and this evil man, a dabbler

---

* Superscript numbers refer to notes that have been placed at the end of this chapter.

in magic, was interested in her primarily as a tool for him to employ in his search for immortality. Although she is by no means a sympathetic character, she is well-drawn. When, at twenty-three, she marries the 38-year-old Edward Derby, a weak man who is also interested in the arcane, she is "dark, smallish, and very good-looking except for over-protuberant eyes." However, she is of suspicious Innsmouth stock, which causes "average folk to avoid her." She envies the maleness of her husband, and ages rapidly, becoming repulsive in appearance. It is, nevertheless, the malevolent influence of her father acting within her; he had taken her as a "trusting, weak-willed, half-human child," and through her would attempt to take over the body of her husband. On subsequent occasions, there is strong inference that her persona has actually exchanged bodies with her husband, and, eventually, her fate is directly associated with the fascinating and grotesque climax of the story.

Continuing the Innsmouth saga, "The Shadow Over Innsmouth" treats of the intermingling of human and sea folk. An early inhabitant of the town, Captain Obed "took a second wife that nobody in the town never see." Significant to the narrator, who had never before been in the town, is the discovery that his grandmother was the daughter of an Innsmouth woman, his first realization of possible contamination within himself.

One of the finest of Lovecraftian genealogies is to be found in "The Shunned House," which follows the fate of a family, servant, and tenants in the ill-starred house. The common path in a Lovecraft horror tale is for the narrator or for the subject to find within themselves the taint which will destroy them. In "The Shunned House," however, the horror is not in the genes of the family, but in certain remains buried beneath the foundation of the house. It is a vampire-like thing, once a French immigrant, and plays no active role in the story; however, it influences others, particularly women. William Harris, who had built the house, dies, after which it is primarily a matriarchal home. His ailing, mad widow, Rhoby, screams in a French she could never have learned, and is survived by her sister, Mercy Dexter, who lives a "useful, austere and virtuous life." They are real women, as are their children, some of whom barely survive or fail to survive birth. The resolution of the evil is finally accomplished by others, but the reality of the Harris family makes the story credible.

Lavinia Whateley is one of the prominent women in the Lovecraft canon, although primarily for giving birth to her remarkable progeny in "The Dunwich Horror." Not prepossessing physically, she is a "somewhat deformed, unattractive albino woman." She has "no known husband" but is seen with a son, and "according to the custom of the region, made no attempt to disavow the child." On the other hand, "she seemed strangely proud of the dark, goatish-looking infant who formed such a contrast to her own sickly and pink-eyed albinism."

This is scarcely sentimental writing, but it is direct and honest, free of moralizing by the author. Lovecraft explains that she is a "lone creature given to wandering . . . [that] she had lost her mother when she was twelve," and grew fond of "wild and grandiose day-dreams."

However, the author's interest is in her son, and before long, without pathos, love, or sympathy, Lavinia simply vanishes. Her funeral, if it may so be called, is a "kind of pandaemonic cachinnation" of vast flocks of whippoorwills, whose significance according to local legend is that her soul has been caught and will never rest. It is a grim climax to an unloved life.

If these are not the women of a sentimental or romantic literature, they, and their sisters in the genealogies, do reflect the cold and austere granite of Lovecraft's New England. To ignore them for not being something else is to be unfair to the writer and his vision of the world, in which their part is as certain, if less important than the male characters.

Most of the gods who populate the Cthulhu Mythos are male in origin (several of a female nature have been added to the Mythos by other writers), but one of the major deities is unquestionably female: Shub-Niggurath, "the Black Goat of the Woods with a Thousand Young." Although imprisoned in an unknown place by the Elder Gods, "it is foretold in *The Necronomicon* that (she) shall come forth and multiply in all her hideousness."[5]

In a lighter vein, in his mock-classical poetry, as in the Elizabethan-style tragedy, "Alfredo," Lovecraft was willing and able to adopt a traditional romantic tradition, although, characteristically, his women eschew the wistful dream of love of a Juliet for the sharp tongue of a Katherine. One must not place undue importance on this trifle, but it is worth a glance inasmuch as it does reveal a different aspect of the author.

The play is basically a satire on the Elizabethan tragedy, and HPL even outdoes William Shakespeare's *Hamlet* in eliminating nearly an entire cast in a poker-faced but farcical ending. Before this, however, the play is wry and amusing, with a heroine at least as pretty and headstrong as Kate and equally shrewish. When she hears a serenade of pretentious folderol, Margarita snaps: "Of such suppliance I am sick. . . . Content thyself," she tells her swain, "with sovereignty and art/ And leave to the sprightlier swains the female heart." HPL knows the tricks of Love: his hero, Alfredo, is advised by an older man, "This much I know of nymphs, that poets say/ They shun the ardent swain, but follow him/ Whose fancy they have cause to think engag'd/ Upon another nymph." The older man perhaps mirrors HPL's own sentiments as he continues: "Here were a maid well-suited to thy life/ A wise companion and discerning friend./ Who like to thee enjoys the bookish moment,/ When Margarita, being thy wife, would yawn/ Or fret thee with those naggings known to wives,/ Which make Celibacy an heav'nly boon."

In "Sweet Ermengarde," a frank farce not only on old theatrical melodrama, but possibly on the new realism of such writers as Norris and Dreiser, Lovecraft has fun with women, their vanity about age and willingness to put a few things — such as gold — before "true love."

At the height of his brief happiness as the husband of Sonia Davis Greene, he wrote: "SHG is the most inspiring and encouraging influence which could possibly be brought to bear upon me . . . that most inspiring, congenial, tasteful, intelligent, solicitous and devoted of mortals and co-workers. . . ."[6] Just a few years later, he decided he had been too old to try "weaving new kinds of nests,"[7] that it was wise for the State to allow an unhappy or unsuccessful marriage to "be cancelled by a sane and benign court action."[8]

It is hardly an impressive list of women characters that Lovecraft created, and perhaps his aristocratic leanings tended him to keep the male characters in dominant roles; nevertheless, those women who are present remain archtypical New England figures, just as firm and hard as the male Pickmans, Dexter Wards, Armitages, and even the Whateleys.

NOTES:

[1] *Lovecraft,* L.S. de Camp, p. 189, Doubleday, 1975.

[2] *Selected Letters,* H.P. Lovecraft, vol. III, p. 134, Arkham House, 1971.

[3] *Selected Letters,* H.P. Lovecraft, vol. I, p. 238, Arkham House, 1965.

[4] *Lovecraft, The Fiction,* Eidolon Press, 1974 (a list of all characters and places in the fiction).

[5] Quoted in "H.P. Lovecraft: The Gods," by Lin Carter, in *The Shuttered Room and Other Pieces,* p. 261, Arkham House, 1959.

[6] *Selected Letters,,* H.P. Lovecraft, vol. I, p. 320–322.

[7] *Selected Letters* H.P. Lovecraft, vol. III, p. 5–9 (including many interesting and enlightened views on divorce).

[8] Ibid.

WHEN THE STARS ARE RIGHT

by Richard L. Tierney

On the evening of February 28, 1925, the monstrous, alien-angled fane
of Great Cthulhu rose above the waters of the Pacific, beneath which it
had slumbered for millions of years. For slightly over a month it remained
above water, allowing the thoughts of Cthulhu and His minions to beam
nightmares and madness to sensitive human minds all over the world.
Then, on April 2nd, the madness abruptly ended; cultists and asylum-in-
mates became relatively quiescent. Cthulhu's great citadel of R'lyeh had
once again descended to the depths — as abruptly and mysteriously as it
had arisen.

The narrator in Lovecraft's story, "The Call of Cthulhu," later discovered that the Cthulhu-spawned could rise and become active only "when
the stars were right." However, just exactly what stellar configuration
was necessary was never disclosed.

Astrologers have traditionally referred to the influences of the "stars"
on a certain event while meaning primarily the influence of the sun, moon,
and planets, although the stellar background is granted some slight
importance.

I am indebted to Ken Faig for obtaining for me the exact time of the
rising of R'lyeh. It occurred to me that, since Lovecraft based many of his
tales on actual events and places (for instance, the discovery of Pluto and
the Vermont floods in "The Whisperer in Darkness"), he just might have
based "The Call of Cthulhu" on the actual earth-tremor occurring on the
stated evening. Ken checked the files of *The Providence Journal* and, to
the surprise of both of us, found that the quake had not only occurred, but
had made the headlines. On checking out the files of *The San Jose
Mercury,* I discovered that it was front-page news even on the west coast!
It had severely rocked the whole north Atlantic seaboard and was reported
to be the strongest quake in that area for decades. Its epicenter was some
distance out at sea (probably not far from Y'ha-nthlei) and the time was
exactly 9:25 P.M Eastern Standard Time.

No tremor was reported for the vicinity of R'lyeh in the south Pacific,
but this is not surprising considering its remoteness from all populated

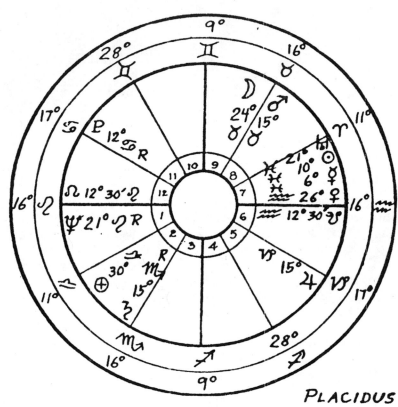

PLACIDUS

Horoscope Data Sheet

Name..C.t.h.ú.l.h.u.........

Place....R.'.l.y.ch...........

....

Lat. ..47.°..9.'..S.

Long. ..126.°..43.'..W.

~~Birth~~ date { Month...Feb........

Rising { Day.....2.8.

{ Year...1.9.2.5.....

Hr...6...Min..23....A.M. / (P.M) (Std. Time)

Std. Time— Eastern / Central — Mountain / (Pacific)

Cross out all time zones except your own

True Local Time..5.:.5.6..P.M...

Calc. Sid. Time.....................

Nearest Sid. Time....................

Greenwich Mean Time................

Adj. Calc. Date.....................

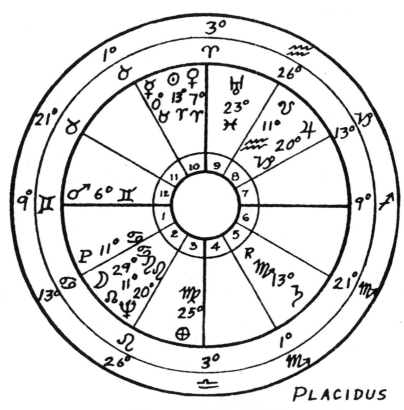

PLACIDUS

Horoscope Data Sheet

Name .. *Cthulhu* ......

Place .... *R'lyeh* ......

....

Lat. .. 47° 9' S ......

Long. 126° 43' W .....

~~Birth~~ date {
Month .. *April* ....
Day .... 2 ......
Year .. 1925 ......
}
Sinking

Hr. 12 .. Min. .. 0 .... A.M. *Noon* / P.M. (Std. Time)

Std. Time— Eastern / Central / Mountain / (Pacific)

Cross out all time zones except your own

True Local Time.. 11:33 AM.

Calc. Sid. Time ....

Nearest Sid. Time ....

Greenwich Mean Time ....

Adj. Calc. Date ....

by Richard L. Tierney

areas. The coordinates Lovecraft gives place it in the Pacific Standard Time zone, about half way between New Zealand and Chile, not far north of the Antarctic Circle, with Easter Island being possibly the nearest inhabited location at more than a thousand miles away. HPL chose his coordinates wisely.

Assuming (safely, I think!) that the Y'ha-nthlei tremor was activated by the same stellar configuration that induced the rising of R'lyeh, we find that Cthulhu rose from the deeps at exactly 6:23 P.M., Pacific Standard Time. From this datum we are able to construct an astrological chart showing exact planetary configuration.

The chart for the *sinking* of R'lyeh is based on the assumption that it coincided with the cessation of Wilcox's mad dreams in Providence, R.I., at 3:00 P.M, Eastern Standard Time, which would be noon at R'lyeh, Pacific Standard Time.

There are several striking features about the "rising" chart. The sun, considered the single most powerful factor in any horoscope, is in the sign Pisces, indicating that the event in question will be of a watery and occult nature with probable supernatural overtones. Pisces also contains Uranus, which deals with sudden and unexpected happenings and is often associated with earthquakes. However, the fact that Pisces happens to be "suppressed" in this chart (that is, squeezed between two other signs in such a way that no part of it touches a house-cusp) may indicate why the rising of R'lyeh turned out to be such a short-term event. The stars were right, but not *quite* right.

A second striking pattern in the chart is that the "Ascendant" (the point rising on the eastern horizon) at 16° of Leo (a sign often associated with rulership and the rise to power) is bracketed by Neptune (the ruler of Pisces) and the "ascending lunar node" at 21° and 12° respectively.

As if this weren't enough, Jupiter (the other planet ruling Pisces and the indicator of good fortune) is exactly in the center of Capricorn, and the sign of ambition and attainment of one's goals. Probably the most significant factor in the chart, however, is that the Midheaven (that point corresponding to Capricorn's influence concerning the culmination of ambition) falls at 9° Gemini — the exact celestial longitude of Aldebaran and the Hyades, that is to say, of dark Carcosa where dwells that monstrous and abominable half-brother of Cthulhu, Hastur the Unspeakable!

Surely, even those so densely skeptical as to doubt the significance of the foregoing cannot fail to be impressed by the equally striking features to be found in the "sinking" chart. Here the moon, which is in the "rising" was above the horizon in the earth-sign Taurus, is now below the horizon and has plunged into the watery sign of Cancer. Neptune, also, is well below the horizon, while Jupiter is well past the mid-point of Capricorn, indicating that the influences combining for the attainment of good fortune are waning. The "part of fortune," formerly in the second house, indicating opulence, is now in the third house very close to the nadir.

Pisces is still "suppressed," and moreover, the sun has not moved out of it into the fire-sign Aries.Most striking of all, that same 9 of Gemini indicating the influence of Carcosa, formerly at the Midheaven, is now exactly on the Ascendant in close conjunction with Mars. The full significance of this is not completely clear to me, but obviously Carcosa must somehow be the most important factor in triggering the rising and sinking of R'lyeh. When taken together with all the foregoing, the chances of this being a mere "coincidence" are roughly one in a jillion.

Probably Mars is somehow the crucial factor that tipped the scales against the possibility of R'lyeh remaining above the water. At the "rising," Mars was in the earth-sign of Taurus and in trine (a very favorable aspect) with Jupiter. It was in so special aspect at all with either the Ascendant of the Mid-heaven. At the "sinking," however, it was on the Ascendant (formerly the Midheaven at the "rising") in Gemini, an air-sign naturally ruled by Hastur, and evidently reinforcing the influence of Aldebaran. Ptolemy says, in his *Tetrabiblios*: "Of the stars in the head (of the Bull), that one of the Hyades which is bright and ruddy, and called Facula (Aldebaran), has the same temperament as Mars." Evidently, as Mars approached the celestial longitude of Aldebaran, reinforcing that star's radiation while moving out of harmony with Jupiter and, perhaps most importantly, into trine with the descending lunar node in Aquarius, the "stars" went more and more "wrong" — until, finally, on the 2nd of April, as Mars rose above the eastern horizon, the strain became too much. The ascending lunar node was now in square (the worst possible aspect) with Saturn (the most restrictive planet) and, as the sun and Venus (representing light and beauty respectively, and therefore terrifically adverse to Cthulhu and His minions) culminated in conjunction at the Midheaven, R'lyeh, in a titanic finale of earthquake, storm, and thunder, was plunged once more beneath the roaring waves.

Cthulhu still waits dreaming, however, and those who have read too much in the ancient records cringe with the knowledge that he shall rise again. None knows, though, just when that rising shall be — for, as every astrologer is aware, there are more ways than one for the "stars" to be "right."

Addendum: It would be a mistake to try to infer any of the *characteristics* of Great Cthulhu from the charts here presented. Only characteristics regarding the *events* they pertain to — that is, the rising and sinking of R'lyeh — can be validly inferred from them. To know the personal traits of Cthulhu more intimately, we would need a chart made for the time of His birth — and this is doubtless impossible. Cthulhu's origin millions of years ago, perhaps near the very dawn of the universe, could not have resembled a "birth" in any sense that we can conceive of. At any rate, the planetary configurations in our puny solar system, even if it existed at the time of His origin, could have had no effect on his genesis in realms so remote that the very laws of time and space are different from those of the universe we know.

by Richard L. Tierney

LOVECRAFT AND LORD DUNSANY

by Darrell Schweitzer

No knowledgeable critic has ever tried to deny that the writings of Lord Dunsany were a major influence on those of H.P. Lovecraft. The reason for this is that Lovecraft's letters are so thickly laden with statements to this effect that one simply has to believe him. Also, the Dunsanian elements in some of Lovecraft's stories are unmistakable to anyone who knows their Dunsany. So no one doubts the influence, but few have tried to actually determine the nature and extent of it, where it appears in the Lovecraft canon and from what works by Dunsany it derives.

Lovecraft first encountered Dunsany's work in "the autumn of 1919" according to his own account in a letter to Clark Ashton Smith dated July 20, 1923 (Letter no. 139, p. 242 in *Selected Letters I*). Sprague de Camp, in his biography of HPL, says that in September of that year Lovecraft first read Dunsany's *Time and the Gods* and quotes him as saying, "The first paragraph arrested me as if with an electric shock" (p. 139). Unfortunately, de Camp fails to give the source of the quotation or the information itself, but presumably took it from a Lovecraft letter, perhaps an unpublished one. It is quite likely, then, that this was the first sample of Dunsany HPL encountered. How he was led to it I don't know, but would venture to guess that either he was paging through a copy in a bookstore or library and was attracted by the fantastic illustrations of Sidney Sime which adorn most early editions of the book, or a correspondent recommended it to him. By 1919 Lovecraft already had many correspondents.

In early November of the same year Dunsany was making a tour of the United States and gave a public lecture in Boston. Lovecraft attended in the company of a Miss Hamlet and some others. He describes the affair in a letter to Reinhardt Kleiner dated November 9, 1919 (no. 56 in *Letters I*).

Dunsany spoke briefly about ideals and methods of writing, then gave a reading of his short play, "The Queen's Enemies" (from *Plays of Gods and Men*), "Why the Milkman Shudders When He Sees the Dawn," (from *The Last Book of Wonder*), the latter of which Lovecraft and the audience perceived to be a parody by Dunsany of his own work. Lovecraft came away with a very favorable impression, and neither he nor Miss Hamlet got up their nerve sufficiently to ask Dunsany for his autograph, but she at least didn't give up so easily. The next day she sent Dunsany a letter of appreciation along with a gift of an autograph letter by Abraham Lincoln (which must have been worth a great deal even then), and received Dunsany's signature appended to a kind note by return mail. Lovecraft rationalized that he had not sought an autograph because "I detest fawning upon the great." This is the first mention of Dunsany in his published letters.

Now then, what books by Dunsany did HPL read, and when did he read them? In the very next letter in the same volume he mentions expectantly purchasing the newest Dunsany book, *Unhappy Far-Off Things.* He must have been disappointed when he actually read it, because that volume is a collection of World War I propaganda, not ethereal fantasies. He also says he "recently" read *Time and the Gods.* This is December 3, 1919. We can also infer that he had read at least *A Dreamer's Tales* by this time, because in the same letter to Kleiner he is answering comments on "The White Ship," which, as I shall demonstrate later on, bears a heavy resemblance to one of the stories in that volume. (In letter no. 116, January 11, 1923, to Clark Ashton Smith, he cites *A Dreamer's Tales* as his favorite of all Dunsany's books.)

Details beyond this can't be made out from the published letters, and I don't have access to the unpublished ones, but even without such confirmation it seems reasonable that after Lovecraft discovered Dunsany and became enthusiastic about him, he read all of the books of the Irish master he could get his hands on. Dunsany was older than Lovecraft (born 1878, Lovecraft 1890), and he began his literary career with the publication of *The Gods of Pegāna* in 1905, when Lovecraft was fifteen and about to commence writing astronomy articles for the local newspapers. By the time Lovecraft began to write his serious fiction, Dunsany was an established author with an international reputation. His books were easily available in the United States. The Luce company of Boston had reprinted all the early fantasy collections, *The Gods of Pegāna, Time and the Gods, The Sword of Welleran, A Dreamer's Tales, The Book of Wonder, The Last Book of Wonder* (called *Tales of Wonder* in the British editions) and also *Plays of Gods and Men* by around 1918. *Five Plays* appeared from Little, Brown in 1917, followed by the two war books, *Tales of War* and *Unhappy Far-Off Things* in 1918 and 1919. Michael Kennerly published *Fifty-One Tales* in 1915 and about the same time the Modern Library produced two inexpensive double volumes, *A Dreamer's Tales* (containing also *The Sword of Welleran*) and *The Book of Wonder* (with *Time and the Gods*) making the best of the early fantasies even more available to the always impecunious Lovecraft. Finally, in 1919 the last collection of Dunsany's first, pure-fantasy phase appeared, *Tales of Three Hemispheres,* published by Luce, but without the Sime illustrations found in all the others of their uniform edition.

by Darrell Schweitzer 73

Lovecraft's Dunsany-influenced stories, by general agreement go as far as *The Dream-Quest of Unknown Kadath,* finished in January, 1927, so we should at least consider in passing the Dunsany publications up till the end of 1926, although by then Dunsany was no longer writing of enchanted kingdoms by the edge of the world and he seems to have held less appeal for Lovecraft.

In 1922 Dunsany's first novel appeared. This was *Don Rodriguez: The Chronicles of Shadow Valley,* a meandering fantasy set in a mostly imaginary version of roughly sixteenth century Spain. It was published by Putnam's in this country, and in his letter to Smith dated January 11, 1923 (no. 116) Lovecraft expresses an intention to read it, and a hope that it will make a return of Dunsany's earlier mode. It didn't. More to Lovecraft's taste was probably *The King of Elfland's Daughter* (1924), Dunsany's last and most elaborate imaginary-land extravaganza. In November of that year the editor of *Weird Tales* paid off a debt to Lovecraft by giving him credit at a bookstore, and Lovecraft, according to his account in letter no. 178 (to Mrs. F.C. Clark, November 6, 1924) obtained, among other things, four volumes by Dunsany, *The King of Elfland's Daughter, Fifty-One Tales, Plays of Near and Far* (another collection of short plays, first published in 1922), and *Five Plays.* Dunsany had been having considerable success on the stage, and in 1921, *If,* his first book-length play appeared, followed by *Alexander and Three Small Plays* in 1925. In 1926 came another fantasy novel, *The Charwoman's Shadow,* a vastly superior half-sequel to *Don Rodriguez,* which contains some of the best descriptions of magic and the doings of magicians in literature.

These then comprise all the books that Lovecraft could have read during his Dunsanian period. *Supernatural Horror in Literature* shows him to have been familiar with most of them, and with the help of a library there's no reason why he couldn't have read them all. In any case the only ones that left any detectable mark in HPL's fiction are the early fantasies published by Luce.

Lovecraft probably had the Luce editions, not the Modern Library, because he refers in his letters to the Sime illustrations, which appear nowhere else.

That being settled as best it can be, I move on to Lovecraft's "Dunsanian" stories. By these I mean stories which have clearly borrowed some concept or stylistic element from Dunsany, not those that merely make an offhand reference to some name found in his work.

"The Whisperer in Darkness" contains a long list of occult and otherwise eldritch persons, places, and things (mostly Things), many culled from other writers such as Robert W. Chambers. One of these is Bethmoora, the city hastily abandoned before the strange curse of the emperor Thulba Mleen in a story in *The Dreamer's Tales,* but that does not make "Whisperer" Dunsanian, nor does the fact that the title *At The Mountains of Madness* comes from "The Hashish Man" (same collection) qualify that effort. In this latter case the reference was in fact an unconscious one, and was only brought to Lovecraft's attention by a correspondent.

Lovecraft was a strict realist in many ways, and he admired realism above all other forms of writing, or so he claimed. It was his usual method, especially later in his career, to give his tales a firm basis in reality by setting them in places he had actually seen, such as Providence, various small towns in Massachusetts, Boston, and Brattleboro, Vermont. Most of his stories set in imaginary lands or in otherwise unrealistic places tend to be of the Dunsanian cast, although one has to be careful in saying this because the first one of this type he wrote, "Polaris," predates his knowledge of Dunsany by one year. (This is confirmed by letter no. 265, *Letters II*)

"Polaris" seems to have been based on a dream Lovecraft had in the spring of 1918, which is related in some detail in letter no. 34. The tale itself is one of Lovecraft's better earlier efforts, not written in the first person delirious mode of "Dagon" or the verbose style of "The Tomb," both of which preceded it, but in a relatively uncluttered manner. The narrator, in our world, dreams of a strange city in which there are grave faces carven atop pillars. He first moves about as a disembodied presence, then becomes an inhabitant of the place, which is called Olathö and located in the land of Lomar, somewhere near to the North Pole in aeons past, when the icecaps had not yet expanded to cover the site. Lomar is menaced by the savage Inutos and everybody is drafted into the army except for the hero, who, like Lovecraft, is so sickly and frail he is useless as a fighter. So he is given the post of look-out, and as he watches from atop a tower the evil spirit of the star Polaris bewitches him (with a few lines of better than average Lovecraftian verse) and he falls asleep, dreaming of another life. The "dream" of the Lomarian is, of course, the life of the man in the contemporary United States, and each is as real as the other, echoing the ancient paradox of Chuang Tzu and the butterfly. (The sage dreamed he was a butterfly, and when he awoke had no way of proving he wasn't a butterfly dreaming he was a man.) The hero is in great distress because he has fallen asleep at his station and the barbarians are coming, and he can't seem to "awaken" into his "true life" and warn the city. The people in this world naturally think him mad.

"Polaris" is much the sort of thing Dunsany wrote, but it lacks the biblical rhythms of his style and the various eccentricities which marked his prose, the numerous sentences beginning with "And," and the long strings of clauses linked together with semi-colons. It is taken almost entirely from Lovecraft's dream, with only a few rationalizations added by the conscious writer. The proper names were arrived at independent of Dunsany, despite one coincidence almost too powerful to be believed. In *The Last Book of Wonder* Dunsany wrote of the city of Loma ("The Loot of Loma" was the tale) which sounds very much like Lovecraft's Lomar. It can only be a matter of chance — though it must also be noted that there is a Point Loma in California — but the nature of the story itself

by Darrell Schweitzer

shows that Lovecraft was working in similar directions before he discovered the Irish fabulist, and was heavily influenced by him because he saw in Dunsany a more polished form the sort of fiction he had been trying to write in the first place.

Lovecraft said such in a letter to Frank Belknap Long dated June 3, 1923 (no. 134)(The italics are HPL's.):

> But *Dunsany* is closer to my own personality and understanding. Machen has an hysterical intensity which I neither experience nor understand — a seriousness which is a philosophical limitation. But Dunsany *is myself,* plus an art and cultivation infinitely greater. His cosmic realm is the realm in which I live; his distant, emotionless vistas of the beauty of the moonlight on quaint and ancient roofs are the vistas I know and cherish.

When he first read Dunsany's fantasies, Lovecraft promptly produced a number of Dunsany-influenced tales, not imitations in the strictest sense of the word (i.e., designed to cash in on the readership of somebody else, the way *The Man from U.N.C.L.E.* is an imitation of James Bond) or deliberate pastiches, but simply stories resulting from an inexperienced writer trying to use another man's voice to say what he (the inexperienced writer) intends to say, not having found a distinct voice of his own. This is a very common early development among novice writers, and eventually, when they have their own style, they grow out of the other author's. They often come to despise their less original work, as Lovecraft did after a few years had passed. Lovecraft was keenly aware of the limitations and dangers of using another writer as a model. He wrote to Maurice Moe in March 1931:

> What every guy has to say, is what's in him — and every fresh combination of a guy and wot he's got on his chest calls for a distinctly individual use of the language. If anybody feels perfectly at home in some other bimbo's shiny coat and pants, that's proof of one or two things — either that he is, by accident, a dead ringer for the other guy; or that he hasn't a damn thing of his own to say.
>
> (letter no. 467, *Selected Letters III*

Lovecraft certainly had something original to say, so for him, as for many fantasy writers, imitating Dunsany was a learning experience, sort of literary training-wheels, and it had to be discontinued after a while, once it had served its purpose and before it began to stifle further development.

Lovecraft wrote two recognizably Dunsanian tales by the end of 1919, "The White Ship" and "The Doom That Came to Sarnath." In the former, Lovecraft had for the first time copied Dunsany's sentence-structure. After he had abandoned his strictly biblical style, by the time he got to

The Sword of Welleran, Dunsany continued to have long rolling sentences tied together with semi-colons and commas. The initial *Ands* decreased in number but remained present. This is the Dunsanian manner that most shaped Lovecraft. It is found also in HPL's favorite, *A Dreamer's Tales.* In the first two paragraphs of "The White Ship" Lovecraft wrote:

> . . . In the days of my grandfather there were many; in the days of my father not so many; and now there are so few that I sometimes feel strangely alone, as though I were the last man on the planet.
> From far shores came those white-sailed argosies of old; from far Eastern shores where warm suns shine and sweet odors linger about strange gardens and gay temples.

Word-use and word-choice aside, Lovecraft is here trying to recapture the luxuriant phantasmagoria of Dunsany's mostly imaginary "East." Compare Lovecraft's opening to this one, from Dunsany's "Idle Days on the Yann":

> So I came down through the wood to the bank of Yann and found, as had been prophesied, the ship *Bird of the River* about to loose her cable.
> The captain sat cross-legged upon the white deck with his scimitar lying beside him in its jeweled scabbard, and the sailors toiled to spread the nimble sails to bring the ship into the central stream of Yann, and all the while sang ancient soothing songs. And the wind of evening descending cool from the snowfields of some mountainous abode of distant gods came suddenly, like glad tidings to an anxious city, into the wing-like sails.

This particular story was written by Dunsany in expectation of wonders he would see on his first trip up the Nile, and it is merely a long, plotless travelogue describing a voyage through the lands of fancy, with stopovers at points of particular interest.

The story exists only for the sake of its brilliant inventions, and when they run out it stops. It was one of Dunsany's favorites and was reprinted in two subsequent collections. *Tales of Three Hemispheres* contains two sequels to it.

The story seems to have made a strong impression on Lovecraft. There is a note on it and on one of the sequels ("The Shop in Go-By Street") in his *Commonplace Book,* although he used neither in his own fiction. One of the more ingenious toss-off devices, an ivory gate carven out of a single tusk, particularly struck his fancy, and he not only used the same idea (changing it to a throne out of a single piece) in *The Dream-Quest of Unknown Kadath,* but brought it to the reader's attention when discussing Dunsany in *Supernatural Horror in Literature.*

In the other sequel, "The Avenger of Perdóndaris" Dunsany extended

by Darrell Schweitzer   77

the motif further himself, using the whole tusk as a bridge and introducing the mighty hunter who killed the beasts with the big teeth.

In "The White Ship" Lovecraft gives us his version of the whole story. The parallels are obvious. Both deal with voyages on fabulous ships through imaginary lands. Lovecraft skirts seacoasts while Dunsany floats along the river Yann, but both see towering cities and periodically stop, or at least expend a lot of wordage describing the splendors passed. Dunsany tends to be more inventive, while Lovecraft rhapsodizes about exotic architecture and hopes the reader will take his word for it. In Dunsany, the ship is called *Bird of the River* while Lovecraft's White Ship is led on by a mystical "Bird of Heaven," which flies in front of the vessel. I can't help but suspect that one of the illustrations Sime drew for "Idle Days on the Yann" provided some of Lovecraft's inspiration for this. The picture looks vaguely like a Japanese block print and shows the *Bird of the River* under partial sail on a rather stormy river Yann with seagulls behind, strange black fish leaping out of the water in front, a bird's head figure on the bowsprit, and what looks to me like a stylized flying fish embroidered on the mainsail. The mixture of bird and ship predominates, and when you take into account the oriental flavor of both the tale and the artwork, and the traditional Eastern preoccupation with Heaven, the mental associations producing the "Bird of Heaven" are quite clear.

The main difference between the two stories is that Lovecraft's has a plot. Dunsany goes on until his idea supply is used up, while Lovecraft weaves an allegory. Dunsany never took allegorical figures or situations seriously. In *The Sword of Welleran* there's a story about a river located at the junction of the rivers of Myth and Fable, but for Dunsany it was just colorful rhetoric. Lovecraft goes a lot further when his ship encounters lands which are concrete manifestations of abstract principles or ideals, such as the City of a Thousand Wonders wherein can be found "all those mysteries that man has striven in vain to fathom," the city of Zar "where dwell all the dreams and thoughts of beauty that come to men once and then are forgotten," Xura, "The Land of Pleasures Unattained," and ultimately Cathuria the Land of Hope, which lies in the unreachable west. The White Ship seeks the land of Cathuria and falls to doom in a huge cataract, reminiscent of Dunsany's edge of the world, and loses forever the countries of marvel. The moral is that if you ask too much you lose everything. Lovecraft never wrote moralistic fiction before or after; so one can easily doubt his seriousness with allegory also. I think he was just playing with the elements for their own sake, as an excuse for all the magic and fancy, which is something many writers are tempted to do, only to find in later years that scholars have read profound meanings into their stories. I don't think there is any great philosophical depth in "The White Ship."

"The Doom That Came to Sarnath" takes its title, says Lovecraft in a letter reproduced in Ben Indick's Esoteric Order of Dagon fanzine *Ibid,* from the works of Dunsany, but quite frankly I can't find it. Was

Lovecraft wrong? But the closest I can come up with is a shepherd boy in *Time and The Gods* named Sardinac, from whom the name "Sarnath" might have derived. There is, incidentally, a real city of Sarnath in India. The story itself is un-Dunsanian in many ways, containing more of a horror element than Dunsany's stories usually do. Despite Lovecraft's inclusion of him in *Supernatural Horror in Literature*, Dunsany rarely wrote weird-horror fiction and would have found Arthur Machen and Algernon Blackwood strange literary company indeed, and would have more likely found kindred spirits in William Morris, James Branch Cabell, J.R.R. Tolkien and other romancers of the imaginary. Dunsany didn't like overt horror, and once even insisted that a Sime drawing not be used in one of his books because he found the monster in it "unwholesome."

Still, there are traces of Dunsany in "The Doom that Came to Sarnath," one of the most interesting being Lovecraft's name "Kadatheron" which may have come from Dunsany's Sardathrion, the city slain by Time in *Time and The Gods,* and evolved into Unknown Kadath of infamous and more eldritch repute. As for the plot, consider first the idol of Bokrug taken from the destroyed city of Ib by the men of Sarnath. The figure walks off its altar in the middle of the night, leaving the high priest Taran-Ish dead of fright. The next morning the "sign of DOOM" is found scrawled on the altar in Taran-Ish's hand. This is quite reminiscent of the mysterious message left on the city gates in Dunsany's *The Golden Doom* (in *Five Plays*), the walking idols in *The Gods of the Mountain* (same) which impressed Lovecraft enough for him to mention them in *Supernatural Horror in Literature,* the lingering and dreaded END which the gods fear in *The Gods of Pegāna,* and the nastily ironic behavior of the death god Mung in that same book. Mung had a habit of sneaking up on unwary persons, making the Sign of Mung over them, and sending their souls off to drift among the worlds. One might also remember the image of Ranorada, also in *The Gods of Pegāna,* which has a cryptic sentence carved on its base.

The ending is quite Dunsanian. Dunsany was fond of wiping impressive and allegedly eternal cities off the face of the earth without trace, demonstrating the vanity of world striving. Babbuklund, Zaccarath, and even the divinely wrought Sardathrion meet this fate, as does Lovecraft's Sarnath, and the sudden frantic evacuation of the place is very similar to the doom that came to Bethmoora in *A Dreamer's Tales.*

More original Lovecraftian elements are present in this story than in "The White Ship." The frog-like beings of Ib have no precedent in Dunsany, and may be the forerunners (or fore-hoppers?) of the Deep Ones and other Cthulhuvian unspeakables, and the attempts to tie the events into prehistory, along with some of the racial ideas (frog men overthrown by dark men with black hair, overthrown in turn by blonde Aryans) are definitely un-Dunsanian. These things Lovecraft pursued when he was no longer writing like Dunsany at all.

1920 was a good year for Lovecraft. He wrote six tales, and of them two show the influence of his Irish mentor, "The Cats of Ulthar" and "Celephais." Of the former little can be said. It has no obvious parallels in any Dunsany story, but in mood and execution resembles him. The prose style is much more restrained than was usual for Lovecraft, and might have passed off for a minor Dunsany story from around 1910, save that Lovecraft wrote it to express his enthusiasm for cats and Dunsany preferred dogs.

"Celephais" is a different matter. It, like "The White Ship," and perhaps even more so than that tale, is a direct rewrite of something by Dunsany, in this case a story from *The Book of Wonder* called "The Coronation of Mr. Thomas Shap." For once, when the two are compared, Lovecraft comes out ahead. "Thomas Shap" is not Dunsany at his best, in my opinion at least, and Lovecraft improved on it. In the original Mr. Shap is a shrewd, very ordinary businessman who discovers his imagination. He begins to explore the realms of his fancy until eventually he does it too much and work begins to suffer. Eventually he withdraws entirely into his dream, is made King over all the Land of Wonder, while back on Earth his physical self is locked away in a mental hospital. Lovecraft tells exactly the same story, even to the point of having his hero live in London, which HPL had never seen, of course, but which served as a starting point for many of Dunsany's pieces. The essential difference is that Lovecraft's character is alone, penniless, the last of his line, and forgotten in a teeming city of millions, so that his fantastic delvings are not merely something to relieve boredom, but the product of desperation. The story gains intensity because of this. Where Dunsany's Mr. Shap was placed safely in the loony-bin after becoming king of his dreams, Lovecraft's Kuranes (his dream name — real name never given) enters the dream city of Celephais only after the death of his body, as he steps off a cliff while his soul goes soaring into the clouds. There is more psychological power in Lovecraft's story, and the character has deeper motivations for what he does. The result is closer to tragedy than to whimsey. Lovecraft also linked the magical city of dreams with childhood, a concept he explored in more detail when he wrote *The Dream-Quest of Unknown Kadath*. The actual writing of "Celephais" includes some of Lovecraft's best prose. His style, modeled on Dunsany, is lucid, economical, and uncluttered.

The following year saw two more Dunsanian tales, "The Quest of Iranon" and "The Other Gods." By this time Lovecraft was beginning to find his own voice, and was simultaneously composing such major stories as "The Music of Erich Zann," "The Outsider," and "The Nameless City." The Cthulhu Mythos was beginning to shape itself, with Abdul Alhazred introduced in "The Nameless City" and the abhorred *Necronomicon* in "The Hound" a year later. Still, HPL continued to base some stories on Dunsany.

"The Quest of Iranon" is Dunsany's old story of the impossible search. Two examples that come to mind immediately are "The Land of Time" from *Time and The Gods,* wherein a king and his army seek out and assault the castle of Time, only to be felled by the decades hurled against them, and "Carcassonne" in *A Dreamer's Tales,* about another king who is led on by a minstrel to find the city of Carcassonne despite a prophecy which says he never will. In the end the army is gone, the king an old man, and the minstrel's inspiration has fled. The two of them still go forth, into a dangerous swamp, and the author suggests they didn't get far.

"Iranon" is the most Dunsanian of all Lovecraft's stories both in content and in language. It is a very close imitation of the sort of story one finds in *Time and The Gods* with its archaisms, poetic prose modeled on the King James Bible, frequent sentences beginning with "And," and dialogue consisting mostly of speeches rather than realistic conversation. The only thing Lovecraftian at all about "The Quest of Iranon" is that the hero is seeking beauty and comfort found in the past, in the glittering lost land of his childhood.

Dunsany never showed such preoccupations, but the theme recurs constantly in HPL's writing. Here it is given one of its more pessimistic conclusions. . . . Iranon meets an ancient shepherd who tells him about a beggar boy who imagined himself an exiled prince and went off in search for his imaginary kingdom. Iranon is that boy, kept artificially youthful by his idealism, and when he learns that his dreams are false, he becomes a decrepit old man and wanders off into a marsh where the quicksand claims him.

This, of course, calls to mind "Carcassonne" and also the appropriately entitled "The Sorrow of the Search" (from *Time and The Gods*) which also has an aged hero sinking into the mud after his life work has proven itself folly.

"The Other Gods" is a bit more original. Dunsany wrote many stories about supposedly wise men who meet their ends seeking the gods or otherwise trying to know what they shouldn't, but Lovecraft's version can't be linked to any one story. His style here is very Dunsanian in that it tends to tell rather than show, to be synoptic and yet image-filled at the same time (the secret of doing such a thing without being boring, imitators please note) and still the dialogue consists of rhetorical speeches rather than exchanges, but in content the piece is considerably less derivative. There is something decidedly malevolent about the Other Gods, and when Barzai the Wise actually beholds them he calls down through a conveniently placed mist to his assistant, more in the manner of an earthly Lovecraftian victim in some later story:

The Gods of the outer hells that guard the feeble gods of earth. . . . Look away. . . . Go backs . . . Do not see! The vengeance of the infinite abysses . . . That cursed, that damnable pit . . . Merciful gods of earth. I am falling into the sky!

Dunsany never would have ended a story like that. He seldom leaned that far into outright horror, and when he did there was always a trace of sophisticated irony present.For example, in "The Hoard of the Gibbelins" one minute the knight is doing well and the next minute he gets what's coming to him:

> And without a word, *or even smiling,* they neatly hanged him on the outer wall — and the tale is one of those that have not a happy ending.

Never would a Dunsany character cry out, as Barzai the Wise is in effect doing, "Help! Help! The monster got me!" Also, Dunsany's gods tend to be capricious, playful, and at times a little foolish, but they are always completely indifferent to humanity (with the possible exception of Mung, who may very well *enjoy* making the Sign of Mung over people), never overtly hostile and frightening. Lovecraft's *forte* was slithering horrors out of the nameless abyss, and he was soon to learn that they worked better when contrasted with mundane, everyday reality. When he came to that conclusion, he stopped writing Dunsanian stories. In fact he did not return to the Dunsanian mode for five more years after he completed "The Other Gods." In 1926 he did return, and got it out of his system entirely.

His letters from the middle to late 1920s indicate that he regarded these final Dunsany-like stories as exceptions to his usual methods, and he didn't plan on doing any more. The last stories were "The Strange High House in the Mist," "The Silver Key," both completed in 1926, and the short novel *The Dream-Quest of Unknown Kadath,* which took him until January, 1927 to finish. (He announces having done so in a letter to Smith, January 21, 1927, no. 257 in *Selected Letters II.*)

"The Strange High House in the Mist" and "The Silver Key" are both concerned with modern dreamers who are dissatisfied with contemporary life and seek escape into something more romantic and wonderful. Both stories are written in a decreasingly Dunsanian style and tend to be a bit more wordy. Lovecraft on his own never had the compactness of Dunsany and could to get bogged down in excess verbiage. He wrote with great care, choosing each word painstakingly, so the only conclusion we can draw is that with great care he made the wrong aesthetic decisions, and failed to trim his prose down. Both the stories are too long, and have descriptions which tend to repeat or slightly expand upon something described previously. In "Strange High House" Lovecraft hit on a phrase with a nice ring to it, "the solemn bells of the buoys tolled free in the aether of faery." Once this is quite effective (although he could have dropped "bells of the" and made it "the solemn buoys"), and once again it is fine, giving the story a cyclical feeling, but when Lovecraft can't resist using this precious and highly noticeable construction for a *third* time it becomes no longer effective, but redundant. The story is Dunsanian only in concept — the spirit of the dreamer is carried off by the gods, while his body returns to the world — and there are some very good incidental happenings in it, but certainly there's very little if any Dunsany in the style.

In "The Silver Key," the Dunsanian style has become a vestige. Where Dunsany would have deftly summed up the hero's dissatisfaction with contemporary life in a single sentence, or, at most, a paragraph, Lovecraft goes on for several thousand words. The result is more a philosophical essay than a narrative, and not without interest for its exposition of Lovecraftian views on the impersonal nature of the material cosmos, and even on the aesthetics of fantasy. Randolph Carter, in his youth, it seems, wrote and published Dunsanian-style fantasies, but as he grew older and "hardened" into middle age, the spirit left him:

> Ironic humour dragged down the twilight minarets he reared, and the earthy fear of improbability blasted all the delicate and amazing flowers of his faery gardens. The convention of assumed pity spilt mawkishness on his characters, while the myth of an important reality and significant human events and emotions debased all his high fantasy into thin-veiled allegory and cheap social satire. His new novels were successful as his old ones had never been; and because he knew how empty they must be to please an empty herd, he burned them and ceased writing. They were very graceful novels, in which he urbanely laughed at the dreams he lightly sketched; but he saw that their sophistication had sapped all their life away.

(*At the Mountains of Madness*, p. 412)

Lovecraft found many of the same faults in later Dunsany, from *The Book of Wonder* onward, and the entire passage can be read as a critique of the fantasies of James Branch Cabell, which were very popular when "The Silver Key" was written, but of which Lovecraft was never fond, for the reason stated in the last sentence above.

Once the story starts, it's quite poignant. Randolph Carter, who lost a friend in an eldritch manner due to occult dabblings in a previous adventure, is now jaded with life and tired of everything. The only thing he desires, in a typically Lovecraftian manner, is a return to the happy world of his childhood. As he has grown older he has ceased to dream, and can no longer visit marvelous worlds of the imagination, all of which are linked in his mind to childhood.

So he obtains (literally) the key to dreams to help him regain his dreams and cease being prosaic, adult, responsible, and otherwise dull. He goes back to the site of his ancestral manse and, by means of the key, twists time and vanishes into the past. The transition is very skillfully handled, as Carter catches glimpses of scenes from his past, an old church tower that was torn down, and so on. Ultimately he meets his old servant who ushers the now youthful Carter into the house where he is scolded for being out so late.

by Darrell Schweitzer 83

The tale is related to Dunsany only in concept, with its literalization of dreams, its romantic search for something alternative to mundane reality, and its easy slipping from the real world into another. Then, if we consider it, it also resembles some Ray Bradbury stories and a few *Twilight Zone* episodes to be written decades later. By this point the Dunsanian influence in HPL had been almost entirely assimilated.

Last came *The Dream-Quest of Unknown Kadath.* This work was never given final polish, never submitted, or even typed, as Lovecraft had no confidence in it and abhorred typing. For a first draft it is an astonishing effort, a dreamland story, set in the alternate world of "Celephais," "The Other Gods," et al. and containing references to them and frequently characters from them, but far more ambitious than anything Dunsany ever did in this area. Dunsany wrote a pure fantasy novel, *The King of Elfland's Daughter,* but it is more of an imaginary-land romance akin to *The Lord of the Rings.* Dunsany's own dreamland fiction tended to break down over length. His early fantasies which so impressed HPL never held out for much more than five thousand words at a stretch. Lovecraft in *The Dream-Quest of Unknown Kadath* expanded the basic plot of "Celephais" into a short novel. Dunsany did nothing of the sort for "The Coronation of Thomas Shap" or anything else like it.

Dream-Quest does resemble "Celephais" in that it too concerns a man who glimpses a marvelous city in his childhood dreams and as an adult seeks to find it. This time, it turns out, after an extended journeying through the secondary universe of the unconscious, that the city is none other than a nostalgia-embossed version of Randolph Carter's own native Boston. (Yes, this is inconsistent with "The Silver Key," which says he grew up on a country estate.)

The most remarkable thing about *Dream-Quest* is that Lovecraft managed to keep it going for such a length. It does drag in spots, as the wonders pile atop each other until they seem a little less wondrous, but whenever this starts to happen events suddenly speed up, and the plot carries us through. The writing is uniformly fine, and while it might have benefitted from judicious trimming, even Lovecraft would have found the task difficult. No section is conspicuously below the others in quality.

The central concepts of *The Dream-Quest of Unknown Kadath* are a curious blend of Dunsany and Lovecraft. Dunsany tossed off beautiful vignettes of impossible places, and said casually that they were taking place in "dreamland" or "at the edge of the world." He never explored the matter in any depth or tried to define his terms in relation to living experience. Lovecraft does, even though he isn't totally consistent about it. Much of the time the land of dreams for Carter seems to be what science fiction writers would call "another dimension." When Randolph Carter's spirit ignores the warnings of the priests of Nasht and Kaman-Thah and descends the seven hundred steps to the Gate of Deeper Slumber, and passes into the Haunted Wood, he is entering a place as real as the waking world, where perils can't be escaped by waking up. Dreamland is more than just a mental state. It is an objective reality. The only Dunsany story to touch on this possibility is "The Shop in Go-By Street."

Sometimes Dreamland begins to resemble either the Christian Hell or the Hades of Hellenic mythology, although it is not always unpleasant. It seems that the ghouls and some people who have become ghouls, like Pickman from "Pickman's Model," are able to move from the edges of perception into the waking world through graveyards. There is a scene in the *Aeneid* which is relevant here, in which Aeneas and the Sybil are passing through the underworld and they come to two gates, through which dreams enter into the upper world. One gate, of ivory, is for false dreams, and another, made of horn, is for true dreams. They go through the ivory one, suggesting that some things are more important than truth. Lovecraft's character doesn't face such a choice, but the parallel to the Gate of Deeper Slumber is obvious. Vergil's gates may also be the origin of Dunsany's ivory gate in "Idle Days on the Yann." Dunsany, like Lovecraft, was infatuated with classical writings and thoroughly familiar with Greek and Roman literature. The particular passage with the two gates impressed him, because he mentioned it in his third volume of memoirs. (*The Sirens Wake*, Jarrolds, 1946, p. 83.)

Ultimately the world of dreams becomes a complete universe, in which Carter can go to the moon on a galley rowed by moonbeasts, and be rescued by an army of cats. This secondary cosmos is more hospitable than that of the waking world, as even the night-gaunts who plagued Lovecraft's childhood nightmares are enlisted by Pickman to aid him. The psychological significance of this seems to be that Lovecraft dwelled so long on the fears of his youth that after a while they became familiar, no longer frightening, and ultimately he fell in love with them. He seems quite fond of ghouls in spots in *Dream-Quest*. The story can be regarded as semi-allegorical, both as an exercise in sheer imagination and as something harboring deeper meanings. (Maybe. It is always dangerous to say what was "meant" by a piece of writing, especially in fantasy where things are made deliberately bizarre.) Carter's journey is a weird phantasmagoria, perhaps comparable to a nightmarish recasting of *Alice in Wonderland* or the dream fantasies of George MacDonald. It certainly extends beyond anything Lovecraft picked up from Dunsany, and goes on to become uniquely his own.

There are flaws in the work, most of them probably due to the lack of final revision. At one point it seems off to a false start when Carter descends into the Haunted Wood, them comes up into the world again, and has to begin all over. The story still has recognizable bits from Dunsany, most noticeably the aforementioned gigantic tooth from "Idle Days on the Yann" which here is carved as a throne, but most of the overtly "Dunsanian" elements are taken from Dunsany second hand, having previously appeared in Lovecraft's earlier Dunsanian short stories, then incorporated into the larger work. *The Dream-Quest of Unknown Kadath* is a wholesale exploration of unreality, and if Lovecraft had polished it to the level of his best, the result might have been truly extraordinary. It still opens up new areas into which Dunsany, for all his superior technique, never ventured.

Lovecraft himself never went any further either, as he abandoned this type of writing altogether. The Cthulhu Mythos was by then beginning to take over the large bulk of his original literary efforts, and he shifted away from the purely fantastic into the fantastic grounded in realistic settings, and finally into more rationalized stories bordering on science fiction. There Lovecraft had no use for Dunsany or anything Dunsanian.

In the end, what are we to make of Lovecraft's Dunsanian stories? Certainly they have sufficient merit of their own to be worth reading, derivative or not. For Lovecraft, this phase of his work was certainly a process of growth and training; and, when he had moved beyond it in his own personal evolution as a writer, he didn't go back. Perhaps he could have produced masterpieces of otherworldly fantasy if he had continued in this mode once he had matured as a writer, but he didn't and it's useless to speculate about stories unwritten. Even Dunsany stopped writing that sort of thing as he got older. A simple fact of literary life is that the writer at twenty is not the same writer at forty. His personality changes. He has had new experiences; he sees things differently; and his interests have shifted. Frequently he has exhausted the vein he wrote in during his youth, and if he were to return to it the result would be stale rehash. So Dunsany went from writing of foolish gods and even more foolish men and monsters when he was in his twenties, to writing of that modern Munchausen, Mr. Joseph Jorkens, in his forties and fifties. Lovecraft matured late as a writer, but he did mature, and he did shift into other directions.

If writing Dunsanian fiction was a learning exercise for Lovecraft, what did he learn? Certainly he learned something about style. Dunsany was always an immaculate craftsman, whether he was writing about Pegāna, Elfland, Ireland, robots taking over the world, or dogs. His major failing was an occasional lack of depth — he sometimes wrote about trivial things, albeit splendidly. Lovecraft could hardly have picked up any bad habits from him. He seems to have learned from Dunsany a good deal about restraint, the control of his technique. Lovecraft's Dunsanian period produced some of his best prose. At worst Lovecraft's writing is overly and poorly descriptive (what Damon Knight calls "overdescription of the almost seen"), and laden with unnecessary adjectives, sort of a cumbersome, hysterical gibber. His later, post-Dunsanian stories sometimes degenerate into gibbering at the end, as the Ultimate Shocking Revelation, which the reader has figured out half way through, is made hideously clear; but the best of his stories, such as "The Dunwich Horror" and "The Colour Out of Space" start out very well indeed and maintain some degree of control all the way through. They're a big improvement over such efforts as "Arthur Jermyn," "The Hound," "From Beyond," and "The Horror at Red Hook," which gibber from start to finish. This polish in the later stories I would attribute to Dunsany, and I would guess that if Lovecraft had never discovered the works of the Irish master he still might have written the same stories, but they wouldn't have turned out as well.

The irony of all this is that Dunsany in his lifetime (died 1957) never heard of Lovecraft until introduced to his work by August Derleth in the late '40s. Dunsany, whose *Fourth Book of Jorkens* had ust been published by Arkham House, inquired after this Lovecraft fellow, who was reputed to have written stories "in my style," as Dunsany put it. Derleth sent Dunsany some Lovecraft fiction; and so, Dunsany read "Celephais," "The Silver Key," etc., a quarter of a century after they were written. Dunsany was by then so far removed from his own early manner that he remarked that Lovecraft was "welcome to it." At the time, Lovecraft was still primarily known to a select few. He was a cult figure in American science fantasy fandom. But in the next twenty or so years Lovecraft's reputation and readership expanded enormously, until he not only overtook Dunsany but Machen, Blackwood, M.R. James, and all the other "real authors" he never dared to compare himself to. He is rapidly closing in on Poe, and today it is more likely that a college literature teacher will have heard of Lovecraft than Dunsany, despite the fact that Dunsany was a world-renowned figure in his own time, who had five plays running on Broadway simultaneously in 1915 and was often cited in drama textbooks as an example of How To Do It.

Some while ago, I was paging through a book on Irish literature, and there was a page devoted of Dunsany. It ended with a statement to the effect that Dunsany's "primary importance was his influence on the American master, H.P. Lovecraft." Maybe that's going a bit far, but the reversal of roles is undeniable. Dunsany was arguably the most brilliant fantasy writer who ever lived, but in fame Lovecraft has eclipsed him. Lovecraft sells millions of copies, while Dunsany sells thousands. Hopefully, the two of them will be read and appreciated together in the years to come.

by Darrell Schweitzer   **87**

H.P. LOVECRAFT AND PSEUDOMATHEMATICS

by Robert Weinberg

One of the strongest points in the Cthulhu stories by H.P. Lovecraft is the skillful blending of the unreal and the real. True and false are juggled together until one is undistinguishable from the other. Probably the most mentioned example of this work is Lovecraft's invention of a number of fictitious books complete with quotes, mysterious authors and histories. However, little attention has ever been given to the mathematics, or in reality, the pseudomathematics used in several of the Cthulhu tales. In this chapter, I hope to cover this area, however briefly.

In the period that Lovecraft did his writing (1920–1935) science was just emerging from the greatest traumatic period in all history. At the turn of the century, the Michaelson-Morley experiment had all but destroyed the notion of an all-pervasive ether. Einstein and Planck had completely disrupted all of classical physics with the theory of General Relativity and their restructuring of the physical universe. Heisenberg's Uncertainty Principle had completely reshaped the idea of what we know, and more important, of what we can learn. Research done by half-a-dozen famous scientists had determined the structure of the atom. For the first time in history, modern man was exposed to what is now being called "Future Shock." Man tried, with little success, to grasp *all* that was occurring about him. Popular science articles in the Sunday papers were quite common, as well as many books proclaiming "Mathematics for the Millions" and "Relativity Made Easy." The unfortunate fact is that without a strong background and training such concepts are not easy. Nor are they simple. Most simplistic views of the subjects were no more than a thin gloss of a much deeper idea.

Most of the writers in the fantasy-science fiction field of this time were not scientists. The few that were, were not associated with the fields of major advances. There were exceptions, of course, like John Campbell, but even he did not use a strong straight science background in his stories. Most of the tales in the period employed what can be loosely called pseudo-science. That is, made-up science which had very little or no relation to the real work of the period. The speed of light, which was just then being recognized as an absolute upper boundary on speed, was ignored by every writer who used a FTL drive. Structural impossibilities in construction of super cities were common (and still are). Biological impossibilities (such as violations of the square-cube law) were the order of the day. Though the claim has been made that this was the period of **science** fiction (i.e., the science emphasized while the fiction was not), this statement is not true. Anyone competent in the sciences could tell otherwise. It was a time of **pseudoscience**-fiction. In other words, a time when impossible science was emphasized. Not speculative science, with a possibility of reality someday (as in *Ralph 124C41+*), but just sheer nonsense masquerading as science. This is not to say that some of these stories were not entertaining, but just to point out that they were straight fantasy. Any speculation they contained was false and misleading. (A fine example of such work is Ray Cummings's stories about "The Girl in the Golden Atom." These are fairly entertaining tales, but Cummings's basic premise that the structure of an atom is somewhat similar to a solar system is utter nonsense, and was known to be nonsense long before most of the series appeared.)

The revolution in mathematics had taken place sometime before the revolution in physics, though the two events are closely interrelated. Cantor's work with infinite sets was a major breakthrough from finite to infinite mathematics. Work in non-Euclidian geometry, showing that structure was possible as long as an axiomatic system was maintained, produced a minor breakthrough. Again, popular science articles tried, with little success, to convey the meanings of such breakthroughs to the public. Misconceptions immediately arose.

Lovecraft's misunderstandings in both geometry and quantum physics are therefore nothing uncommon for the time he wrote. Even if he had (or did) consulted various reference works of the period for information, it is doubtful that the references to mathematics in his stories would have been very different.

In nearly all of the Cthulhu stories, some mention is made to the alien geometry, encountered (as in "The Call of Cthulhu," "The Shadow Out of Time," and others). Instead of going over every story, I will attempt to note the pseudo-mathematics used in one story, and thus avoid repetition. The mistakes in one are common throughout all of the Mythos stories (including work by others, such as "The Hounds of Tindalos" by Frank Belknap Long). The story I have chosen to study is "Dreams in the Witch House."

The story is the one in which HPL makes his greatest use of mathematics. The protagonist of the story is Walter Gilman, a mathematics student at Miskatonic University. Gilman is very interested in non-Euclidian calculus, we are told, as well as quantum physics. Needless to say, no such subject as non-Euclidian calculus exists, nor does such a name make any real sense. While calculus does have a strong background in geometry, an in-depth study of the subject reveals the relative unimportance of the field in which the actual limitation process takes place. The name of the subject sounds good, but means nothing. Quantum physics is a fancy name for the study of quantum mechanics, i.e., the motion of the universe as related by the theory developed by Planck and Einstein.

Lovecraft's pseudomathematics we might call pseudo-geometry. That is, the notion that certain geometric shapes could be constructed that might not be entirely of this dimension. In the story itself, Gilman speculates on the possibility of creating a hole in the space-time continuum by a geometric construction, so that a person could step in through the hole at one place and emerge in another. It is much the same idea that was popular around the same time and after about a space warp. Space, we know, is curved. If, we are told by the pseudoscientists, we were able to bend space, then we could step from one spot in space to another without traveling the intervening distance. This concept of curved space is easily explained for the curious in the book entitled *Sphereworld* (the author I've forgotten).

This idea, unfortunately, is not quite true. The existence of higher dimensions should be of little concern to this world as any contact with such dimensions is impossible. Lovecraft's angles and curves that vanish into some other space is absolute nonsense. The reason for this is that geometry is a closed system. It is impossible (not unlikely or not yet possible, but impossible, actually shown to be never possible) to construct a higher dimension from a lower one. A quick reading of *Flatland* by Abbott will suffice to convince the reader. A two-dimensional being which lives on a flat surface cannot grasp the concept of "up" and "down." Such flatworlders cannot understand the meaning of height, or depth, or thickness, as no such thing exists, nor can it exist, in their two-dimensional world. As I do not want to belabor this point, I would strongly advise all of those interested to read *Flatland,* a book quite easy to understand and readily available in most libraries.

The same facts, thus, also apply to a three-dimensional world. There is no way that we can construct a four-dimensional object. Nor can such a thing even exist in our world. Since our perceptions are only three-dimensional, we could not see the fourth dimension extension of the object even if it had one. As all of our building material is only three dimensional, it would be impossible to construct anything of a higher dimension out of it. A quick way to grasp this impossibility is this. A straight line segment defines one dimension. Put another line segment perpendicular to this first line segment (getting something in the form of an L) and you have defined two dimensions (length and width). A third line, sticking out from the paper at a right angle, defines depth. Now, to define a fourth dimension of measurement (as we are talking of instantaneous occurrences, we ignore time measurements in our argument) take another line segment and put it at right angles to all of the other three. This will give you a fourth dimension. This is also quite impossible in our physical universe.

We are also told in the story of Gilman stating that time could not exist in certain belts of space, so that one could live forever in such regions. This fact would surprise a number of scientists.

In conclusion, Lovecraft was a master craftsman who used whatever knowledge he could in the furtherance of his story. Unfortunately, while his grasp of science and mathematics might have been greater than the average layman, it was not strong enough to present a convincing picture to the careful reader. Further, Lovecraft made the cardinal mistake of speculation of the impossible. While to the non-scientist, this may not sound like much of a sin, it is the cardinal mistake of the uninformed.

TEXTUAL PROBLEMS IN LOVECRAFT

A Preliminary Survey

by S.T. Joshi

It is now known to the majority of Lovecraft scholars that the printed texts of Lovecraft's work — particularly the editions of his fiction published by Arkham House, from which all other editions derive[1] * — are notoriously corrupt and misprinted; some texts bearing over 1000 errors, including the omission of whole passages. The reasons for this state of affairs are manifold, and stem both from Lovecraft's idiosyncratic use of English and from the oftentimes curious transmission of his texts. The fact that Lovecraft did not, as with Bierce, live to supervise an edition of his work, and the fact that his posthumous editors August Derleth and Donald Wandrei were not authorities in textual scholarship and (in Derleth's case) were oftentimes very careless in the preparation of their editions,[2] has resulted in a textual chaos from which only a whole new edition — founded on the extensive number of manuscripts of Lovecraft's fiction still preserved, thanks largely to the diligence of R.H. Barlow — can rescue Lovecraft's work. Such an edition has now been prepared by the author of this essay, but an examination of the nature of the textual problems in Lovecraft's work may not be out of order. For the sake of simplicity only Lovecraft's prose shall be dealt with in this article, as his poetry involves wholly different textual problems of a rather less complex nature.

The reasons for the plethora of errors in the published texts of Lovecraft's work stem, as has been noted, both from Lovecraft's own style and from vagaries in the textual history of individual works. Let us consider the former.

Lovecraft, nurtured upon the old books in his grandfather's library, gained from youth an archaic, complex style of writing which never wholly left him, in spite of his later attempts to exorcise the most extreme of the archaisms. (The actual archaism of Lovecraft's mature style has

---

* Superscript numerals refer to notes at the end of this chapter.

perhaps been exaggerated by critics, and certain of his spelling preferences — e.g. *shew*[3], *phantasy, connexion*[4], *whilst*, etc. — were common not only in his day but afterwards.) Lovecraft, however, never abandoned his usage of British spellings, in spite of the fact that most magazines in which he appeared did not allow them in their "style sheets." The most common of Lovecraft's British spellings are these:

-our for *-or*: *honour, colour*, etc.
At times Lovecraft would use the improper *glamourous*, but he knew that *honorary* and *vaporise* are the proper forms.[5]
-ise for *-ize*: *rationalise, recognise*, etc.
Curiously, *Weird Tales* would sometimes alter *surprise* (so both in British and American orthography) to the unintentionally Elizabethan *surprize!*
-xion for *-ction*: *connexion*.
Lovecraft never uses the form *reflexion* (*complexion* is so both in England and America).
-ae or *-oe* for *-e*: *palaeontologist, daemon, mediaeval, foetor*, etc.
Primaeval occurs intermittently, but *primeval* is more common. And *aera* for *era* is rare in the fiction (less so in the letters).
-re for *-er*: *centre* (hence *centring, centred*), *lustre, mitre*, etc.
-ce for *-se*: *defence* (but *defensive*), *licence* (not consistent in Lovecraft), *pretence*, etc.
Lovecraft always used the American *practice*, although *Weird Tales* paradoxically changed this to *practise*.
-ll for *-l*: *travelling, jewellery* (for *jewelry*, etc.
Individual words: *programme, shew* (for *show* — only as verb; not wholly consistent in Lovecraft) *plough, despatch* (for *dispatch*), et al.

Certain non-British spellings used regularly by Lovecraft are *practice* (for *practise*), *judgment* (although *judgement* is not exclusively British) *inquiry* (for *enquiry*[6]); *eery* occurs more often than *eerie*. Lovecraft did not employ the British mode of abbreviating personal titles (e.g. *Mr* for *Mr.*) or of telling time (*3.10* for *3:20*).[7] Lovecraft employed certain archaisms of syntax and spelling which have not always been preserved in his printed texts. In particular we may speak of his use of punctuation. Note the comma in the construction "He affirms (or knows or says), that" found regularly in eighteenth-century prose;[8] the use of the serial comma (*apples, pears, and bananas*) — even now not wholly out of fashion; *an* (not *a*) before some words beginning with an *h* or a consonantal vowel (in *At the Mountains of Madness* alone we find *an Euclid, an hypothesis, an hundred,* and the formerly common *such an one*); the use of a semicolon before a present participle ("The Dunwich Horror": " . . . they rode around Dunwich; questioning the natives . . .") or before an adversative clause ("The Whisperer in Darkness": "But while . . . the creatures would appear to have harmed only those trespassing on their privacy; there were

later accounts . . .") or before a clause beginning with *for* ("The Festival":
"The nethermost caverns . . . are not for the fathoming of eyes that see;
for their marvels are strange and terrific"); the use of a semicolon for a
colon (*The Case of Charles Dexter Ward*: "The new withdrawals were all
modern items; histories, scientific treatises, [etc.]"); and numerous other
forms. Lovecraft hyphenated many words and compounds in which
hyphenation has now been abandoned. All cases where the suffix *-like* is
used are hyphenated in Lovecraft (save very common words such as
warlike or *godlike*); hyphens are used for the prefixes *pre-, trans-, post-,
half-, ultra-, extra-, sub-, semi-* (save only *semicircle*), some words with
non-, and some verbs with *re-*. Other hyphenated words in Lovecraft
are *breath-taking, far-away, first-hand, burying-ground, copy-book,* and
words with compound *-place* (e.g. meeting-place). The diaeresis is used in
such words as *coördinate, coöperate, reënter,* and the like (an earlier form
in Lovecraft is *co-operate* [cf. *The United Co-operative,* edited by Love-
craft] or *coöperate*.) Lovecraft has a tendency not to italicize certain
foreign words which he felt were sufficiently incorporated into English;
hence the non-italicization of *fantaisiste, en masse, facade* (without the
cedilla), *outré, cul de sac,* and others. Latin is usually italicised (cf. *ex
nihilo nihil fit* from "The Whisperer in Darkness").

There are a number of other idiosyncratic or archaic syntactical ar-
rangements employed by Lovecraft which have caused difficulties for his
editors; moreover, there are indications that certain of these idiosyncrasies changed toward the end of his career, so that we can speak definitely
of a "late" orthographical or syntactical style in Lovecraft. One feature
alone is the replacement of a semicolon by a dash; note "Dreams in the
Witch House": "The other three were what sent him unconscious — for
they were living entities. . . ."

Another point of difficulty in Lovecraft's texts is his handwriting. The
illegibility of his handwriting has perhaps been exaggerated by some
(certainly Clark Ashton Smith's is infinitely worse), and after a certain
interval his hand becomes actually fairly effortless to read; albeit his
handwriting became smaller and smaller toward the end of his life.
This initial difficulty in reading Lovecraft's hand, compounded with the
fact that he often allowed associates to prepare typescripts of his work
through his own disinclination to type, have resulted in curious misreadings.[9] Both *The Dream-Quest of Unknown Kadath* and *The Case of
Charles Dexter Ward* remained in manuscript until after Lovecraft's
death. August Derleth and Donald Wandrei have spoken of their difficulty in preparing the latter for publication: "Lovecraft's handwriting
was not easy to read under the best of circumstances; he had his own
peculiarities of spelling, often used Latin and Greek phrases [but there is
no Greek in *Ward*], and often used coined words of his own. These made
the problem of deciphering his complex puzzle-pages even more difficult."[10] The results are often amusing. The Arkham House text of the
novel bears such readings as "wholly" for "vitally," "sad" for "and,"

TEXTUAL PROBLEMS IN LOVECRAFT

"contacts" for "contents," "wrested" for "arrested," "here" for "well," "ruins" for "rims," and others. Neither Derleth nor Wandrei seemed to know Latin (this is certainly borne out in some wild misreadings in the *Selected Letters*),[11] although Wandrei knew Greek; and both editors' lack of knowledge of archaic English caused them to be unaware of such things as the archaic doubling of the lower-case *f* to indicate a capital *f* (e.g. *ffortunes*, not *Fortunes*); hence in the Arkham House text such words are — in the epistles between Curwen and his cohorts — repeatedly spelled with one *f*, save when the word happens to be at the beginning of a sentence (where the capital *f* is improperly used). Other errors are the failures to capitalize nouns. Indeed, Derleth, as if in some sort of frenzy, has *added* archaisms in these letters where they do not belong (e.g. *calle* for *call*).

Problems in *The Dream-Quest* stem partly from Lovecraft's coining of place names: hence "Inquanok" is actually "Inganok" (the editors misread the *g* as a *q*, then inserted the *u* after the *q*, in spite of such Middle Eastern place names as *Qatar*); and all the species names (*gug, zoog, shantak*, etc.) ought to be in lower case. Other comical misreadings are "air out" for "an ant," "beings" for "priests," "goodly" for "grisly," "putrid" for "foetid," and others.

A final matter concerns the deliberate tampering of Lovecraft's texts by his editors. This is a comparatively rare phenomenon, and the reasons for it are usually obvious. When R.H. Barlow published "Cats and Dogs" (retitled "Something about Cats" by Derleth) in *Leaves* (1937), he removed certain of Lovecraft's attacks upon democracy and his praises of fascism and aristocracy; hence "aristocratic" becomes "unshackled," "even the fascist sentiment" becomes "any hand," and — in a similar light — "negroes" becomes "tradesmen." The date of original publication must always be kept in mind. Similarly, when Derleth printed "Observations on Several Parts of America" (not "North America") in *Marginalia* (1944), he altered "oily Jews" to "foreigners."

A more culpable instance of tampering occurs in Lovecraft's revisions of Zealia Bishop's "The Mound" and "Medusa's Coil."[12] Both these stories lay in manuscript (or, rather, in typescripts prepared by Frank Belknap Long, then Bishop's agent) after Lovecraft's death; and Derleth, in an effort to sell them to a pulp market, decided to alter and abridge both texts. (As it was, "The Mound" was published in a still more abridged form in *Weird Tales*, although fortunately no subsequent edition followed this text). His changes in "The Mound" amount to excisions of about 500 words, and countless changes in spelling and punctuation (some resulting in incoherence; hence in a sentence reading "And if any room for doubt remained, that room was abolished. . . ." Derleth changed the second "room" to "crypt," destroying the idiom and producing nonsense).[13] "Medusa's Coil" fared still worse under Derleth's pencil, and whole sections have been removed and abridged.

In the majority of Lovecraft's texts (particularly the fiction), textual errors have crept in not so much through the bungling of any particular editor, as in the fossilization of errors through repeated publications. Hence to account for all textual errors in a work, we must ascertain the details of the *transmission of the text,* beginning with the autograph manuscript and proceeding to the latest edition. In such a procedure we often need not examine all publications of a work; very often the text is transmitted through a relatively small number of publications, rendering other publications textually irrelevant. Hence, since the Arkham House editions usually derive from the first *Weird Tales* appearance of a story, the second or third *Weird tales* appearance of that story is textually irrelevant. (This is not the case "Under the Pyramids" [commonly known as "Imprisoned with the Pharaohs"], where the Arkham House text derived from the second *Weird Tales* text, textually much inferior to the first.) After examining all relevant publications and extant manuscripts of a work, we can, in most cases, readily determine the order and process of transmission. In some instances we must hypothesize the existence of manuscripts not now extant to account for all textual derivations; and, in cases where no manuscript of a work survives, more weight must be given to those publications which seem closer to the source (i.e. the original manuscript) than to those which are secondary (i.e. derive from other publications). For "The Beast in the Cave," there survive the autograph manuscript, a typescript (prepared by Barlow), and published versions in *The Vagrant* (June, 1919) and the Arkham House editions beginning with *Marginalia.* (The appearance in *The Acolyte* of Fall 1943 is textually irrelevant.) Since the *Vagrant* appearance reveals a text revised from the original manuscript, a now non-extant typescript (presumably by Lovecraft) must be postulated, so that the *stemma* or textual genealogy of the tale would be as follows (bracketed text represents the hypothetical T.Ms. [typed manuscript]):

A.Ms.

T.Ms. (by Barlow)   [T.Ms.] (revised

V   = *The Vagrant*
AH = Arkham House editions   AH   V

We have noticed that many of Lovecraft's manuscripts — particularly his long later works — were typed by other hands, whose ability to read Lovecraft's hand varied widely. An unspecified revision client typed "The Dreams in the Witch House" (surprisingly accurately); Donald Wandrei (the best of Lovecraft's amanuenses) typed (or probably retyped) many of Lovecraft's earlier stories, e.g. "The Quest of Iranon,"[14] "The Other Gods," etc.; R.H. Barlow typed a great many of Lovecraft's texts, including the T.Ms. (non-extant) of "The Shadow out of Time" (see below) and the partial T.Mss. of *The Case of Charles Dexter Ward* and *The Dream-Quest of Unknown Kadath* (the latter followed by Arkham House until it ceased; the former ought to have been followed by Arkham House, since Lovecraft had written some revisions on the T.Ms.); E. Hoffmann Price prepared a T.Ms. of "The Picture in the House" (very poor) for use in an anthology which he was planning (cf. *Selected Letters* IV. 112f.); Lovecraft writes that "a delinquent [revision] client"[15] typed "The Thing on the Doorstep" (the T.Ms. is very bad, confusing Lovecraft's chapter divisions of the tale; unfortunately it has been followed in all publications), but I have not ascertained who this is (perhaps Hazel Heald).

If a story has emerged relatively unscathed textually at this level, it must begin its ventures into print; here is where the majority of textual errors arise. Lovecraft had to be content to appear in the lowest and humblest of venues — amateur journals, pulp magazines, "fan" journals, cheap anthologies, and the like. The result is not pleasant to behold. Surprisingly, some of his soundest publications are found in the amateur journals, in spite of the unprepossessing appearance of many of them. Thus the appearance of "The White Ship" in *The United Amateur* (November, 1919; typeset by W. Paul Cook) is word-for-word perfect with the surviving T.Ms. (by Lovecraft); although in an A.Ms prepared by Lovecraft at a later time, [16] he has made some apparent revisions which must be incorporated in any text claiming to be definitive.

Unfortunately, the value of many of these amateur journal appearances is lessened by the fact that Lovecraft often revised many of his earlier tales for subsequent publications; hence a *double tradition* arises which makes the establishment of the text sometimes difficult, especially when a reliable manuscript for the tale is not extant. The *stemma* for "The Picture in the House" is as follows (texts in brackets indicate non-extant manuscripts):

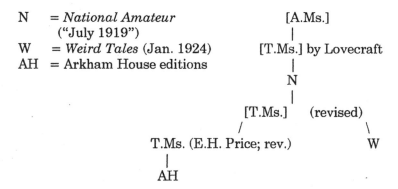

N = *National Amateur* ("July 1919")	[A.Ms.]
W = *Weird Tales* (Jan. 1924)	[T.Ms.] by Lovecraft
AH = Arkham House editions	N
	[T.Ms.] (revised)
	T.Ms. (E.H. Price; rev.) W
	AH

This text was apparently revised twice; first for the *Weird Tales* appearance, then for the appearance in Price's anthology (which, of course, never appeared). Many other stories were similarly revised after initial publication.

When we turn to appearances in the pulp magazines, we find not only that certain standard alterations were made in Lovecraft's texts —

Americanization of his British spellings, simplification of his punctuation, etc. — but also that there were some bizarre alterations or errors hard to account for. Thus in the appearance of "The Call of Cthulhu" in *Weird Tales* (followed by Arkham House), the long newspaper article from the *Sydney Bulletin* hinting of Johansen's encounter with Cthulhu, which in Lovecraft's text consists of four long paragraphs, has been broken up into thirteen paragraphs; apparently Farnsworth Wright, editor of *Weird Tales,* felt that these short paragraphs were more in keeping with journalistic style. *Weird Tales* almost always spelled out Lovecraft's abbreviated forms "Mr.," "Prof.," "St." (street), "Dr.," and the like. Lovecraft notes some bewildering printer's errors in "Dreams in the Witch House": "love" for "lore," and "human element" for "known element." Lovecraft is correct when he remarks that such errors cause the author (and not his editors) to become "laid open to the suspicion of rambling feebleness and semi-illiteracy."[17] Lovecraft had, indeed, when submitting his first manuscripts to *Weird Tales* in 1923, laid down the dictum that "If the tale cannot be printed as written, down to the very last semicolon and comma, it must gratefully accept rejection"[18] but the injunction was never followed. *Weird Tales* actually made few typographical errors (here it bested the amateur journals); most of the textual changes were quite deliberate. The textual problems encountered in the science-fiction journals in which Lovecraft appeared — *Amazing Stories, Astounding Stories* — must be considered later.[19]

The "fan" magazines — *The Fantasy Fan, Fantasy Magazine, Fanciful Tales, The Phantagraph,* etc. — were the poorest of all in the presentation of texts: Lovecraft remarks that the appearance of "The Nameless City" in *Fanciful Tales* had "59 bad misprints . . . surely something of a record!"[20] *The Fantasy Fan* perpetrated the horrible misreading "seven cryptical books of earth" for "seven cryptical books of Hsan" in "The Other Gods," leading L. Sprague de Camp to believe that the latter title (used in *The Dream-Quest*) was a deliberate change by Lovecraft to make the title sound "more impressive."[21] Unfortunately, when Derleth and Wandrei came to prepare their Arkham House editions, they ordinarily picked the very worst printed texts to follow — indeed, they seemed to have an uncanny knack for so doing. The reason for this circumstance is simply that they usually used the printed text most readily available to them; this generally happened to be the latest appearance, wherein the greatest number of errors had encrusted. Hence the stemma for "The Doom That Came to Sarnath" appears on the facing page.

This is one of the tales revised after its initial appearance; the T.Ms. by Barlow introduced a number of errors, and each publication added new errors. Moreover, the later Arkham House edition — *Dagon and Other Macabre Tales* (1965) — introduced many errors from its own predecessor, *Beyond the Wall of Sleep* (1943).

Arkham House did in certain instances follow Lovecraft's typescripts where they existed; but, save in the prose poem "What the Moon Brings,"

TEXTUAL PROBLEMS IN LOVECRAFT

avoided following the A.Ms. [author's manuscript] if any published appearance at all, however poor, survived. The following are some of the more important stories followed from the T.Ms. (hence relatively accurate): "The Dunwich Horror," "The Whisperer in Darkness," "He," "The Horror at Red Hook," "Pickman's Model," "The Silver Key," and some others.

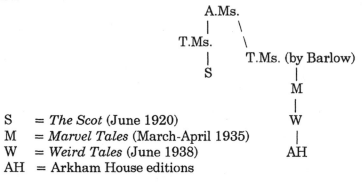

S   = *The Scot* (June 1920)
M = *Marvel Tales* (March-April 1935)
W = *Weird Tales* (June 1938)
AH = Arkham House editions

Arkham House often failed to realize that some published versions of a tale were better than others. Lovecraft rarely remarked upon the relative textual accuracy of the published versions of his work (save, as in the cases of "The Nameless City" and *At the Mountains of Madness,* where the appearances were extremely bad), so that Derleth and Wandrei had no way of distinguishing textually poor from textually sound printed versions — a distinction which only actual collation with manuscripts could elicit. Thus Arkham House followed the poor *Weird Tales* appearance of "The Call of Cthulhu," not realizing that the appearance in Harré's *Beware After Dark!* (1929) had followed the T.Ms., hence was notably superior to the *Weird Tales* text. As noted earlier, the first *Weird Tales* appearance of "Under the Pyramids" is much superior to the second *Weird Tales* appearance, but Arkham House followed the latter.

Vagaries in the transmission between various Arkham House editions themselves exist. For *The Outsider and Others* Derleth and Wandrei followed Derleth's T.Ms. for "Dreams in the Witch House," but in the appearance in *At the Mountains of Madness and Other Novels* (1964) Derleth used the poor *Weird Tales* text; one is at a loss to understand why he did not follow his own earlier text rather than return to another one which had much less authority. In the 1964 reprint of "The Statement of Randolph Carter" from *The Outsider and Others,* part of a paragraph is curiously omitted;[22] part of the second paragraph has been dropped in the 1964 reprint of "The Silver Key," which completely reverses the meaning of the passage. T.G.L. Cockcroft has at various times pointed out certain lines dropped from one Arkham House edition to another: two celebrated instances occur in the text of "The Dunwich Horror" in *The Dunwich Horror and Others* (1963); although one exists in the first paragraph of the 1963 edition of "The Whisperer in Darkness," hitherto unknown.

The task of restoring the texts of Lovecraft's fiction is in essence simple, thanks to the survival of manuscripts for nearly all of his original tales and even some of his revisions. Some of these manuscripts are, of course, typescripts not by Lovecraft, but they have a certain value in any case. (Lovecraft was not notably careful in correcting blunders made by his typists, and rarely if ever made any word-by-word collation between his A.Ms. and the T.Ms.) Important tales for which no manuscripts exist are: "The Alchemist," "The Tomb," "Polaris," "The Temple," "The Street," "The Moon-Bog," "The Outsider," "The Music of Erich Zann," "Hypnos," "The Rats in the Walls," "The Unnamable," and "The Shunned House." Even here we have some published versions which are quite reliable: Cook's pamphlet of *The Shunned House* and his *Vagrant* text of "The Tomb"; Galpin's text of "Polaris" in *The Philosopher* (although the tale was subsequently revised); and others. In the *Weird Tales* text of "The Rats in the Walls," however, there may have been some tampering with the paragraphing of the tale, as there was in the second *Weird Tales* appearance of "Under the Pyramids." In the one instance of "From Beyond," we have a manuscript which is *not* the final or revised text: in its appearance in *The Fantasy Fan* the text bears some divergences from the A.Ms. (the T.Ms. is non-extant) which are manifestly revisions by Lovecraft (e.g. the addition of phrases), but other divergences may be printing errors.

Aside from countless minor problems involved in establishing a definitive text of Lovecraft's work, two problems stand out foremost — the texts of *At the Mountains of Madness* and "The Shadow out of Time." These were the two tales published in *Astounding Stories,* and their textual histories are so bizarre (although in certain respects wholly different from each other) that enormous difficulty may be had in establishing their texts. Let us first consider *At the Mountains of Madness.*

The tale was conceived in late 1930. Clark Ashton Smith wrote to Lovecraft on December 18, 1930, (Ms., John Hay Library): "I think your idea for an Antarctic story would be excellent, in spite of 'Pym' and subsequent tales. . . ." The A.Ms. records that the actual writing took place from February 24 to March 22, 1931. Lovecraft then himself prepared the 115-page T.Ms., finishing it (as he notes on the last page) on May 1, 1931. The tale of its submission to *Weird Tales* and its rejection there (causing Lovecraft an enormous psychological setback which "did more than anything else to end my effective fictional career")[23] is well known. It lay in manuscript for five years, until (through the agency of Julius Schwartz) it was accepted by *Astounding Stories* and published in a three-part serial in the February, March, and April, 1936 issues. In the interim, however, had occurred Admiral Byrd's expedition to the Antarctic (1933–35); and among its results was the confirmation that a hypothesis made by Lovecraft in his novel (that the antarctic continent was actually two continents divided by a frozen sea) was incorrect. Lovecraft was apparently concerned with correcting this error (which is alluded to three times in his novel); but he must have made the correction on the carbon copy of the novel (assuming that one was made), for no such revisions are found either on the existing T.Ms. or the A.Ms., although the revisions (clearly the work of Lovecraft) appear in the printed text. This carbon copy must have been sent to *Astounding* for publication; it has, I have discovered, now been destroyed.[24] When the tale was actually published, however, hundreds if not thousands of deliberate alterations and deletions appear to have been made in the text by the editor F. Orlin Tremaine (whom Lovecraft once called a "god-damned dung of a hyaena").[25] Apparently Tremaine considered Lovecraft's text too difficult for easy comprehension by his readers, so that he felt compelled to simplify Lovecraft's English and extensively alter his paragraphs. Lovecraft was forced laboriously to pencil in corrections in his own copies of *Astounding*; but unfortunately, he seems to have corrected only a fraction of the errors, since even after his corrected text there remain hundreds of divergences between the *Astounding* text and the original T.Ms. The problem becomes: How much did Lovecraft revise the text of his tale when submitting it to *Astounding*? Did he revise not merely his scientific hypothesis, but other portions (particularly the punctuation of the tale, which accounts for most of the divergences between *Astounding* and the T.Ms.) as well? The point is a delicate one, although I tend to doubt that Lovecraft revised his text much: the punctuational forms found in the *Astounding* text seem less typical of Lovecraft's normal punctuational style (although it is unfortunately exactly at this time when Lovecraft's style shifted to the "late" punctuational style noted earlier), and we know (see below) that *Astounding* altered the punctuation of "The Shadow out of Time." In his copies of *Astounding* (still extant in the John Hay Library) Lovecraft has failed to correct certain obvious errors (e.g. the Americanization of his British spellings), a thing accountable only by oversight or by Lovecraft's unconcern about these lesser errors. Lovecraft has in almost every case corrected the misparagraphing of the tale in *Astounding* — a point of considerable importance in our examination of the text of "The Shadow out of Time" — as well as most of the actual omissions of passages. Two passages, however, omitted in the first part of the serial were not pencilled in by Lovecraft; and the question again arises as to whether Lovecraft had deleted the two passages in his revised T.Ms. or whether he had failed to notice their omission in the printed text. The latter is — in spite of the relative bulk of the omitted passages — not improbable; since Lovecraft did not appear to realize the extreme corruption of the printed text until he examined the third part of the serial, where by far the most omissions occurred. Moreover, the second of the two omitted sections seems so important to the smooth transition of the passage that its absence is difficult to endure;[26] I claim, therefore, that both passages are authentic and must be restored.

There are, however, additional complications at this stage. Lovecraft wrote[27] that he corrected the *Astounding* text from his A.Ms., not having the T.Ms. at hand. Now in his T.Ms. Lovecraft had made certain revisions — usually phraseological — as is normal when any writer prepares a typescript of his own work. Unfortunately, in the five years between the preparation of the T.Ms. and the publication of the tale, Lovecraft seems to have *forgotten* some of these revisions when correcting the *Astounding* text with his A.Ms., hence the following oddity:

At the beginning of Chapter IV there occurs the phrase "mountains of madness" in the A.Ms.; this was changed to "frightful mountain wall" in the T.Ms., presumably because the phrase "mountains of madness" had just appeared in the last paragraph of Chapter III. In *Astounding Stories* the text reads "awful mountain wall"; this appears to be a deliberate alteration (probably by Tremaine rather than by Lovecraft) from the T.Ms.; but Lovecraft has corrected his copy of *Astounding* here to read "mountains of madness" again, and the Arkham House editions follow this reading. Lovecraft seems to have forgotten his revision of the phrase in the T.Ms., and has restored what is actually an incorrect reading in terms of what appear to be his final wishes for the wording of the passage. Hence a proper text of the tale should here read "frightful mountain wall"; this reading, at least, has some manuscript authority, and the possibility that Lovecraft changed "frightful" to "awful" in the T.Ms. sent to *Astounding* is too dim and uncertain for reliance (Lovecraft, in any case, normally used "awful" as an archaic synonym for "awesome"). Similar problems occur elsewhere in the text. It thus appears that the existing T.Ms. should be followed in nearly all instances where a deliberate revision has not taken place, and that Lovecraft's "corrected" copies of *Astounding* must not be allowed to carry great weight save as corroboration.

Unfortunately, Derleth and Wandrei, when preparing the first Arkham House edition of the tale — *The Outsider and Others* (1939) — based their text on Lovecraft's copies of *Astounding*.[28] They apparently knew that Lovecraft had revised his text after preparing the T.Ms. and that the *Astounding* version was not at all reliable; hence they felt that Lovecraft's corrected copies of *Astounding* would provide as secure a text as could easily be obtained. That the current Arkham House edition (very little different from the 1939 edition) still contains some 1500 errors need not strictly be attributed to Derleth and Wandrei; for only an enormously laborious collation of all existing manuscripts and publications of the novel can produce a text that has even a modest claim to authority. In the end there shall always remain doubt as to what Lovecraft's final wishes for the novel were, and which of the uncorrected divergences between *Astounding* and the existing T.Ms. are the result of deliberate revision by Lovecraft and which the result of editorial alteration.

The textual status of "The Shadow out of Time" has been radically altered since the discovery, in 1994, of the original autograph manuscript of the story. That discovery itself is a saga as bizarre as anything Lovecraft ever imagined. It is well known that R. H. Barlow surreptitiously typed the story for Lovecraft when the latter was visiting him in Florida in the summer of 1935;[29] in gratitude, Lovecraft gave the manuscript to Barlow as a present,[30] and it is the only manuscript that Barlow did not turn over to the John Hay Library of Brown University after Lovecraft's death. When Barlow moved to Mexico in the early 1940s, he took the manuscript with him; prior to his own death in 1951, he gave the manuscript to a female student of his at Mexico City College. This student eventually retired to Hawaii, and upon her own death her sister came upon the manuscript and, learning that the John Hay Library had an extensive Lovecraft collection, offered it as a gift. The library accepted it with alacrity, and I was the first scholar to be allowed to examine it in detail.

My examination conclusively proved that the text as published in *Astounding Stories* (June 1936) is severely corrupt. Although Lovecraft inexplicably stated that "this story was not intentionally mangled,"[31] there are in fact more than 400 divergences between the autograph manuscript and the printed text. Most of these errors concern the paragraphing of the tale: as with *At the Mountains of Madness*, the long paragraphs of "The Shadow out of Time" have been chopped up into short paragraphs of the sort common in pulp magazines. Other errors are apparently the result of Barlow's inability to read Lovecraft's crabbed handwriting. This manuscript is one of the most exhaustively revised and interlined of any of his autograph drafts, with insertions sometimes written vertically in the narrow margins of the text. One error toward the beginning is of importance in regard to the protagonist Nathaniel Wingate Peaslee's background. The current Arkham House text (*The Dunwich Horror and Others*, p. 370) reads: "I . . . did not go to Arkham till I entered Miskatonic University as instructor of politicy economy in 1895." Lovecraft's text reads: "I . . . did not go to Arkham till I entered Miskatonic University at the age of eighteen. That was in 1889. After my graduation I studied economics at Harvard, and came back to Miskatonic as Instructor of Political Economy in 1895." Barlow's eye no doubt skipped from the first citation of "Miskatonic" to the second, so that the intervening passage was inadvertently omitted.

My corrected text of "The Shadow out of Time" has not yet been published, although I hope it will be in the near future. It might be possible to conjecture why Lovecraft was not more vociferous in his complaints of editorial tampering with this text. Two reasons can be offered. First, Lovecraft may have felt so grateful to his friends R. H. Barlow (who typed the manuscript) and Donald Wandrei (who sold it to *Astounding* without asking for any agent's commission) that it would have seemed churlish to cast aspersions on the publication of the story. Second, the death of Robert E. Howard on June 11, along with several other personal traumas that Lovecraft was suffering at this time, may have forced this matter to take an insignificant place in his emotional horizon.

My corrected texts of Lovecraft's fiction and revisions have now been published in four volumes by Arkham House, and my edition of his collected poetry has only recently been issued by Night Shade Books. All that remains is the issuing of Lovecraft's voluminous essays and letters, and plans are underway to prepare this body of work for publication, possibly as a CD-ROM. Once that occurs, Lovecraft's entire corpus will be available to scholars in textually corrected editions. All aspects of scholarship are affected by textual study; and it is certain that the analysis of Lovecraft's work will rise substantially in quality once we are aware of what he actually wrote.[32]

NOTES:

[1] The Arkham House editions of Lovecraft's fiction date from *The Outsider and Others* (1939) to *The Horror in the Museum and Other Revisions* (1970). The earlier Arkham House editions were the source for the early British editions from Gollancz, while the later Gollancz editions derive from (and in some cases are facsimile reprints of) the later Arkham House editions beginning with *The Dunwich Horror and Others* (1963), itself largely a photocopy reprint of the *Best Supernatural Stories of H.P. Lovecraft* (1945). The Ballantine editions derive from the newer Arkham House editions (the two paper editions originally published by Lancer Books and later by Zebra and Jove derive from the earlier Arkham House editions, hence are somewhat securer textually), while the Panther editions stem from Gollancz.

The earlier foreign editions (especially the French), as noted by Derleth in "H.P. Lovecraft: The Making of a Literary Reputation, 1937–1971" *(Books at Brown* 25 (1977) 19), were largely triggered by the earlier Gollancz editions.

[2] The question of how competently R.H. Barlow would have edited Lovecraft's work had he been given a chance is an interesting one, but in all probability he would have done even worse than Derleth: Barlow could not read Lovecraft's hand as well as Derleth could (as the manifold errors in his edition of the *Commonplace Book* [Futile Press, 1938] indicate), although he was more respectful of Lovecraft's work and less interested in presenting it in an "orthodox" format excluding Lovecraft's many idiosyncrasies of orthography, grammar, and the like. Barlow's main importance to Lovecraft textual studies is simply in the assiduity with which he collected and preserved Lovecraft's original manuscripts so that textual reparation could, however belatedly, be made.

[3] Regularly used by Evelyn Waugh (d. 1966); cf. the Chapman & Hall editions of his novels.

[4] Still employed by many British writers.

[5] Cf. *Selected Letters* III. 101.

[6] *Enquiry* occurs very rarely in Lovecraft: cf., e.g., letter to W.F. Anger, 14 August 1934 (Ms., University of Minnesota Library).

[7] The only exceptions are the astronomy articles for the *Pawtuxet Valley Gleaner* (1906) and the juvenile fiction.

[8] Cf. the "Note on the Text" of the Oxford edition (1966) of Radcliffe's *Mysteries of Udolpho* (ed. Bonamy Dobree), p. xvii.

[9] I have pointed out many misreadings made by Tom Collins (due to his inability to read Lovecraft's handwriting) in his edition of Lovecraft's poetry, *A Winter Wish* (1977); cf. "A Textual Commentary on *A Winter Wish*," *The Miskatonic*, 6, no. 2 (May 1978) [11–21]; revised as "An Errata List to *A Winter Wish*," *Crypt of Cthulhu* No. 20 (Eastertide 1984): 31–45.

[10] *H.P. Lovecraft in "The Eyrie"* (1979) p. 58.

[11] Cf., e.g., the butchery of Vergil at *Selected Letters* III. 313 *(Aeneid* 6.847–853).

[12] Cf. my article, "Who Wrote 'The Mound'?" *Nyctalops*, 14 (March 1978) 41–42; revised in *Crypt of Cthulhu* No. 11 (Candlemas 1983): 27–29, 38.

[13] "Crypt" appears in the *Beyond the Wall of Sleep* (1943) text; in the *Horror in the Museum* (1970) text the word "doubt" is substituted for "crypt," a makeshift change which at least preserves the sense.

[14] See. *Selected Letters* II. 211.

[15] See. *Selected Letters* IV. 310.

[16] Prepared in 1934 for Alvin Earl Perry; published in facsimile in *Whispers,* July 1974.

[17] See. *Selected Letters* IV. 213.

[18] *H.P. Lovecraft in "The Eyrie,"* p. 15. "Accept rejection" is as succulent an oxymoron as anything in Lovecraft.

[19] I have not had an opportunity to examine the extant T.Ms. (not by Lovecraft) of "The Colour out of Space" (in private hands), hence cannot remark on the textual accuracy of its appearance in *Amazing Stories.* The fact that the British spelling of "colour" in the title was preserved (as it has not been in some anthology appearances) may lead us to assume relatively little corruption in this text.

[20] *Selected Letters* V. 368.

[21] *Lovecraft: A Biography* (1975), p. 167.

[22] Pointed out by R. Alain Everts in his edition of the tale (Strange Co., 1976).

[23] *Selected Letters* V. 224.

[24] In a recent talk with Kirby McCauley, who discussed this matter with Stanley Schmidt, current editor of *Analog* (formerly *Astounding*), I learned that the old files of *Astounding* were destroyed ca. 1960.

[25] Cf. Lovecraft to R.H. Barlow, 4 June 1936 (Ms., John Hay Library).

[26] The second passage (here indicated by brackets) would occur on p. 36 of the 1964 Arkham House edition: "The whole general formation, it must be made clear, seemed abominably suggestive of the starfish-head of the archaean entities; and we agreed that the suggestion must have worked potently upon the sensitised minds of Lake's overwrought party. [Our own first sight of the actual buried entities formed a horrible moment, and sent the imaginations of Pabodie and myself back to some

of the shocking primal myths we had read and heard. We all agreed that the mere sight and continued presence of the things must have cooperated with the oppressive polar solitude and daemon mountain wind in driving Lake's party mad.]

"For madness — centering in Gedney as the only possible surviving agent — was the explanation spontaneously adopted by everybody as far as spoken utterance was concerned. . . ." The word *for* beginning the new paragraph must obviously refer to a previous mention of madness — a mention which we find precisely in the omitted section.

[27] Lovecraft to Barlow, *loc. cit.*

[28] Cf. August Derleth to R.H. Barlow, 21 March [1937] (Ms., John Hay Library).

[29] See "The Wind That Is in the Grass," in *Marginalia* (1944), p. 348–349.

[30] Lovecraft to E.H. Price, 21 August 1935 (Ms., John Hay Library).

[31] Lovecraft to Duane Rimel, 20 June 1936 (Ms., John Hay Library).

[32] I am grateful to Prof. Edward S. Lauterbach for suggestions on the revision of this paper.

H.P. LOVECRAFT: THE BOOKS

by Lin Carter

[as annotated by Robert M. Price, and S.T. Joshi]

[H.P. Lovecraft employed all the devious imagination of a hoaxer, he once admitted, in order to lead readers on such a merry chase that, for the duration of the story, they might become unsure whether the grim and terrible myths to which he gave literary life might not actually be based on genuine ancient lore. Might there truly be a cult of the Old Ones, a *Necronomicon*? More than once he had to disabuse young readers of such notions, which he himself had planted in their heads.

[As far as we know the young Lin Carter never believed in the reality of the esoteric tomes of the Cthulhu Mythos, but he became a scholarly curator of the Lovecraftian library nonetheless, combing all the relevant stories for any bit of data on the contents, authors, and publishing histories of the forbidden books. The product of his enthusiasm was the following glossary, "H.P. Lovecraft: The Books."

[August Derleth chanced upon Carter's glossary of the Mythos books when it was serialized in *Inside and Science Fiction Advertiser* for March, May, and September 1956. He decided to include it in his Arkham House potpourri volume *The Shuttered Room and Other Pieces* (1959). Fittingly, that volume and Carter's glossary itself would become an official Mythos tome once Brian Lumley had a character refer to it in his tale "The House of the Temple."

[Inevitably, there were a few errors in Carter's compilation, and other Lovecraftian bibliophiles did not hesitate to point them out. The first of these was New Zealander T.G.L. Cockcroft, whose "Addendum: Some Notes on the Carter Glossary" followed on the very heels of Carter's "H.P. Lovecraft: The Books" in *The Shuttered Room* itself. And then in that volume's sequel, *The Dark Brotherhood and Other Pieces* (1966), there followed William Scott Home's helpful "The Lovecraft 'Books': Some Addenda and Corrigenda."

[Yet even these glosses on the original do not correct all Carter's errors. And various important bits of information have come to light in unpublished letters and other sources in the intervening years. Doubtless the job shall have to be done again some day, but for the time being we have ventured to update Lin Carter's most fascinating scholarly work.

[We present Carter's essay as it appears in *The Shuttered Room,* silently correcting minor typographical errors and adding corrections and additions of our own. We have also appended a discussion of seven authors and titles found in Lovecraft's stories or letters in addition to the fifty-nine covered by Carter. No attempt has been made to discuss books created by later writers, or the further use by these writers of the books included in this listing. Our notes appear in brackets throughout the text, incorporating the findings of Cockcroft and Home while at the same time correcting the mistakes they themselves made. We hope that this augmented and corrected edition of Carter's essay will be of interest to those who wish to delve into the minutiae of Lovecraft's work.]

[— Robert M. Price & S.T. Joshi]

One of the most interesting and original features of the Cthulhu Mythology, that unique body of fiction and verse that was the combined product of some dozen or so writers, is the library-full of demonological texts and reference books frequently mentioned and quoted in the various stories. There are some fifty-nine of them in all, volumes of ancient magical lore, fragmentary works surviving from lost and semi-mythic cultures such as Atlantis and Hyperborea, modern works of research and commentary, curious testaments of personal experience, archaeological compilations, compendiums of verse, and so on. Each volume contributes to and supports the numerous points of the Mythos, and lends an air of authenticity and scholarly research to it. Some of these books actually exist; others were the invention of one or another of the authors who contributed to the Mythos; still others are legendary tomes drawn from extant mythology and actual mystical cults.

The "lay" reader, steeped in H.P. Lovecraft's references to such occult volumes as the *Book of Dzyan* or *De Furtivis Literarum Notis,* who chances upon copies of them in bookshop or library, may be persuaded that the Mythos does actually have a basis in fact, and might conceivably seek for copies of such other books as the *R'lyeh Text* or the fabulous *Necronomicon* itself. I know, personally, of two such gullible HPL-ophiles who have diligently advertised for copies of Abdul Alhazred's work in learned journals.

For some years I have indulged in the hobby of collecting works on demonology and the allied arts. Continually coming across data on some of the books referred to in the Cthulhu Mythos, I made notes of them, eventually compiling such a body of interesting information that I conceived of the present essay, and began studying the Mythos more deeply. The result is this present work. I have here gathered into place every item of information given in the Mythos to the books, arranging them in alphabetical order, indicating, wherever possible, the origin of the book in question, i.e., was it the invention of August Derleth or H.P. Lovecraft, was it an actual book, and if so, giving some information upon it. During the preparation of this article I have had the assistance of many authorities. August Derleth, Robert Bloch, Frank Belknap Long, and Clark Ashton Smith have been most helpful, as have such Lovecraftian scholars as George Wetzel. Others, versed in the esoterica of one or another of the occult arts, such as Hannes Bok and Jack Grill, have given me valuable aid in establishing which of the books were actual and extant. Members of the respective staffs of the Special Collections Library at Columbia University, the Rare Books Room of the New York Public Library, too numerous to acknowledge by name, have helped greatly.

Listed, as I have said, alphabetically, the books are given in full title, followed either by the author ascribed, or, in parentheses, the Mythoswriter who devised them; following this is any data on edition, translations, editors, and houses, places, and dates of publication. Following this head is a paragraph on the book in general, sometimes (where possible) describing its physical appearance, in other cases, listing the places were copies are preserved. I have also incorporated into this essay, under its respective book, every quotation given in the entire body of the Mythos, feeling that it will be of considerable value to any future critics and students of Lovecraftian lore to have all such quotes preserved in one place for quick and easy reference. Whereas, on some occasions, the same quotation is given in two different stories in the Mythos, I have noted any divergence between the two.

All this lore has been checked for accuracy, and, by this time, I am reasonably confident that every datum is correct.

— Lin Carter

THE BOOKS

1. *Al Azif, the Book of the Poet* (see 37. *Necronomicon*).

2. *An Investigation into the Myth-Patterns of Latter-Day Primitives with Especial Reference to the R'lyeh Text*, Dr. Laban Shrewsbury (Derleth).

A non-existent work by Derleth's mysterious blind scholar, hero of *The Trail of Cthulhu*, specifically in "The Watcher from the Sky" and other chapters (see 17. *Cthulhu in the Necronomicon*).

3. *Ars Magna et Ultima*, Raymond Lully.

This book, which is referred to variously in the Mythos, as in Derleth's "The Whippoorwills in the Hills," actually exists. Raymond Lully, who wrote under the name of Raymundus Lullus, and was born 1235 and died in 1315, was an alchemist and scholar. Born in Majorca, he was stoned to death by angry Arabs in Tunis, whom he had sought to convert to Christianity. The *Ars Magna*, which is one of the few works attributed to the Spanish martyr that is believed to have actually been written by him, contains little of magical lore — and even less about Cthulhu — as it is a scholarly treatise on the conversion of Moslems by intellectual argument. The title may be rendered roughly into English as *Universal Art.*

[The proper title of this work is *Ars Magna, Generalis et Ultima* (first published 1517). It was first cited by Lovecraft in *The Case of Charles Dexter Ward.* Raymond Lully is now more commonly referred to as Ramón Lull.]

4. *Atlantis and The Lost Lemuria,* W. Scott-Elliot.

This book is mentioned rarely in the Mythos (you will find it referred to, for instance, in "The Call of Cthulhu"). It actually exists, and the copy in my collection, called more fully *The Story of Atlantis and The Lost Lemuria,* was published by the Theosophical Publishing House, Ltd., London, 1954. Scott-Elliot, an English Theosophist, first published it in 1896. In his scholarly study of the Atlantis story, *Lost Continents,* L. Sprague de Camp reprints some of the maps of the antediluvian world from it, and outlines the theories therein.

[*The Story of Atlantis and The Lost Lemuria* (1925) is a combined reprint of two works, *The Story of Atlantis* (1896) and *The Lost Lemuria* (1904), both by the Theosophist W. Scott-Elliot, whose name Lovecraft misspells "W. Scott-Elliott."]

5. *Azathoth and Other Horrors.* Edward Derby (Lovecraft).

A book of verse which is referred to in "The Thing on the Doorstep"; it was written by a friend of the mad poet Justin Geoffrey (see 41. *People of the Monolith*).

6. *The Black Book* (see 57. *Unaussprechlichen Kulten*).

7. *The Black Rites,* Luveh-Keraphf (Bloch).

Robert Bloch's "The Suicide in the Study" mentions this book as written by "the mad poet Luveh-Keraphf, priest of Bast." It is mentioned again in "The Grinning Ghoul" — "the grotesque *Black Rites* of mystic Luveh-Keraphf, the priest of cryptic Bast," who, Bloch says in *The Acolyte,* Spring 1944, "is apparently contemporaneous with Klarkash-Ton." The distortion of Lovecraft's name is not too successful. The book does not exist.

["Luveh-Keraphf," with the redundant "f," is the spelling of the name in Bloch's "The Suicide in the Study," while the simpler "Luveh-Keraph" appears in "The Grinning Ghoul." Lovecraft frequently signed his letters to Bloch using the latter name.]

8. *Book of Dzyan.*

This book is referred to quite frequently in the Mythos, yet never quoted from, nor are any data given on translations or editions. The only information I have been able to unearth is that a copy is preserved in the Miskatonic University Library and in the ruined church on Federal Hill, Providence, where the "Starry Wisdom Sect" once flourished. The book does exist, and purports to be an ancient Sanskrit document of the

Theosophists. According to de Camp, Madame Blavatsky says the book was originally composed in Atlantis in "the forgotten Senzar language." The copy in my collection is published by the Hermetic Publishing Company, San Diego, 1915, and has commentary by Dr. A.S. Raleigh.

[*The Book of Dzyan* is today published by the Theosophical Publishing House and represents the extracted text upon which Madame Blavatsky's massive tome *The Secret Doctrine* poses as a commentary. "Dzyan" apparently represents the Sanskrit word from which *dyhana, ch'an,* and *zen* (all meaning "meditation") are derived. The text seems to be a cobbling together of material from the *Rig Veda* and other Oriental sources. Lovecraft also mentions the book in his revision of "The Diary of Alonzo Typer."]

9. *Book of Eibon,* translated into medieval Latin by Gaspard du Nord of Averoigne (Clark Ashton Smith).

This book is the work of the great Hyperborean wizard, Eibon of Mhu Thulan (the ultimate peninsula of the Hyperborean continent) who was a worshiper of Tsathoggua. We know little of his life, save how it ended: fleeing from the jealous priests of the goddess Yhoundeh, he flew to Saturn by means of a "door of ultra-telluric metal," in the last century before the onset of the great Ice Age. The book contains the oldest incantations and the forgotten lore of Tsathoggua and Yog-Sothoth: "it was a collection of dark and baleful myths, of liturgies, rituals and incantations both evil and esoteric." The French translator of it, Gaspard du Nord, rendered the title as *Liber Ivonis,* and as such it is occasionally mentioned.

We have two quotations from the *Book of Eibon,* both of which occur in C.A. Smith's story, "Ubbo-Sathla":

> . . . for Ubbo-Sathla is the source and the end. Before the coming of Zhothaqquah or Yok-Zothoth or Kthulhut from the stars, Ubbo-Sathla dwelt in the steaming fens of the new-made Earth: a mass without head or members, spawning the gray, formless efts of the prime and the grisly prototypes of terrene life. . . . And all earthly life, it is told, shall go back at last through the great circle of time to Ubbo-Sathla.

> This wizard, who was mighty among sorcerers, had found a cloudy stone, orb-like and somewhat flattened at the ends, in which he could behold many visions of the terrene past, even to the Earth's beginning, when Ubbo-Sathla, the unbegotten source, lay vast and swollen and yeasty amid the vaporing slime. . . . But of that which he had beheld, Zon Mezzamalech left little record; and people say that he vanished presently, in a way that is not known; and after him the cloudy crystal was lost."

[As Cockcroft noted, Gaspard du Nord, translator of Eibon into Norman French (as *Livre d'Eibon,* which is a French title, not a Latin one as

Cockcroft correctly notes), is probably to be identified with the character du Nord in Clark Ashton Smith's "The Colossus of Ylourgne." In a letter to Clark Ashton Smith (c. 28 January 1932) Lovecraft supplies the missing information that the Latin *Liber Ivonis* is the translation of one C. Philippus Faber. Though it is not stated as such in the text, Smith once jokingly claimed that the entire tale "The Coming of the White Worm" was a chapter of the *Book of Eibon.*]

10. *Book of Hidden Things.*

This is one of the numerous titles which are only referred to in passing, without any elucidation or additional information.

[*The Book of Hidden Things* is the creation of William Lumley in the draft version of "The Diary of Alonzo Typer." Lovecraft retained it. It is certainly some sort of grimoire, as it told Claes van der Heyl the hidden way to Yian-Ho as well as the manner of obtaining there some sort of familiar spirit to which he was thenceforth indissolubly bound.]

11. *Book of Thoth.*

While this book does not actually exist, it was not an invention of any member of the Lovecraft Circle. It is a legendary book, originating in Egyptian mythology, and has a curious and interesting history. According to Seligman's *History of Magic,* the early alchemists believed Hermes Trismegistus to be the master of their art. This "Thrice-Greatest" Hermes, the Greek god whom the Romans knew as Mercury, was imported into Egypt, where the Egyptians equated him with their own god, Thoth, the inventor of magic, of writing, and of speech. Eventually, Thoth-Hermes became regarded as the absolute authority on alchemy, and was thought of as a mythical king who had reigned over three millennia and written 36,525 books. . . . These books were, actually, simple anonymous texts on magic and philosophy and alchemy. Iamblichus brought the fantastic number down to twenty thousand, and Clement of Alexandria reduced it to a mere forty-two.

Later on there seems to be a division: Hermes Trismegistus becomes separate from Thoth, and fourteen short texts (such as *The Poimandres*) are extant and ascribed to him; the *Book of Thoth*, however, is something else again.

Some commentators have stated it is simply a book of arcane symbols which survive today as the Tarot cards used in fortune-telling. It is, however, mentioned briefly in the *Necronomicon* (as quoted in "Through the Gates of the Silver Key"): "And while there are those . . . who have dared to seek glimpses beyond the Veil, and to accept HIM as a Guide, they would have been more prudent had they avoided commerce with HIM; for it is written in the Book of Thoth how terrific is the price of a single glimpse," from which we may ascertain Lovecraft conceived of the book as a written document of some sort. The "HIM" Alhazred is talking about, incidentally, is 'Umr at-Tawil, the Most Ancient One.

[It is worth noting that the mention of the Book of Thoth in the

Necronomicon passage in "Through the Gates of the Silver Key" was the work of E. Hoffmann Price, though Lovecraft did retain it from Price's draft when he could have omitted it. He did edit the "quote" slightly.]

12. *The Cabala of Saboth* (Bloch).

This book is twice referred to in the Mythos. In Robert Bloch's "The Secret in the Tomb," it is only mentioned by name; in "The Mannikin" by the same author, we learn that this "almost priceless" book was published in a Greek translation, circa 1686. "Cabala," or, more properly, "the Kabballah," is a body of esoteric lore compiled by Hebrew mystics who sought certain magical knowledge they thought had been concealed by cipher in the Pentateuch (see 59. *Zohar*). "Saboth" is a Hebrew word connected with "sabbath" and the "sabbat" of the medieval witch-covens. There is some mention of the "Aklo Sabaoth" here and there in the Mythos, as, for instance, in "The Dunwich Horror," and, as we know Aklo to be the name of a pre-human language, perhaps something may be deduced from the title. The "cabala of saboth" — the hidden lore ciphered in the ritual called the 'Aklo Sabaoth'? Perhaps this is what Bloch meant.

[Carter is correct in connecting Cabala with the Hebrew "Kabbalah," meaning "tradition," and denoting a vast body of esoteric interpretation of the Torah and the mystical system thus grounded. However, he fails to discern the meaning of "Saboth." It has nothing to do with "sabbath," but rather surely reflects "Sabaoth," part of the divine epithet Yahweh Sabaoth, "Lord of Hosts." This name was used widely in magical incantations (cf. "The Kabbalists . . . derived the 'Most Potent and Holy Names of God'; these names form much of the foundation of magical lore since their day" [Carter's entry under *Zohar*]). Perhaps Bloch was better informed. The title would seem to denote a mystical treatise on angelology, the study of the Heavenly Hosts. Something of the kind is attested at Qumran, as the Dead Sea Scrolls contain lists of the esoteric names of the angels.]

13. *The Celaeno Fragments* (Derleth).

Celaeno is a star in the Pleiades Cluster (in the constellation Taurus), between Alcyone and Electra on one side, and Maia and Taygeta on the other. In Derleth's stories he mentions that Dr. Laban Shrewsbury disappeared mysteriously from the Earth, and lived for some time on Celaeno — or, I suppose he means, a planet revolving about the star. There are references to "the library on Celaeno," a building of monolithic stone where the books, manuscripts, and hieroglyphics stolen from the Elder Gods by the Great Old Ones are now. The *Celaeno Fragments,* I am informed by Derleth, are broken stone tablets, and not a printed or even a manuscript book.

We have only one quotation from the *Fragments,* given in *The Trail of Cthulhu*:

> The golden mead of the Elder Gods renders the drinker insensible
> to the effects of time and space, so that he may travel in these

dimensions; moreover, it heightens his sensory perceptions so that he remains constantly in a state bordering upon dream.

14. *Clavis Alchimiae,* Fludd.

The *Clavis* ("Key") is listed in *The Case of Charles Dexter Ward* as being among the books in the library of Joseph Curwen, Providence, Rhode Island, around 1746. Mr. Jack Grill of Brooklyn, N.Y., informs me that the book exists, and mentions a two-volume folio edition, *Clavis Philosophiae et Alchymiae,* Frankfort, 1633. Robert Fludd (1574–1637) was perhaps the greatest English student of the Kabballah; among his works are the *Summum Bonum,* which is an *apologia* of the Rosicrucians, and a defense of alchemy and kabbalistic teachings, and the highly entertaining *Integrum Morborum Mysterium,* which claims all disease is caused by demons and evil spirits, thus preceding Mary Baker Eddy by about three centuries.

15. *Commentaries on Witchcraft,* Mycroft (Bloch).

Mentioned only in "The Mannikin," this book seems to be solely the product of Bloch's imagination. The author, "Mycroft," may be derived from Sherlock Holmes's brother, Mycroft. Derleth borrowed his cognomen for one of his publishing imprints, Mycroft & Moran.

16. *Cryptomenysis Patefacta.* Falconer.

I am informed that William Falconer, physician to the General Hospital at Bath, England, wrote many books, largely on medical subjects. His book, *Cryptomenysis Patefacta, or the Art of Secret Information Disclosed without a Key,* exists. The second edition was printed "for Daniel Brown, at the Black Swan and Bible without Temple Bar," London, 1685.

[The author is actually John Falconer, and the first edition of the book also dates to 1685. Lovecraft found this title, as well as the other cryptographical titles mentioned in "The Dunwich Horror" (see 21, 30, 43, 55), in the entry on "Cryptography" in the 9th edition of the *Encyclopaedia Britannica.* See Donald R. Burleson, "Lovecraft and the World as Cryptogram," *Lovecraft Studies* No. 16 (Spring 1988): 14–18.]

17. *Cthulhu in the Necronomicon,* Dr. Laban Shrewsbury (Derleth).

This book, the manuscript of which resides in the Library of Miskatonic University, was never completed or published. It is listed in *The Trail of Cthulhu.*

18. *Cultes des Goules,* the Comte d'Erlette (Lovecraft).

This book was invented by H.P. Lovecraft and attributed to an ancestor of Derleth, after Lovecraft learned that the original family name was d'Erlette, which was changed to Derleth, as a result of the family's flight to Bavaria from France during the French Revolution. The title of Count was hereditary in the Derleth line up to that time. A copy is preserved in the Miskatonic, others elsewhere. No further data have ever been given on it, nor do quotations exist.

[*Cultes des Goules* was the literary invention neither of Lovecraft, as Carter thinks, nor of Derleth, who erroneously claimed paternity (e.g., in his introduction to *Tales of the Cthulhu Mythos*), but of Robert Bloch. Obviously, Comte d'Erlette is a reference to Derleth and his supposed armigerous ancestry, but it is a friendly salute by Bloch. (Carter thought this title ought to be pronounced "Kultez dez Goolez," but actually it is "Koolt day Gool.")]

19. *Daemonolatreia,* Remigius.

Nicholas Remy (1530–1612), who wrote under the Latin form of his name, Remigius, was a notorious French judge who tried many persons accused of witchcraft and condemned around nine hundred to death in his fifteen years of presiding over such trials. The book *Daemonolatreia* (or *Demonolatry*) was first published in Lyons in 1595; there was an edition of it published at Hamburg in 1693, and in 1930 an English translation was published with an introduction by Montague Summers. It is similar to the famous *Malleus Maleficarum,* being a compendium of data on witches and witchcraft, with especial reference on evidence against them: i.e., a sort of reference text for would-be judges of witchcraft trials. M. Remy fits perfectly into the Mythos, as he seems to be the sort of person Cthulhu could enlist in his cause.

20. *The Daemonolorum* (Bloch).

This is another of the imaginary books, the invention of Robert Bloch. It is mentioned in his story, "The Dark Demon"; he informs me it contains "nightmare arcana."

21. *De Furtivis Literarum Notis,* Giambattista Porta.

Giambattista della Porta (1541–1615) was an Italian scholar who contributed heavily to the then new sciences of human thought. He invented various optical instruments (such as the lens for the *Camera obscura* — for which reason he is called "the father of photography"); the modern science of ophthalmology is greatly indebted to him for his pioneering study of the human eye; his vast collection of botanical and mineral rarities in Naples was one of the first of its kind. He wrote books on astrology, geometry, architecture.

De Furtivis Literarum Notis exists, although I do not know its subject. I have seen a copy bound in wrinkled and yellowed vellum, but it is in Italian black-letter.

[The work, which deals with ciphers, was first published in 1563. The author is Giovanni Battista della Porta (1535?–1615). The title translates to "On the Secret Symbols of Letters." See note on 16.]

22. *De Lapide Philosophico,* Trithemius.

This work is listed as one of the books in the collection of Joseph Curwen, Providence, c. 1746 (see *The Case of Charles Dexter Ward*). Its author, Johannes Trithemius (1462–1516), who was the abbott of a monastery at 22, wrote a large number of ecclesiastical treatises, and a few books of commentary on the arcane arts. In one of his books he discussed the *Lapis Philosophicus* ("the Philosopher's Stone" — one of the Four Arcana of Alchemy), and in another book of that title he expands upon the subject. *De Lapide Philosophico* was published in an edition of 1611.

[A 1611 edition cannot be verified. The title of the 1619 edition of this work is *De Lapido Philosophorum.*]

23. *De Masticatione Mortuorum in Tumulis,* Ranft, 1734 (Bloch).

This book, another of the purely imaginary texts, was given mention in "The Mannikin." No further information on it has been published.

[As Home notes, there are actually two books with this title, one by Michael Raufft (1728), the other by Philip Rehrius (1679). The premise of both (as the title implies: "On the Eating of the Dead in the Tomb") is that corpses in their graves are hungry and chew their burial shrouds and even their own putrefying flesh. Legends had it that corpses, once exhumed, were found to have eaten parts of their own bodies, exactly as in Donald R. Burleson's tale "The Last Supper," which is thus perhaps even more Lovecraftian than its author knew.]

24. *De Vermis Mysteriis,* Ludvig Prinn (Bloch).

Ludvig Prinn, according to Bloch, was a Flemish sorcerer, alchemist, and necromancer who was burned at the stake in Brussels by the Inquisition. He boasted of having attained miraculous age — having been the sole survivor of "the ill-fated Ninth Crusade"; captured by Arabs, he lived among the Wizards of Syria from whom he learned daemonic lore. He was known to have been in Alexandria at one time. During his declining days he lived in the Flemish lowlands, until his sorcerous activities earned him the attention of the Holy Order. He wrote *De Vermis Mysteriis* (*The Mysteries of the Worm*) while in prison. After his execution, the manuscript was smuggled out past the guards, and was published in Cologne the year after his death.

We have data on several chapters. There was a chapter on divination, according to Henry Kuttner, and a chapter on familiars, according to Robert Bloch, and a famous chapter called "Saracenic Rituals" which speaks of "the symbols on the Gate" and relates the story of Nephren-Ka the Black Pharaoh. We have two brief quotations, one from the chapter on familiars which gives the spell by which Prinn once summoned his invisible servitors from the stars. In the original Latin, it begins:

> Tibi, Magnum Innominandum, signa stellarum
> nigrarum et bufoniformis Sadoquae sigillum. . . .

The other quotation (given in a story by one James Causey, "Legacy in Crystal") goes:

> Never accept a gift from a necromancer or demon. Steal it, buy it,
> earn it, but do not accept it, either as a gift or legacy.

Furthermore, we are told a bit about the contents of the book. Bloch says it mentions Father Yig, "dark Han," and "serpent-bearded Byatis" (both of whom would seem to be lesser deities among the Great Old Ones). A copy of the book is described by Bloch in "Black Bargain" as being bound with "rusty, iron covers" and being printed in German black-letter. Copies of it are preserved in the Huntington Library, California, in the books of the Starry Wisdom Sect on Federal Hill in Providence, and (of course) in the Library of Miskatonic University.

Needless to say, neither the book nor its author ever existed.

[*De Vermis Mysteriis*, it should be noted, is the "original" Latin title supplied by Lovecraft for the grimoire Bloch invented and dubbed simply "Mysteries of the Worm." Lovecraft also composed the Latin "quotation" from the volume, which means "Come, Great One Who Is Not to Be Named, sign of the black stars and sigil of toad-shaped Tsathoggua. . . ." Lovecraft often made use of the book as a prop in his own subsequent stories, always referring to the book by the Latin title he had coined for it, while Bloch virtually always ignored Lovecraft's title, using his own "Mysteries of the Worm." (Carter pronounced it "dee VER-mis mi-STIR-ee-is," but "day VAYR-mees mis-TER-ees" is correct.)]

25. *The Dhol Chants* (Lovecraft & Derleth).

This book is mentioned in the posthumous collaboration, *The Lurker at the Threshold,* and elsewhere, but we have no data on it, save that a copy is preserved in the Miskatonic. According to *The Dream-Quest of Unknown Kadath,* Dhols (or "dholes") are invisible creatures inhabiting those valleys of the Earth's dreamworld beyond the "grey and ominous Peaks of Thok." They are mentioned in the *Necronomicon* as being among the legions of monsters against whom "the five-pointed star of grey stone from ancient Mnar" (i.e., The Elder Sign) has power.

This book, incidentally, may be that "loathsome book in Burmese that reveals ghastly legends of the shunned and hidden Plateau of Leng, the place of the dread Tcho-Tcho people" mentioned in Derleth's "Beyond the Threshold," as both the Dhols and Leng are in the Dreamworld.

[*The Dhol Chants* is the creation of Lovecraft and appears first in "The Horror in the Museum" (although it is not printed in italics, hence may not be a published book but rather a collection of ancient fragments, like the Eltdown Shards and the Pnakotic Manuscripts). It does not appear in the minute portion of *The Lurker at the Threshold* actually penned by Lovecraft, which amounts only to a few scraps, a couple of pages' worth. The implied connection to the creatures of *The Dream-Quest of Unknown Kadath* is based on a mistranscription of Lovecraft's text in that novella: he has no references to "Dhols" or "dholes" but only to "bholes," which thus have no connection either to Machen's Dôls. ("The White People") or to Frank Belknap Long's doels ("The Hounds of Tindalos"), which, however, HPL does mention along with the Hounds in "The Whisperer in Darkness." Bloch mentions them in "The Mannikin." Carter's identification of *The Dhol Chants* with the source of Tcho-Tcho lore seems gratuitous.]

26. *The Eltdown Shards,* translated by the Rev. Arthur Brooke Winters-Hall, 1912 (Lovecraft).

In "The Shadow out of Time," we learn that "the disturbing and debatable Eltdown Shards" give the name of the planet from which the Great Race made their migration-of-mind. It is Yith. The ancient book also tells much of the history of the Great Race, i.e., the complete tale of their tremendous voyages through time and space. The implication seems to be that the Shards were carven and inscribed stone tablets in fragmentary form, preserved in the city of the Central Archives of the Great Race, which has been discovered to be in the deserts of Australia.

The translator was a Sussex clergyman.

[The Eltdown Shards (of which Lovecraft first heard in correspondent Richard F. Searight's tale "The Sealed Casket") were already in Lovecraft's work the object of much confusion, thanks to Lovecraft himself. First, as Cockcroft pointed out, Lovecraft has the Shards already translated as a book left in the old van der Heyl house since 1872 ("The Diary of Alonzo Typer"), while in "The Challenge from Beyond" we read that the Shards remained a collection of clay tablets until translated by Rev. Arthur Brooke Winters-Hall in 1917. A harmonist might suggest that the "conjectural" translation of the learned Sussex clergyman with occult leanings was not in fact the first, that Claes van der Heyl had a copy of an earlier version from another source. But this, at any rate, cannot have been Lovecraft's intent, as it is plain in "The Challenge from Beyond" that Winters-Hall is understood to provide the modern world's first glimpse into the mysteries of the ancient text.

A more serious confusion, acknowledged by HPL himself, arises from the fact that, intrigued by the evocative title (itself coined by Searight on the basis of the Piltdown Man "discovery"), he charged off enthusiastically and supplied lore concerning the Shards, their description, and their translation utterly at odds with a set of details simultaneously created by Searight. In Searight's then-unpublished tale "The Warder of Knowledge," we learn that the Shards were twenty-three in number, "slabs of iron-hard grey clay, of all shapes, and ranging in size from the fifth shard, an oblong piece about four inches by eight, to the fourteenth, a jagged, roughly triangular tablet nearly twenty inches across." These artifacts were translated by Gordon Whitney, who recognized their language as the ancestor of Amharic and Arabic.

Lovecraft had advised Searight to locate the writers of the Shards way back in the Eocene or the Miocene, before the earliest attested human remains. Searight proceeded to place their origin in the Triassic, but as the product of a human civilization, while Lovecraft treated them as a product of pre-human erudition, like the older, indecipherable portions of his own Pnakotic Manuscripts. Carter's ascription of them to the Great

Race of Yith is out of the question. It is an unfounded inference from Lovecraft's remarks in "The Shadow out of Time" that the Eltdown Shards happened to mention Yith and in "The Challenge from Beyond" that the conflict between the Great Race and its caterpillar-like foes was chronicled (but long afterward) in the Shards.

A fragment from the Eltdown Shards originally prefaced Searight's story "The Sealed Casket," but this epigraph was omitted in the *Weird Tales* publication (March 1935).

Carter was, of course, mistaken in ascribing the creation of this fascinating book to Lovecraft. Rather, like Smith's Tsathoggua, it was someone else's (Searight's) invention, which HPL liked so much that he adopted it into his own collection of props. Incidentally, in a letter to Searight, Lovecraft notes that von Junzt made extensive use of the Shards in his own *Unaussprechlichen Kulten*. In the revision "The Tree on the Hill" with Duane W. Rimel, Lovecraft had von Junzt make similar use of Rudolf Yergler's *Chronicle of Nath* (see 62).]

27. *Image du Monde*, Gauthier de Metz (Lovecraft).

The "delirious *Image du Monde*" is mentioned in "The Nameless City," but nowhere else in the Mythos. I am unable to state whether or not the author or the work exists, but several friends of mine acquainted with French literature recognize neither it nor its author. The title may be translated as *Picture of the World.*

[*Image du Monde*, as Home describes, is a real book, widely translated and still extant. It is a "didactic primer" composed in 6594 rhyming octosyllables, and later rendered into prose. It is an encyclopedia of ethnology, astronomy, geography, and the animals of exotic lands. The text is largely lifted from classical Latin authors, and mostly from Honorius Augustodunensis, *Imago Mundi*. It was translated into English as *Myrrour of the World* by Caxton in 1481.]

28. *Invocations to Dagon* (Derleth).

In "The Black Island," the concluding chapter of *The Trail of Cthulhu*, by August Derleth, this manuscript is mentioned, and apparently consists of prayers and ritual verses in the worship of Dagon. This sea-deity, actually worshipped by the Philistines, was incorporated into the Mythos by Lovecraft, who had his degenerate inhabitants of Arkham, Innsmouth, etc., belong to a cult known as The Esoteric Order of Dagon. The followers of the Order worshipped Father Dagon and Mother Hydra, two minor members of the Great Old Ones, subservient to Cthulhu, and both drawn from actual myth.

We have one quotation from the *Invocations*, given in the above-mentioned Derleth story:

> By all the depths of Y'ha-nthlei —
> and the dwellers thereof, for the
> One Over All;

By the Sign of Kish — and all who
    obey it, for its Author;
By the Door to Yhe — and all who
    use it, who have gone before and
    who shall come after, for Him to
    Whom it Leadeth;
By Him Who Is To Come . . .
"Ph'nglui mglw-nafl Cthulhu R'lyeh
wgah-nagl fhtagn."

Of the symbols here given, Y'ha-nthlei is the "many-columned"
sunken city off Innsmouth, inhabited by the subhuman Deep Ones who
serve Cthulhu; Yhe is a submerged continent in the Pacific; and one of
the titles of Cthulhu is "Him Who Is To Come." The last line is from the
R'lyeh Text, and is slightly inaccurate: the hyphens in the second and the
second-to-last words should be apostrophes. This line has been translated
as "In his house at R'lyeh dead Cthulhu waits dreaming" (see 45. *R'lyeh
Text*).

29. *Key of Wisdom,* Artephius.
    In *The Case of Charles Dexter Ward,* this book is listed as being among
the collection of Joseph Curwen of Providence. Beyond author and title,
no further data were given, nor was the book mentioned elsewhere
in the Mythos. Artephius was a real alchemist (see Waite's *Lives of the
Alchymystical Philosophers*); a twelfth-century adept whose *Clavis
Sapientiae* was first printed in Paris in 1609, later at Frankfort in 1785.
    [The full title of the 1609 edition is *Clavis Maioris Sapientiae*; the
edition of 1618 bears the title *Clavis Sapientiae.*]

30. *Kryptographik.* Thicknesse.
    Among the books in the library of Dr. Jean-François Charriere, as
described in the posthumous collaboration "The Survivor," is to be found
this book. Phillip Thicknesse published *A Treatise on the Art of Decypher-
ing and of Writing in Cypher* (sic) in London, 1772, which looks like a
case of Lovecraft borrowing part of the truth and making up the rest.
    [*Kryptographik,* as Cockcroft shows, is indeed misascribed to Thick-
nesse, but was nonetheless a real book on cipher-writing and its decipher-
ment, but one by J.H. Klüber (1809). Klüber's work is correctly cited in
"The Dunwich Horror," but a line of text containing the title was dropped
in the tale's appearance in *Best Supernatural Stories* (1945), perhaps
leading to Derleth's error. See also 16.]

31. *Liber-Damnatus* (Lovecraft).
    This book is only mentioned in *The Case of Charles Dexter Ward,* and
we are given little information about it. In a letter quoted in the novel,
the phrase "ye III Psalme in ye Liber-Damnatus holdes ye Clauicle. With
Sunne in V House, Saturne in Trine, drawe ye Pentagram of Fire, and
saye ye ninth Uerse thrice. This Uerse repeate eache Roodemas and

Hallow's Eve; and yᵉ Thing will breede in yᵉ Outside Spheres." Whether this astrological instruction is an English rendering of Psalm III or not is never clearly explained.

Elsewhere in the novel a Latin passage is quoted which, from its context in the story, would seem to be this Ninth Verse:

> Per Adonai Eloim, Adonai Jehova,
> Adonai Sabaoth, Metraton Ou Agla Methon,
> verbum pythonicum, mysterium salamandrae,
>   conventus sylvorum, antra gnomorum,
>   daemonia Coeli Gaod, Almousin, Gibor, Jehosua,
>   Evam, Zariatnatmik, veni, veni, veni."

This is said in the story to be closely similar to a passage in Eliphas Levi. My copy of Levi is in English, so I cannot be sure. The passage above is a jumble of bad Latin and Hebrew Names of Power from the Kabballah.

[Lovecraft cribbed the Latin incantation from Eliphas Lévi's *The Mysteries of Magic* (1886; rev. ed. 1897), a compendiun of Lévi's writings selected and translated by A.E. Waite. In Lévi the incantation appears as prose. This volume does not provide a translation, but another volume by Lévi, *Trancendental Magic*, trans. A.E. Waite (1896), does: "By Adonai Eloim, Adonai Jehova, Adonai Sabaoth, Metraton on Agla Methon, the Pythonic word, the Mystery of the Salamander, the Assembly of Sylphs, the Grotto of Gnomes, the demons of the heaven of God, Almousin, Gibor, Jehousa, Evan, Zariatnatucik, come, come, come!"]

32. *Liber Investigationis,* Geber.

This book is mentioned in *The Case of Charles Dexter Ward.* Geber, as he was known to the Latin scholars who annotated and commented upon his works, is more correctly known as Abu Musa Jabir ibn Hayyan, an Arab alchemist called "the most celebrated chemist of medieval times" by the *Encyclopaedia Britannica.* He was born around A.D. 721 or 722 at Tus near present-day Meshed. Banished from Baghdad in 803, he set up his laboratory in Kufa near the Damascus Gate, and is believed to have lived at least until 813. Of his many works about one hundred treatises are extant, but not all have been translated. The *Liber Investigationis* is not listed among his works. It may be a combination of two books (incorrectly) attributed to him, *De Investigatione Perfectionis* and *Liber Fornacum.*

[There is a *Liber Investigationis Magisterii* attributed to Geber, although it was never published separately. It first appears in an omnibus of Geber's work, *Incipit Liber Geber* (1475?).]

33. *Liber Ivonis* (see 9. *Book of Eibon*).

34. *Magyar Folklore.* Dornly (Howard).

This book, briefly mentioned in Robert E. Howard's "The Black Stone," has no existence that I have been able to discover.

35. *Marvells of Science,* Morryster (Lovecraft).

Morryster's "wild *Marvells of Science*" is mentioned only once or twice in the Mythos, as in "The Festival."

[This title is not Lovecraft's creation, Home points out, but rather that of Ambrose Bierce in his story "The Man and the Snake" (in his collection *In the Midst of Life*).]

36. *Mysteries of the Worm* (see 24. *De Vermis Mysteriis*).

37. *Necronomicon*, Abdul Alhazred; translated from the Arabic into the Greek by Theodorus Philetas, A.D. 950; from the Greek into the Latin by Olaus Wormius, A.D. 1228; Black-Letter Edition, Germany, ca. 1400; Greek Text Edition, Italy, ca. 1500–1550; Spanish Edition of the Latin Text published 1622; translated into English by Dr. John Dee in the early seventeenth century (Lovecraft).

This is, of course, the single most famous book in the Mythos; the one most often mentioned and the one upon which we have the largest amount of information, as well as the one most deeply significant to Cthulhu, his cult, and his history. Luckily, it is also the one book from which we have the largest number of quotations, some of them of considerable length. While the book itself and most of its translators, and its author, are all imaginary, Lovecraft here employed most effectively his technique of inserting actual historical fact in the middle of large areas of purely imaginary lore. The Latin translator, for instance, actually lived. Olaus Wormius was a Danish scholar and clergyman, born 13 May 1588 in the village of Arbus, Jutland. He studied Greek and Latin at Luneborg and during his life wrote many highly important books on the history, politics and literature of Denmark. A section devoted to him is in Vol. 45 of the *Biographie Universelie*.

Abdul Alhazred of Sanaa (in Yemen), called "the Mad Poet" or "the Mad Arab," is said to have lived during the era of the Ommiade Caliphs, ca. A.D. 700. Like many poets, he was not very orthodox in his professed religion. An indifferent Moslem, he secretly worshipped dark gods and demons like Yog-Sothoth and Cthulhu.

Seeking lost lore of black magic and demonology, he visited ruined Babylon and burrowed through the subterranean caverns under Memphis. Then he sought a city older than Memphis or Babylon — the Nameless City in Turkistan which the Arabs have called Beled-el-Djinn ("the City of Devils"), the Turks know as Kara-Shehr ("the Black City"), and which he, himself, later names in the *Necronomicon* as "the City of Evil."

For ten years he dwelt alone in this silent city of black stone in the southern desert the ancients know as Roba El Khaliyeh ("the Empty Space") and modern Arabs know as the Dahna, or "Crimson Desert."

Here, in this desert believed haunted by evil spirits and monsters, he found the annals and terrible secrets of a race older than mankind. After his return to civilization, he said he had been in Irem, the City of Pillars, a city of Arabic myth as legendary as Camelot or El Dorado.

He dwelt in Damascus during his last years, and there, about A.D. 730, composed his famous book, which he called *Al Azif* — a word used by Arabs to denote the nocturnal sound of insects, which they believe to be the howling of demons.

He died (or disappeared) in 738, and, according to his twelfth-century biographer, Ibn Khallikan, he was seized in broad daylight by invisible monsters and devoured horribly in front of many witnesses.

The *Azif* gained a considerable reputation among the wizards and philosophers of the time during the next two centuries, and was copied and circulated in manuscript secretly. In 950, Theodorus Philetas of Constantinople made a secret Greek translation from the original Arabic and retitled the book *Necronomicon,* a title whose meaning has been widely disputed. The Lovecraftian critic and scholar George Wetzel has translated the name as "the Book of the Names of the Dead"; Manly Bannister translates it as "the Book of the Laws of the Dead," but as to which version is the most correct I can give no opinion, as I do not know the language. (Incidentally, Charles Tanner informs me that the Greeks often translated works and gave them a new title, taking the title from the first few words of the text. If this is correct, then we may assume the first line of the *Necronomicon* is "The book of the names [or laws] of the dead. . . .") The Arabic text was lost by 1050, when the Patriarch Michael had all known copies of the Greek translation burned. However, a copy of the Arabic text is believed to have been in San Francisco and perished there in the Great Fire.

After the Greek translation was banned, it is heard of only furtively. Olaus Wormius made his famed Latin version from a rare copy of it in 1228 — which was printed only twice — first in Germany during the fifteenth century, secondly in Spain during the seventeenth century. In 1232 the Greek translation and the Latin version were banned by Pope Gregory IX. The last copy of the Greek translation was destroyed in the burning of a certain home in Salem, in 1692, unless we credit the vague rumor that a copy was in the possession of the Boston family of Richard Upton Pickman, the artist, which was lost when he vanished in 1926.

In the early seventeenth century, the *Necronomicon* was translated into English by Dr. John Dee. The Dee translation was never published, but circulated in manuscript, copies of which are now believed incomplete and fragmentary. This is the second place where truth enters into the history of the *Azif* and its author. Dr. John Dee actually lived; he was born in London on 13 July 1527, and studied at Cambridge, from which he received the degree of Bachelor of Arts, and Louvain. While a Fellow of Trinity College, Cambridge, he began reading occult literature — probably including Cornelius Agrippa, whom his contemporary, Marlowe, put into *Doctor Faustus* — and later studied astrology, mathematics, philosophy, alchemy, and divination. He left college at the age of twenty-three and was offered posts at Oxford and elsewhere, which implies that he was something of a prodigy in scholastic circles. Accused of magical practices in 1555, he was later acquitted and befriended by Elizabeth I, who occasionally consulted him for horoscopes and such matters. He is said to have selected the date of the Queen's coronation, and is credited with being the inventor of the crystal ball as used for divination. Among his extant works are the *Monas Hieroglyphica,* which is still in print, and other titles on magical subjects. If such a book as the *Necronomicon* had actually existed, he would have been the obvious person to have translated it into English.

Despite statements throughout the Mythos that only five or six complete copies exist, there appear to be about eleven extant. Perhaps some are incomplete. We know one complete copy of the fifteenth-century German edition is in the "restricted" archives of the British Museum, and another copy (perhaps incomplete) is rumored to be in the collection of a celebrated American millionaire. Of the seventeenth-century Spanish edition, one is preserved in the Bibliotheque Nationale at Paris, another known complete copy in the Library of Miskatonic University at Arkham, Mass., a third in the Library of the University of Buenos Aires, a fourth in the Widener Library at Harvard. That makes six in all. Other copies are extant, but in which edition we know not: one in the library of the University of Lima, Peru, a second in the Kester Library, Salem, Mass., and a third was preserved in the ruined church on Federal Hill, Providence, Rhode Island. Still other copies in various editions are only rumored to exist — one secretly in Cairo (probably a private collection), and another is said to be in the Vatican Library at Rome. Eleven in all.

The book is so rare because, unlike many other volumes of demonology and necromancy, it is rigidly suppressed by the authorities of most countries and by all branches of the organized religions.

We have many quotations from the book, some long and some very brief, which I shall now give in full exactly as they were originally published, without any commentary except for a line of information on the story in which the quotation appeared, and the name of its author. Wherever possible, I have indicated the position of the quotation in the *Necronomicon.*

(1) from "The Dunwich Horror," H.P. Lovecraft:

Nor is it to be thought that man is either the oldest or the last of earth's masters, or that the common bulk of life and substance walks alone. The Old Ones were, the Old Ones are, and the Old Ones shall be. Not in the spaces we know, but *between* them, They walk serene and primal, undimensioned and to us unseen. *Yog-Sothoth* is the gate. *Yog-Sothoth* is the key and guardian of the gate. Past, present, future, all are one in *Yog-Sothoth.* He knows where the Old Ones broke through of old, and where They shall break through again. He knows where They have trod earth's fields, and where They still tread them, and why no one can behold Them as They tread. By Their smell can men sometimes know Them near, but of Their semblance can no man know, *saving only in the features of those They have begotten on mankind*; and of those are there many sorts, differing in likeness from man's truest eidolon to that shape without sight or substance which is *Them.* They walk unseen and foul in lonely places where the Words have been spoken and the Rites howled through at their Seasons. The wind gibbers with Their voices, and the earth mutters with Their consciousness. They bend the forest and crush the city, yet may not forest or city behold the hand that smites. Kadath in the cold waste hath known Them, and what man knows Kadath? The ice desert of the South and the sunken isles of Ocean hold stones whereon Their seal is engraven, but who hath seen the deep frozen city or the sealed tower long garlanded with seaweed and barnacles? Great Cthulhu is Their cousin, yet can he spy Them only dimly. *Iä! Shub-Niggurath!* As a foulness shall ye know Them. Their hand is at your throats, yet ye see Them not; and Their habitation is even one with your guarded threshold. *Yog-Sothoth* is the key to the gate, whereby the spheres meet. Man rules now where They ruled once; They shall soon rule where man rules now. After summer is winter, and after winter summer. They wait patient and potent, for here shall They reign again."

The above is a text from the seventeenth-century Spanish edition of the Latin version, as translated by Dr. Henry Armitage of the Miskatonic University. The following quotation duplicates the above, with certain changes, and may be the same passage as given in the Dee translation.

(2) from *The Lurker at the Threshold,* H.P. Lovecraft and August Derleth:

Never is it to be thought that man is either oldest or last of the Masters of Earth; nay, nor that the great'r part of life and substance walks alone. The Old Ones were, the Old Ones are, and the Old Ones shall be. Not in the spaces known to us, but *between* them, They walk calm and primal, of no dimensions, and to us unseen. Yog-Sothoth knows the gate, for Yog-Sothoth is the gate. Yog-Sothoth is the key and the guardian of the gate. Past, present, future — what has been, what is, what will be, all are one in Yog-Sothoth. He knows where the Old Ones broke through of old, and where They shall break through in time to come until the Cycle is complete. He knows why no one can behold Them as They walk. Sometimes men can know Them near by Their smell, which is strange to the nostrills, and like unto a creature of great age; but of Their semblance no man can know, save seldom in features of those They have begotten on mankind, which are awful to behold, and thrice awful are Those who sired them; yet of those Offspring there are divers kinds, in likeness greatly differing from man's truest image and fairest eidolon to that shape without sight or substance which is

Them. They walk unseen. They walk foul in lonely places where the Words have been spoken and the Rites howled through at Their Seasons, which are in the blood and differ from the seasons of man. The winds gibber with Their voices; the Earth mutters with Their consciousness. They bend the forest. They raise up the waves, They crush the city — yet not forest or ocean or city beholds the hand that smites. Kadath in the cold waste knows them, and what man knows Kadath? The ice desert of the South and the sunken isles of Ocean hold stones whereon Their seal is engraven, but who has seen the deep frozen city or the sealed tower long garlanded with seaweed and barnacles? Great Cthulhu is Their cousin, yet can he spy Them only dimly. As a foulness shall They be known to the race of man. Their hands are at the throats of man forever, from beginning of known time to end of time known, yet none sees Them; and Their habitation is even one with your guarded threshold. Yog-Sothoth is the key to the gate whereby the spheres meet. Man rules now where once They ruled; soon They shall rule again where man rules now. After summer is winter, and after winter summer. They wait patient and potent, for here shall They reign again, and at Their coming again none shall dispute Them and all shall be subject to Them. Those who know of the gates shall be impelled to open the way for Them and shall serve Them as They desire, but those who open the way unwittingly shall know but a brief while thereafter.

(3) The following, from the same source, comes after a brief hiatus in this copy of the *Azif,* and may not necessarily come right after the passage above:

'Twas done then as it had been promis'd aforetime, that He was tak'n by Those Whom He Defy'd, and thrust into ye Neth'rmost Deeps und'r ye Sea, and placed within ye barnacl'd Tower that is said to rise amidst ye great ruin that is ye Sunken City (R'lyeh), and seal'd within by ye Elder Sign, and, rag'd at Those who had imprison'd Him, He furth'r incurr'd Their anger, and They, descend'g upon him for ye second time, did impose upon Him ye semblance of Death, but left Him dream'g in that place under ye great waters, and return'd to that place from whence they had come, Namely, Glyu-Vho, which is among ye stars, and looketh upon Earth from ye time when ye leaves fall to that time when ye ploughman becomes habit'd once again to his fields. And there shall He lie dream'g forever, in His House at R'lyeh, toward which at once all His minions swam and strove against all manner of obstacles, and arrang'd themselves to wait for His awaken'g powerless to touch ye Elder Sign and fearful of its great pow'r know'g that ye Cycle returneth, and He shall be freed to embrace ye Earth again and make of it His Kingdom and defy ye Elder gods anew. And to His brothers it happen'd likewise, that They were tak'n by Those Whom They defy'd and hurl'd into banishment, Him Who Is Not to be Nam'd be'g sent into Outermost space, beyond ye Stars, and with ye others likewise, until ye Earth was free of Them, and Those Who Came in ye shape of Towers of Fire, return'd whence They had come, and were seen no more, and on all Earth then peace came and was unbrok'n while Their minions gather'd and sought means and ways with which to free ye Old Ones, and waited while man came to pry into secret, forbidd'n places and open ye gate."

(4) The following, also from *The Lurker at the Threshold*, supposedly follows on the next page. The writer seems to have been copying hurriedly (perhaps under the eye of some watcher), for which reason he uses all manner of abbreviations. (It is also quoted, almost exactly the same, in "The Whippoorwills in the Hills," by Derleth.)

Concern'g ye Old Ones, 'tis writ, they wait ev'r at ye Gate & ye Gate is all places at all times, for They know noth'g of time or place but are in all time & in all place togeth'r without appear'g to be, & there are those amongst Them which can assume divers Shapes & Featurs & any Giv'n Shape & any giv'n Face & ye Gates are for Them ev'rywhere, but ye 1st, was that which I caus'd to be op'd, Namely in Irem, ye City of Pillars, ye city under ye desert, but wher'r men sett up ye Stones and sayeth thrice ye forbidd'n Words, they shall cause there a Gate to be establish'd & shall wait upon Them Who Come through ye gate, ev'n as Dhols, & ye Abomin. Mi-Go, & ye Tcho-Tcho peop., & ye Deep Ones, & ye Gugs, & ye Gaunts of ye Night & ye Shoggoths, & ye Voormis, & ye Shantaks which guard Kadath in ye Colde Waste & ye Plateau of Leng. All are alike ye Children of ye Elder Gods, but ye Great Race of Yith & ye Gr. Old Ones fail'g to agree, one with another, & boath with ye Elder Gods, separat'd, leav'g ye Gr. Old Ones in possession of ye Earth, while ye Great Race, return'g from Yith took up Their Abode forward in Time in Earth-Land not yet known to those who walk ye Earth today, & there wait till there shall come again ye winds & ye Voices which drove Them forth before & That which Walketh on ye winds over ye Earth & in ye spaces that are among ye Stars for'r.

(5) Here occurs a break of some length, "as if what had been written there had been carefully expunged;" and the quotation continues:

Then shal They return & on this great Return'g shal ye Great Cthulhu be fre'd from R'lyeh beneath ye Sea & Him Who Is Not To Be Nam'd shal come from His City which is Carcosa near ye Lake of Hali, & Shub-Niggurath shall come forth & multiply in his Hideousness, & Nyarlathotep shal carry ye word to all the Gr. Old Ones & their Minions, & Cthugha shal lay His Hand upon all that oppose Him & Destroy, & ye blind idiot, ye noxious Azathoth shal arise from ye middle of ye World where all is Chaos & Destruction where He hath bubbl'd & blasphem'd at Ye centre which is of All

Things, which is to say Infinity, & Yog-Sothoth, who is ye All-in-One & One-in-All, shal bring his globes, & Ithaqua shal walk again, & from ye black-litt'n caverns within ye Earth shal come Tsathoggua, & togeth'r shal take possession of Earth and all things that live upon it, & shal prepare to do battle with ye Elder Gods when ye Lord of ye Great Abyss is apprised of their return'g & shal come with His Brothers to disperse ye Evill.

(6) Also from the same book is the following paragraph, "in the midst of the first passage" of the *Necronomicon*:

Ubbo-Sathla is that unforgotten source whence came those daring to oppose the Elder Gods who ruled from Betelgeuze, the Great Old Ones who fought against the Elder Gods; and these Old Ones were instructed by Azathoth, who is the blind, idiot god, and by Yog-Sothoth, who is the All-in-One and One-in-All, and upon whom are no strictures of time or space, and whose aspects on earth are 'Umr at-Tawil and the Ancient Ones. The Great Old Ones dream forever of that coming time when they shall once more rule Earth and all that Universe of which it is part. . . . Great Cthulhu shall rise from R'lyeh; Hastur, who is Him Who Is Not To Be Named, shall come again from the dark star which is near Aldebaran in the Hyades; Nyarlathotep shall howl forever in darkness where he abideth; Shub-Niggurath, who is the Black Goat With a Thousand Young, shall spawn and spawn again, and shall have dominion over all wood nymphs, satyrs, leprechauns, and the Little People; Lloigor, Zhar, and Ithaqua shall ride the spaces among the stars and shall ennoble those who are their followers, who are the Tcho-Tcho; Cthugha shall encompass his dominion from Fomalhaut; Tsathoggua shall come from N'kai. . . . They wait forever at the Gates, for the time draws near, the hour is soon at hand, while the Elder Gods sleep, dreaming, unknowing there are those who know the spells put upon the Great Old Ones by the Elder Gods, and shall learn how to break them, as already they can command the followers waiting beyond the doors from Outside.

(See 45. *R'lyeh Text* for parallel passage.)

[When Derleth donned the mantle of Alhazred to pen this passage and wrote "Ubbo-Sathla is that unforgotten source," surely he meant to write instead "the unbegotten source" (cf. the second quotation by Clark Ashton Smith under 9. *Book of Eibon*), though the original A.Ms. does have the nonsensical "unforgotten." Subsequent editions ought to correct this slip of Derleth's hasty pen.]

(7) The next passage occurs "somewhat later," and is from the same source:

Armor against witches and daemons, against the Deep Ones, the Dholes, the Voormis, the Tcho-Tcho, the Abominable Mi-Go, the

H.P. LOVECRAFT: THE BOOKS

Shoggoths, the Ghasts, the Valusians and all such peoples and beings who serve the Great Old Ones and their Spawn lies within the five-pointed star carven of grey stone from ancient Mnar, which is less strong against the Great Old Ones themselves. The possessor of the stone shall find himself able to command all beings which creep, swim, crawl, walk, or fly even to the source from which there is no returning. In Yhe as in great R'lyeh, in Y'ha-nthlei as in Yoth, in Yuggoth as in Zothique, in N'kai as in K'n-yan, in Kadath in the Cold Waste as at the Lake of Hali, in Carcosa as in Ib, it shall have power; yet, even as stars wane and grow cold, even as suns die and the spaces between stars grow more wide, so wanes the power of all things — of the five-pointed star-stone as of the spells put upon the Great Old Ones by the benign Elder Gods, and there cometh a time as once was a time, when it shall be shown that

That is not dead which can eternal lie
And with strange eons even death may die."

[This "unexplainable couplet" was, of course, first cited by Lovecraft in "The Nameless City" (1921); although it is attributed to Alhazred, it is not expressly stated as deriving from the *Necronomicon,* since that title was not cited by name until "The Hound" (1922).]

(8) from "The Salem Horror," Henry Kuttner:

Men know him as the Dweller in Darkness, the brother of the Old Ones called Nyogatha, the Thing that should not be. He can be summoned to Earth's surface through certain secret caverns and fissures, and sorcerers have seen him in Syria and below the black tower of Leng; from the Thang Grotto of Tartary he has come ravening to bring terror and destruction among the pavilions of the Great Khan. Only by the looped cross, by the Vach-Viraj incantation and by the Tikkoun elixer may he be driven back to the nighted caverns of hidden foulness where he dwelleth.

[Kuttner is here guilty of an anachronism, as Alhazred lived well before the reign of the Ghengis Khan. Carter committed similar blunders in his own *Necronomicon* tales, when in "The Vault Beneath the Mosque" (original draft) he had Alhazred visit an already ancient shrine in Cairo, forgetting that Cairo was built centuries after Alhazred's time by the Fatimid Caliph Muhammad Ali. In "Dreams of the Black Lotus" he has Alhazred go into the past in a psychic vision in which he beholds the Crusades, which, however, lay well in the future from Alhazred's perspective.

["Vach-Viraj" seems to come, like much pulp esoterica, from Madame Blavatsky. The terms represent the female and male elements which are potent symbols in Tantric yoga, "Viraj" being another transliteration of the "Vajra" or thunderbolt of Indra, a symbol for the stroke of mystical enlightenment. "Tikkoun" in Hebrew means "purification" and perhaps refers here to the Kabbalistic rituals of mystical piety.]

by Lin Carter

Another version of quotation 7 is given below, and we are told it is from page 177 of the Olaus Wormius Latin version (edition is not mentioned), in a fragmentary English translation by Andrew Phelan.

(9) from *The Trail of Cthulhu,* August Derleth:

For within the five-pointed star carven of grey stone from ancient Mnar lies armour against witches and daemons, against the Deep Ones, the Dholes, the Voormis, the Tcho-Tcho, the Abominable Mi-Go, the Shoggoths, the Valusians and all such peoples and beings who serve the Great Old Ones and their Spawn, but it is less potent against the Great Old Ones themselves. He who hath the five-pointed stone shall find himself able to command all beings who creep, swim, crawl, walk, or fly even to the source from which there is no returning.

In the land of Yhe as in great R'lyeh, in Y'ha-nthlei as in Yoth, in Yuggoth as in Zothique, in N'kai as in K'n-yan, in Kadath-in-the-Cold-Waste, as in the Lake of Hali, in Carcosa as in Ib, it shall have power; but even as the stars wane and grow cold, as the suns die, and the spaces between the stars grow more great, so wanes the power of all things — of the five-pointed star-stone as of the spells put upon the Great Old Ones by the benign Elder Gods, and there shall come a time as once there was a time, and it shall be shown that

That is not dead which can eternal lie
And with strange eons even death may die."

(10) from "The Nameless Offspring," Clark Ashton Smith:

Many and multiform are the dim horrors of Earth, infesting her ways from the prime. They sleep beneath the unturned stone; they rise with the tree from its root; they dwell in the inmost adyta; they emerge betimes from the shutten sepulchre of haughty bronze and the low grave that is sealed with clay. There be some that are long known to man, and others as yet unknown that abide the terrible latter days of their revealing. Those which are the most dreadful and the loathliest of all are haply still to be declared. But among those that have revealed themselves aforetime and have made manifest their veritable presence, there is one that may not openly be named for its exceeding foulness. It is that spawn which the hidden dweller in the vaults has begotten upon mortality.

(11) from "The Keeper of the Key," August Derleth:

Whosoever speaketh of Cthulhu shall remember that he but seemeth dead; he sleeps, and yet he does not sleep; he has died, and yet he is not dead; asleep and dead though he is, he shall rise again. Again it should be shown that

That is not dead which can eternal lie,
And with strange eons even death may die."

(12) from "Fane of the Black Pharaoh," Robert Bloch:

> . . . the Place of the Blind Apes where Nephren-Ka bindeth up the threads of truth . . ."

(13) from "Through the Gates of the Silver Key," H.P. Lovecraft and E. Hoffmann Price:

> And while there are those who have dared to seek glimpses beyond the Veil, and to accept HIM as a Guide, they would have been more prudent had they avoided commerce with HIM; for it is written in the Book of Thoth how terrific is the price of a single glimpse. Nor may those who pass ever return, for in the Vastnesses transcending our world are Shapes of darkness that seize and bind. The Affair that shambleth about in the night, the evil that defieth the Elder Sign, the Herd that stand watch at the secret portal each tomb is known to have, and that thrive on that which groweth out of the tenants within — all these Blacknesses are lesser than HE Who guardeth the Gateway: HE Who will guide the rash one beyond all the worlds into the Abyss of unnamable Devourers. For HE is 'UMR AT-TAWIL, the Most Ancient One, which the scribe rendereth as THE PROLONGED OF LIFE.

[" 'Umr at-Tawil" seems to mean, contra Price, "speaker of allegorical interpretations," i.e., of the Koran. This sense applied to the mysterious reinterpreter of the *Necronomicon*, who, e.g., assures Randolph Carter that the Old Ones are not evil after all, would fit the sense of the passage much better than "the Prolonged of Life."]

(14) from "The Space-Eaters," Frank Belknap Long:

> The cross is not a passive agent. It protects the pure of heart, and it has often appeared in the air above our sabbats, confusing and dispersing the powers of Darkness.

[This passage, used as an epigraph for Long's "The Space-Eaters," has been omitted from some printings of the story.]

(15) from "The Festival," H.P. Lovecraft:

> The nethermost caverns are not for the fathoming of eyes that see; for their marvels are strange and terrific. Cursed the ground where dead thoughts live new and oddly bodied, and evil the mind that is held by no head. Wisely did Ibn Schacabao say, that happy is the tomb where no wizard hath lain, and happy is the town at night whose wizards are all ashes. For it is of old rumour that the soul of the devil-bought hastes not from this charnel clay, but fats and instructs *the very worm that gnaws*; till out of corruption horrid life springs, and the dull scavengers of earth wax crafty to vex it and swell monstrous to plague it. Great holes secretly are digged where earth's pores ought to suffice, and things have learnt to walk that ought to crawl.

by Lin Carter 131

[This is the first attributed citation from the *Necronomicon,* as "The Festival" was written in 1923.]

(16) from *The Lurker at the Threshold,* H.P. Lovecraft and August Derleth:

> . . . be they visible or invisible, to them to maketh no difference, for they feel them, & give voice . . .

The following passage — the last we have from the *Necronomicon* — is from a private, partial translation from the original Arabic text "bound with ebony covers arabesqued with silver and set with darkly-glowing garnets," which occurs "near the middle" of the book. Mr. Smith informs us this passage was wholly omitted in the Latin translation.

(17) from "The Return of the Sorcerer," Clark Ashton Smith:

> It is verily known by few, but it is nevertheless an attestable fact, that the will of a dead sorcerer hath power upon his own body and can raise it up from the tomb and perform therewith whatever action was unfulfilled in life. And such resurrections are invariably for the doing of malevolent deeds and for the detriment of others. Most readily can the corpse be animated if all its members have remained intact; yet there are cases in which the excelling will of the wizard hath reared up from death the sundered pieces of a body hewn in many fragments, and hath caused them to serve his end, either separately or in a temporary reunion. But in every instance, after the action hath been completed, the body lapseth into its former state.

Further on in the same story, we learn of another passage also excluded from the Olaus Wormius translation, "a singular incantory formula for the exorcism of the dead, with a ritual that involves the use of rare Arabian spices and the proper intoning of at least a hundred names of ghouls and demons," or so the narrator insists.

That is the total of quotations from the *Necronomicon* in the Mythos. Lovecraft left no clue as to where the idea was derived (unless, perhaps, in the long-awaited *Selected Letters*), but commentators on Lovecraft have been quick to offer their own interpretations. In an article in *The Arkham Sampler,* George Wetzel tells us that Lovecraft had traced his ancestry back to one Thomas Hazard, a colonist of early New England, and conjectures that "Alhazred" and "Hazard" may thus be similar to "d'Erlette — Derleth." He also conjectures that the Book of Thoth was the original for Alhazred's book. Those familiar with Egyptian folklore will recall this legendary tome was reputedly discovered by an Egyptian scribe in the necropolis at Thebes; also that a warning existed saying all who beheld the book would come "to a ghastly end." My own feeling is that, since Lovecraft incorporated the Book of Thoth into the Mythos wholesale, he would not base another mythical book on it. The most likely candidate is, it seems to me, *The King in Yellow,* the nonexistent play which figures in the Carcosa Mythos of Bierce and Chambers. Like the *Necronomicon,* this book contained wisdom so deadly and evil that it inspired revulsion in all readers; also Chambers, like Lovecraft, studded his stories with quotations from it. Since Lovecraft lifted most of the symbols from the Carcosa Mythos and incorporated them in the Cthulhu Mythos — Hastur, Lake of Hali, the Hyades, even Carcosa itself — but did not touch the play at all, I believe he derived the germ of the idea behind the *Necronomicon* there.

[The *Necronomicon* is indeed Lovecraft's own creation, as he often had occasion to reassure credulous readers. This fact needs to be stated again with all due force today, when many are persuaded of the reality of the book and even circulate spurious works under the famous title. As S.T. Joshi has shown, Lovecraft was wrong as to the meaning of the title. "Necronomicon" came to him in a dream, probably a subconscious reflection of the astronomical treatise of Manilius, the *Astronomicon,* with which he was quite familiar. Lovecraft did not, then, consciously construct the title, but tried to decipher it after the fact, and he erred in his guess that it would have to mean "Book [literally Image] of the Laws of the Dead." *Necros* does mean "dead" or "corpse," but the rest of the title reflects the Greek verb *nemo* and the suffix preserved in English as "-ical." The title means "An Examination the Dead," with a possible connotation of classification.

[The Arabic title of the book, *Al-Azif,* "the Buzzing," is closer to its target, denoting the insect-like buzzing made by the *jinn* or spirits of the desert, made into demons by the Prophet Muhammad, as they imparted revelations to mantic soothsayers such as Alhazred is described as being. Lovecraft derived the term from Samuel Henley's notes to William Beckford's *Vathek.*

[As for the publishing history (derived from Lovecraft's own tongue-in-cheek article "History of the *Necronomicon* "), Olaus Wormius lived three centuries later than Lovecraft places him. Lovecraft evidently assumed that Wormius lived in the thirteenth century as a result of an erroneous inference from a discussion of Wormius found in Hugh Blair's *A Critical Dissertation on the Poems of Ossian* (1763). See S.T. Joshi, "Lovecraft, Regner Lodbrog, and Olaus Wormius," *Crypt of Cthulhu* No. 89 (Eastertide, 1995):3–7.

[Lovecraft later filled in more exact dates for two of the editions. In a letter to Jim Blish and William Miller (13 May 1936), he pinpoints the date of the Spanish edition as 1623, that for the Italian printing as 1567.

[The biographical sketch of Abdul Alhazred comes not from the fiction, but, again, from the "History of the *Necronomicon.* " It is worth noting that the twelfth-century Arab biographer Ibn Khallikan is a genuine historical figure, though of Alhazred he in fact recorded nothing.

[Carter's speculation that the concept of the *Necronomicon* was derived from Chambers's *The King in Yellow* is a little unlikely in view of the fact that Lovecraft did not read Chambers until five years after first

by Lin Carter   133 citing the *Necronomicon.* There are many possible sources for the idea of a mythical book of magical lore — the Gothic novelists, Poe, Hawthorne — but suffice it to say that Lovecraft developed the conception more exhaustively than any of his predecessors and more subtly than any of his contemporaries or successors.]

38. *Night-Gaunt,* Edgar Hengist Gordon (Bloch).

This is a novel by that author of weird fiction mentioned in the Bloch short story "The Dark Demon." Gordon is supposed to have written various short stories such as "Gargoyle," as well as the present book and a novel called *The Soul of Chaos* (see 50) and three other books which were privately published. *Night-Gaunt* was his first book, and it was a failure due to its excessive morbidity.

39. *Of Evill Sorceries done in New-England by Daemons in no Humane Shape* (Lovecraft & Derleth).

A manuscript discovered by Ambrose Dewart in an old house north of Arkham, which is described in *The Lurker at the Threshold* as being "penned in a crabbed hand, and only in parts legible." We have some quotations from it:

> But, not to speak at too great Length upon so Horrid a matter, I will add onlie what is commonly reported concerning an Happening in New Dunnich, fifty years since, when Mr. Bradford was Governour. 'Tis said, one Richard *Billington,* being instructed partly by Evill Books, and partly by an antient Wonder-Worker amongst ye *Indian* Savages, so fell away from good *Christian* Practice that he not onlie lay'd claim to Immortality in ye flesh, but sett up in ye woods a great Ring of Stones, inside of which he say'd Prayers to ye Divell, Place of Dagon, Namely, and sung certain Rites of Magick abominable by Scripture. This being brought to ye Notice of ye Magistrates, he deny'd all Blasphemous Dealings; but not long after he privately shew'd great Fear about some Thing he had call'd out of ye Sky at Night. There were in that year seven slayings in ye woods near to *Richard Billington's* Stones, those slain being crushed and half-melted in a fashion outside all experience. Upon Talk of a Tryall, *Billington* dropped out of Sight, nor was any clear Word of him ever after heard. Two months from then, by Night, there was heard a Band of *Wampanaug* Savages howling and singing in ye Woods; and it appeared they took down ye Ring of Stones and did much besides. For their head Man *Misquamacus,* that same antient Wonder-Worker of whom *Billington* had learnt some of his Sorceries, came shortly into ye Town and told Mr. *Bradford* some strange Things: Namely, that *Billington* had done worse Evill than cou'd well be repair'd, and that he was no doubt eat up by what he had call'd out of ye Sky. That there was no Way to send back that Thing he had summon'd so ye *Wampanaug* wise Man had caught and prison'd it where the Ring of Stones had been.

They had digg'd three Ells deep and two across, and had Thither charmed ye Daemon with Spells that they knew; covering it over with . . . carved with what they call'd ye *Elder Sign.* On this they . . . digg'd from ye Pit. The old Savage affirm'd this place was on no Account to be disturb'd, lest ye Daemon came loose again which it wou'd do if ye flatt Stone with ye *Elder Sign* shou'd get out of Place. On being ask'd what ye Daemon look'd like, *Misquamacus* covered his Face so that onlie ye Eyes look'd out, and then gave a very curious and Circumstantiall Relation, saying it was sometimes small and solid, like a great Toad ye Bigness of many Ground-Hogs, but sometimes big and cloudy, with no Shape, though with a Face which had Serpents grown from it.

It had ye Name *Ossadogowah,* which signifys ye child of *Sadogowah,* ye which is held to be a Frightful Spirit spoke of by antients as come down from ye Stars and being formerly worshipt in Lands to ye North. Ye *Wampanaugs* and ye *Nansets* and *Nahrigansets* knew how to draw It out of ye Heavens but never did so because of ye exceeding great Evilness of It. They knew also how to catch and prison It, tho' they cou'd not send It back whence It came. It was declar'd that ye old Tribes of *Lamah,* who dwelt under ye Great Bear and were antiently destroy'd for their Wickedness, knew how to manage It in all Ways. Many upstart Men pretended to a Knowledge of such and divers other Outer Secrets, but none in these Parts cou'd give any Proof of truly having ye aforesaid Knowledge. It was said by some that *Ossadogowah* often went back to ye Sky from choice without any sending, but that he cou'd not come back unless Summon'd.

This much ye antient Wizard *Misquamacus* told to Mr. *Bradford,* and ever after, a great Mound in ye Woods near ye Pond southwest of New Dunnich had been straitly lett alone. Ye Tall Stone is these Twenty yrs. gone, but ye Mound is mark'd by ye Circumstance, that nothing, neither grass nor brush, will grow upon it. Grave men doubt that ye evill *Billington* was eat up as ye Savages believe, by what he call'd out of Heaven, notwithstanding certain Reports of ye idle, of his being since seen in divers places. Ye Wonder-Worker *Misquamacus* told that he mistrusted not but that *Billington* had been taken; he wou'd not say that he had been eat up by It, as others among ye Savages believ'd, but he affirm'd that *Billington* was no longer on this Earth, whereat God be prais'd."

[This quotation is one of the few items in Derleth's novel *The Lurker at the Threshold* to come from Lovecraft's notes. But Derleth has somewhat embellished the quoted matter, adding, for instance, the beard of feelers on the face of Ossadogowah.]

40. *Occultus.* Heiriarchus (Bloch).

This book was referred to only in Bloch's "The Secret in the Tomb," and apparently does not exist.

41. *People of the Monolith,* Justin Geoffrey (Howard).

The mad poet Justin Geoffrey, a friend of another poet — Edward Derby who wrote *Azathoth and Other Horrors* — visited Hungary and examined the Black Stone, that curious monolith among the mountains of Hungary (see 44. *Remnants of Lost Empires*). He wrote a book of verse and died screaming in a madhouse in 1926. His history is given in more detail in Howard's "The Black Stone," from which we quote the following verse from *People of the Monolith*:

> They say foul things of Old Times still lurk
> In dark forgotten corners of the world,
> And gates still gape to loose, on certain nights,
> Shapes pent in hell . . .

[Geoffrey's manner and date of death were copied by Lovecraft in "The Thing on the Doorstep" from Howard's "The Black Stone."]

42. Pnakotic Manuscripts (Lovecraft).

This rare and esoteric work is the oldest book mentioned in the Mythos, as it is believed "of pre-Pleistocene" origin (according to Lovecraft, who says in "The Shadow out of Time" that it is a relic of the Great Race who ruled the Earth some fifty million years before man). We know little about its contents: Tsathoggua is mentioned in it, and the curious "Pnakotic Pentagram" spoken of in Kuttner's "The Invaders" is probably from it; and in *The Dream-Quest of Unknown Kadath* we are told of the "Other Gods from Outside who set their seal upon Earth's primal granite" according to a drawing in "those parts of the Pnakotic Manuscripts too old to be read."

A copy is preserved in the Library of Miskatonic University in Arkham, Mass., one in the collection of Dr. Jean-François Charriere of Providence, Rhode Island, another in the ruined church on Federal Hill (also in Providence), and a fourth is kept in the Temple of the Elder Ones in Ulthar, which is in the Earth's Dreamworld.

This is the so-called "last copy" which was made by men in the forgotten boreal kingdoms of this world, and carried into the Dreamworld by them when the hairy, cannibal Gnophkehs overcame Olathö and slew the men of Lomar.

[There is absolutely no warrant for Carter's ascription of this work to the Great Race of Yith. All Lovecraft says in "The Shadow out of Time" is that the Yith race flourished in that far-off era from which the Pnakotic Manuscripts form one of the few surviving relics.

[On the other hand, in a letter to William Lumley, he clearly states that the Pnakotic Manuscripts are the work of "the 'Elder Ones' preceding the human race on this planet, and handed down through an early human civilization which once existed around the North Pole," presumably Lomar, perhaps Hyperborea. Who these "Elder Ones" may have been is a puzzle, since the star-headed Old Ones or Elder Ones were located at the opposite pole, while the Great Race, never called the Elder

Ones, are tucked away in Australia. The Yithites are certainly not the authors of the Manuscripts.

[Carter's own story, "The Acolyte of the Flame," modifies his earlier judgment on the matter, making only the earliest, indecipherable portions of the Pnakotic Manuscripts the work of the Yith race. (Carter pronounced the title "na-KO-tik," with a short "a" and a long "o." Others pronounce "nay-KOT-ik," with a long "a" and a short "o." Who knows?)]

43. *Polygraphia.* Trithemius.

Johannes Trithemius was born at Tritenheim, Trier, Germany, in 1462, and became a Benedictine Abbot at the age of twenty-two. He collected a library of two thousand manuscripts and volumes, a record for his era, and was so famous that his erudition was proverbial and he was consulted by Emperors and Queens. He died in 1516 at the abbey of St. James, Wurzburg, where he is buried.

Although most of his works are of an ecclesiastical nature, he wrote many books on alchemy and magic, which influenced Paracelsus and Cornelius Agrippa, and on the Kabballah. His *Polygraphie et Universelle Escriture Cabalistique,* which is mentioned in "The Dunwich Horror" as *Polygraphia,* was published at Paris in 1561. [See note on 16. Cockcroft adds that the work first appeared in Latin in 1518.]

44. *Remnants of Lost Empires,* Otto Dostman, Der Drachenhaus Press, Berlin, 1809 (Howard).

This mythical book, published by an equally fictitious "Dragon's House" press, is mentioned in "The Black Stone" as referring to that curious monolith in Hungary of which Justin Geoffrey wrote (see 34. *Magyar Folklore,* and 41. *People of the Monolith*).

45. *R'lyeh Text* (Lovecraft).

The *R'lyeh Text* is probably a book concerned with the worship of Cthulhu, since that leader of the Great Old Ones lies "sleeping" in the submerged half-cosmic city of R'lyeh, which, we are told in Derleth's *The Trail of Cthulhu,* is under the Pacific Ocean off New Zealand and south of the East Indies at S. Lat. 49° 51', W. Long. 128° 34'. A swift glance at the map tells us that this is quite a ways "off" New Zealand indeed, as it is in the middle of the South Pacific. From another source, Derleth's "The Black Island," we are told it is "off" Ponape, which it is, to the extent of about four thousand miles, if we accept the latitude and longitude above as correct. There Cthulhu lies in his enchanted sleep, served by the "batrachian" Deep Ones who await the time the Elder Sign shall no longer bind him and he shall awake.

The *Text* is probably written in the pre-human language of R'lyehian. Copies are preserved at the Miskatonic, and in private collections. We have two quotations from it. The first is from *The Trail of Cthulhu*:

Ubbo-Sathla is the source, the unforgotten beginning from whom
came those who dared set themselves against the Elder Gods who ruled

from Betelgeuze, those who warred upon the Elder Gods, the Great Old Ones led by the blind idiot god, Azathoth, and Yog-Sothoth, who is All-in-One and One-in-All, and upon whom are no strictures of time or space, and whose agents are 'Umr at-Tawil and the Ancient Ones, who dream forever of the time when once again they shall rule to whom rightfully belong Earth and the entire universe of which it is a part . . . Great Cthulhu shall rise from R'lyeh, Hastur the Unspeakable shall return from the dark star which is in the Hyades near Aldebaran, the red eye of the bull, Nyarlathotep shall howl forever in the darkness where he abideth, Shug-Niggurath shall spawn in turn and take dominion over all wood nymphs, satyrs, leprechauns, and the Little People, Lloigor, Zhar, and Ithaqua shall ride the spaces among the stars, and those who serve them, the Tcho-Tcho, shall be ennobled. Cthugha shall encompass his dominion from Fomalhaut, and Tsathoggua shall come from N'kai. . . . They wait by the gate, for the time draws near, the hour is soon at hand, and the Elder Gods sleep, dreaming, and there are those who know the spells put upon the Great Old Ones by the Elder Gods, as there are those who shall learn how to break them, as already they know how to command the servants of those who wait beyond the door from Outside."

The final quote is from "The Return of Hastur," by Derleth. Apparently in the original R'lyehian, we have an English translation of it:

Ph'nglui mglw'nafh Cthulhu R'lyeh wgah'nagl fhatgn," reads, "In his house at R'lyeh dead Cthulhu waits dreaming."

[The *R'lyeh Text*, contra Carter, is certainly no invention of Lovecraft, who never thought of such a thing. Derleth created it, along with the whole R'lyeh tourist trade implied by it. The citation from "The Return of Hastur" is obviously derived from "The Call of Cthulhu."]

46. *Saducismus Triumphatus*. Joseph Glanvil, 1681.

In "The Festival," Lovecraft refers to "the shocking *Saducismus Triumphatus*," and gives us the above data on author and date. It is all correct — except, perhaps, for the "shocking" part — and a revised edition of the work was published in London in 1681. Glanvil, whom Seligmann has called the last great defender of belief in witches in Britain, originally published the book in 1668 under the title of *Blow at Modern Sadduceeism*.

[*Saducismus Triumphatus* was a defense of witchcraft beliefs and superstition. It is necessary to correct the note of Home that the title means "Sadduceeism Triumphant." As the title of the English translation listed by Carter (*Blow at Modern Sadduceeism*) implies, the work heralds a "triumph *over* Sadduceeism." The sect of the Sadducees are said in the Acts of the Apostles to have believed in neither angels or spirits (23:8), and so were often used as prototypes of rationalism.]

47. *The Saurian Age*. Banfort (Lovecraft & Derleth).

This book was mentioned only once ("The Survivor"), and I have been unable to discover if it exists or not. I should say it does, however, as it is listed among the collection of Dr. Charriere along with other books which actually exist.

[*The Saurian Age,* thought by Carter to be a genuine, though to him untraceable, work of paleontology, is written of by Home as a Derlethian coinage, a fictitious counterpart to Henry Fairfield Osborn's popular *Age of Mammals.* Derleth needed such a book to foreshadow the transformation of the main character in "The Survivor." As plausible as the title sounds, Home notes that it is unknown to authorities in the field. We might also note Derleth's affinity for the word "saurian" in describing the Old Ones. He also tended to lend the Deep Ones reptilian traits, over against Lovecraft, for whom they were "fish-frogs" but did not hop over into a third phylum as well.]

48. The Seven Cryptical Books of Hsan (Lovecraft).

Here Lovecraft wasted a marvelous title, without ever making effective use of it. A copy is in the Miskatonic, according to *The Lurker at the Threshold,* but unhappily we have no further data. It may be a book of prophecy; the title is similar to *The Nine Books of the Cumaean Sibyl.*

[Here one only need note that this title appears in Lovecraft's original where the published texts (until the recent corrected editions) of "The Other Gods" have the similar title The Seven Cryptical Books of Earth. It is a case of editorial tampering or accidental mistranscription.]

49. *The Seventh Book of Moses.*

August Derleth mentions this in "The House in the Valley" as being "notorious." It is a cheap and imitative hex-book like *The Long-Lost Friend,* and purports to be a lost book of the Bible. The copy in my collection is in the Lewis de Claremont edition, still in print at a dollar or so. A pretty sloppy literary forgery: pretending to have been written by Moses, it mentions Christ, the Disciples, and the Four Evangelists.

[*The Seventh Book of Moses* also appears in Derleth's effective tale "Wentworth's Day," a story suggested by one of Lovecraft's Commonplace Book entries, but based on no draft or outline of Lovecraft's despite the almost verbatim copying of passages from "The Colour out of Space" and "The Picture in the House." The reference to the book does not come from any Lovecraft source.]

50. *The Soul of Chaos.* Edgar Hengist Gordon (Bloch).

This was the first of four privately-printed books by the noted supernaturalist, author of *Night-Gaunt.* From Bloch's "The Dark Demon," we have one quotation:

> This world is but a tiny island in the dark sea of Infinity, and there are horrors swirling all around us. Around us? Rather let us say *amongst* us. I know, for I have seen them in my dreams, and there are more things in this world than sanity can ever see.

[The first sentence of the quotation is a blatant borrowing from the opening of "The Call of Cthulhu." Lovecraft read the tale in Ms., but either did not notice or did not bother to comment on the borrowing.]

51. *The Sussex Manuscript* (Pelton).

This book or Ms. is mentioned in Derleth's *The Trail of Cthulhu* with no further reference in the Mythos, but it has a peculiar and interesting history. The *Manuscript* is purely the invention of Lovecraft-enthusiast Fred L. Penton of Lincoln, Nebraska. Pelton actually wrote out the entire book-length *Sussex Manuscript* in the hopes of Arkham House publication, and Derleth was at one time so interested in the project that he mentioned the work in one of his Mythos stories, the above-mentioned, thus making it "canonical."

The quotations I have seen from the *Sussex Manuscript* are largely an expansion of previous quotes from the *Necronomicon* and such, intermingled with new Peltonian additions to the established lore. I shall not quote them all here, not only because the entire Ms. exists, but as no quotations are ever given in the body of the Mythos, and thus any made here could not quite be considered canonical. I shall give one brief quotation here, to convey the average flavor of the others:

> Not unknowingly did the ancients do their magic by the circles for it is of old lore that the ring did evoke and conjure Him who is Nameless. Only when the fools forgot the memory of them did the power of magic fail: only when fools lost the names did the legends fade and men neglect them. The Names were the keys and they were lost.

This is from "Book I, Chapter xxiii."

[Carter does not quite make clear that this manuscript is a fictional attempt at supplying the *Necronomicon* in an English version. Its prose is of the most turgid, and despite Derleth's inexplicable initial enthusiasm for the work, it no doubt was the item he referred to when he once recalled having seen a couple of fan-produced *Necronomicon*s and said that they were pretty disappointing efforts. It has now been published as a special issue of *Crypt of Cthulhu* 63, Eastertide 1989.]

52. *The Tablets of Nhing.*

This book is another of the many that are only mentioned by title in the Mythos, with no further data ever given. It may not be a printed book, but another such group of shards of broken stone tablets, as *The Celaeno Fragments.*

53. *Thaumaturgicall Prodigies in the New-English Canaan,* the Reverend Ward Phillips, Boston, 1801 (Lovecraft).

Invented by Lovecraft, most of our information on this fascinating book comes from the posthumous collaboration, *The Lurker at the Threshold.* Rev. Phillips (the name is another Lovecraft family name) was a pastor of the Second Church in Arkham during colonial times. The book in question, obviously based on Cotton Mather, is a reprint bound in worn leather in imitation black-letter. Our quotation comes from about two-thirds through the book:

> . . . evill of consorting with Daemons, Familiars, and such ilk. But in respect to Generall Infamy, no Report more terrible hath come to Notice, than of what Goodwife *Doten,* Relict of John *Doten* of *Duxbury* in the Old Colonies, brought out of the Woods near Candlemas of 1787. She affirm'd, and her good neighbours likewise, that it had been borne to her, and took oath that she did not know by what manner it had come upon her, for it was neither Beast nor Man but like to a monstrous Bat with human face. It made no sound but look'd at all and sundry with baleful eyes. There were those who swore that it bore a frightful resemblance to the Face of one long dead, one *Richard Bellingham* or *Bollinhan* who is affirm'd to have vanished utterly after consort with Daemons in the New Dunnich. The horrible Beast-Man was examined by the Court of Azzizes and the which then burnt by Order of the High-Sheriff on the 5th of June in the year 1788.

Later in the same book, we are told that Phillips tried to gather up all copies of the *Thaumaturgicall Prodigies* and burn them.

[The title and extract are indeed of Lovecraft's coinage, and are found on some story notes that Derleth discovered amongst Lovecraft's papers; the quotation has, however, been somewhat altered by Derleth.]

54. *Thesaurus Chemicus.* Roger Bacon.

Friar Bacon (1214–1294) was a Franciscan who was imprisoned in England for ten years due to his unorthodoxy, and who died two years after his release. This has been considered one of the greatest crimes of history, as Bacon was one of the supreme intellects of his, or indeed, any other time. He was possessed of a superb and prophetic imagination, and predicted poison gas, diving suits, airplanes, etc. He is credited with the invention of gunpowder, independent of the Chinese, and he experimented valuably with telescopy and lenses.

The *Thesaurus Chemicus* does exist; a correspondent informs me of an edition printed at Hamburg in 1598.

[The major work on alchemy attributed to Roger Bacon (although probably not by him) is generally known as *Speculum Alchemiae* (1541), translated into English as *The Mirror of Alchimy* (1593). The existence of a *Thesaurus Chemicus* — cited in *The Case of Charles Dexter Ward* — has not been verified.]

55. *Traicté des Chiffres,* De Vigenere.

This book is named in "The Dunwich Horror." Jack Grill has reported that a *Traicté de Chifferes ou Secretes d'Escrire* by Blaise de Vigénère was published at Paris in 1586. Vigénère was one of the first European authorities upon cryptography and this book is of historical interest in that it contains the first representation in European history of the Japanese language. For further information on the author, my reader may consult p. 371–372 of Vol. 43, *Biographie Universelle*. [See note on 16.]

56. *Turba Philosophorum.*

This book, which is among those many mentioned in *The Case of Charles Dexter Ward,* is believed actually to exist, and concerns itself with the art of alchemy.

[The *Turba Philosophorum* ("Gathering of Philosophers") was published in Basel in 1613; it is a German translation of a Latin work on alchemy edited by Guglielmo Grataroli (1516?–1568?) entitled *Auriferae Artis [Libri]* (1572). An English translation by A.E. Waite appeared in 1896 under the title *Turba Philosophorum.*]

57. *Unaussprechlichen Kulten,* von Junzt (Howard).

This is perhaps Howard's greatest addition to the Mythos. Von Junzt was a German who traveled all over the world and gained entrance into various secret societies and cults. Born in 1795, he died mysteriously in a locked room shortly after the original Düsseldorf edition was printed in 1840. The first edition, we are informed, was bound in leather with iron hasps, and only a half dozen copies are extant. The so-called "Black Book" (the title really means *Nameless Cults*) was pirated in a cheap, faulty edition, a translation into the English, published by Bridewell in 1845; an expurgated edition was published by the Golden Goblin Press of New York City in 1909.

The only quotation we have from it is both brief and apocryphal. Philip Duschnes, in his tongue-in-cheek hoax ad for the *Necronomicon,* reprinted in *The Arkham Sampler* No. 1, 1948, says that von Junzt, discussing the madness of Alhazred, says on "page ix":

> es steht ausser Sweifel, dass dieses Buch ist die Grundlage der Okkulteliteratur.

[It should be noted that Howard had simply titled the volume *Nameless Cults,* but Lovecraft felt it needed a more ponderous title (he was right) and engaged Derleth, a good German, to provide one. He came up with *Unaussprechlichen Kulten* (which however requires the initial article *die,* or else it should read *Unaussprechliche Kulten*). E. Hoffmann Price thought this to be inaccurate German (he believed *unaussprechlich* to mean "unpronounceable" rather than "nameless" or "unspeakable") and suggested instead *Unnennbarren Kulten,* which had more the ring, he thought, of the shocking and unmentionable. But Derleth's title prevailed. While *Weird Tales* editor Farnsworth Wright sided with Price, the emphatic advocacy of Derleth's version by former *Weird Tales* illustrator C.C. Senf, himself born and educated in Germany, carried the day.

When Robert Bloch sent Lovecraft a version of his never-published story "The Madness of Lucian Grey," Lovecraft responded in a letter (c. late June 1933): "Also — you give Howard's von Junzt the praenomen of *Conrad,* whereas at least one printed allusion (which I put in a story I ghost-wrote for a revision-client!) establishes it as Friedrich. Howard himself, amusingly enough, did not give von Junzt a first name as far as I know. (Am I mistaken?)" Lovecraft is not mistaken as to the latter point, but he apparently is in regard to the appearance of the first name in a ghost-written tale; none has so far come to light. In fact, it appears that Lovecraft supplied the first and middle names of "Friedrich Wilhelm" for von Junzt, the former in the mock death warrant he wrote for himself on 30 April 1935, giving Bloch permission to annihilate him in "The Shambler from the Stars." The document was signed by Abdul Alhazred, Friedrich von Junzt, Gaspard du Nord, and the Tcho-Tcho Lama of Leng. In his transcription of the document in his book *Lovecraft: A Look Behind the "Cthulhu Mythos,"* Carter mistranscribes von Junzt's first name as "Fvindvuf" (p. 117).]

58. *The Witch-Cult in Western Europe,* Murray.

This work is frequently listed in Lovecraft, and is another of those actually extant. Dr. Margaret Alice Murray is an English scholar and the above book was first published, Oxford, 1921. A later work, *The God of the Witches,* would have suited Lovecraft's purposes far more.

Dr. Murray's theory that the witch-covens of medieval times were not just a perverted cult of Satan-worshipers but represented a survival of a primitive and world-wide religion which was in competition with the Roman Church during the Middle Ages and thus condemned, persecuted and practically eliminated, fits in rather nicely with some of the underlying theses of the Cthulhu Mythos, and is, beside the way, taken quite seriously in the field of modern folklore-study and anthropology, where she is sometimes mentioned in the same breath as Frazer and Miss Weston.

[Murray's thesis is not regarded as very likely by modern anthropologists.]

59. *Zohar.*

There is only one reference to "the cabalistic *Zohar*" in the Mythos, but Lovecraft could well have put it to further use. It is not really one book, but a compilation of many books, fragments, biblical commentaries and lore of the Kaballah, first compiled and published in Spain during the late thirteenth century by Moses de Leon, who, seeking the authority of antiquity for his work, attributed it to the Rabbi Simon bar Yohai of second-century Palestine.

The *Zohar* is one of the great works of the Kaballah, that peculiar science which seeks to unravel the secret magical arcana given to Moses on Sinai and hidden by him cryptographically throughout the Pentateuch.

By adding up the arbitrary numerical values given by them to the Hebrew alphabet, the Kabbalists derived new numbers from which, translated back again into letter, they derived the "Most Potent and Holy Names of God"; these names form much of the foundation of magical lore since their day.

A few such names as "Eloim," "Agla," and so on have been used by Lovecraft, as in the quotation from the *Liber-Damnatus* (see 31).

A slim volume called *Selections from the Zohar,* edited by Gershom G. Scholem, was published in New York in 1947, to which I refer those seeking further information.

[The volume is cited in *The Case of Charles Dexter Ward.* "Zohar" is Hebrew for "splendor." Major portions of the vast bulk of the *Zohar* have been published. They include S.L. MacGregor Mathers's translation *The Kabbalah Unveiled* (Samuel Weiser, 1968, 1983); Harry Sperling and Maurice Simon, trans., *The Zohar* (Soncino Press, Vols. 1–5, 1934, 1978); Daniel Chanan Matt, trans., *Zohar, the Book of Enlightenment* (Paulist Press, 1983). The sampling culled by Gershom Scholem is available in paperback from Schocken Books.]

ADDENDA
by S.T. Joshi and Robert M. Price

60. *Book of Invaders*

Home has a lengthy note on this title, cited in "The Moon-Bog." It is a real work chronicling the legendary invasion and population of Ireland.

61. *Book of Iod* (Kuttner).

Mentioned in various of Henry Kuttner's early Mythos tales, the tome is of course young Kuttner's *Necronomicon* analogue, at least one of which seems to have been created by each member of the Lovecraft Circle. Lovecraft never got around to mentioning the *Book of Iod* in any of his stories, but he assured Kuttner that he intended to do so: "Sometime I'll quote darkly from your *Book of Iod* — which I presume either antedates the human race like the Eltdown Shards and the Pnakotic Manuscripts, or repeats the most hellish secrets learnt by early man in the fashion of the *Book of Eibon, De Vermis Mysteriis,* the Comte d'Erlette's *Cultes des Goules,* von Junzt's *Unaussprechlichen Kulten,* or the dreaded & abhorred *Al Azif* or *Necronomicon* of the mad Arab Abdul Alhazred" (letter of February 16, 1936).

As Kuttner himself describes the book in "Bells of Horror," it is an "abhorrent and monstrous volume of ancient esoteric formulae about which curious legends still cling. Only a single copy of the original volume, written in the prehuman Ancient Tongue, is said to exist." There is an English translation, in an expurgated edition, the work of one Johann Negus. Here is a passage of Negus's *Iod* from "Bells of Horror":

> The Dark Silent One dwelleth deep beneath the earth on the shore of the Western Ocean. Not one of those potent Old Ones from hidden worlds and other stars is He, for He is the ultimate doom and the undying emptiness and silence of Old Night.
>
> When earth is dead and lifeless and the stars pass into the blackness, He will rise again and spread His dominion over all. For He hath naught to do with life and sunlight, but loveth the blackness

and the eternal silence of the abyss. Yet can He be called to earth's surface before His time, and the brown ones who dwell on the shore of the Western Ocean have power to do this by ancient spells and certain deep-toned sounds which reach His dwelling-place far below.

But there is great danger in such a summoning, lest He spread death and night before His time. For He bringeth darkness within the light; all life, all sound, all movement passeth away at His coming. He cometh sometimes within the eclipse, and although He hath no name, the brown ones know Him as Zushakon.

62. Borellus

Cockcroft points out Carter's omission of this author (cited as the epigraph to *The Case of Charles Dexter Ward*), and Home identifies Borellus with Giovanni Alfonso Borelli (1608–1679). Although this identification was elaborated upon by Roger Bryant ("The Alchemist and the Scientist: Borellus and the Lovecraftian Imagination," *Nyctalops* 2, No. 3 [January-February 1975]: 26–29, 43), it is incorrect. Borellus, as Robert Marten has informed me, is the chemist and physicist Pierre Borel (1627–1689), author of *Bibliotheca Chemica* (1654), *Discours nouveau prouvant la pluralité des mondes* (1657), and other works. Lovecraft found the citation from Borellus in Cotton Mather's *Magnalia Christi Americana* (1702), as Barton L. St. Armand established ("The Source for Lovecraft's Knowledge of Borellus in *The Case of Charles Dexter Ward*," *Nyctalops* 2, No. 6 [May 1977]: 16–17). Lovecraft had a copy of the first edition of the *Magnalia* in his library. The citation from Borellus in *The Case of Charles Dexter Ward* is in fact Mather's translation or paraphrase of a passage from Borellus, probably the *Historiarum et Observationum Medicophysicarum Centuriae IV* (1656), quoted earlier in the *Magnalia*.

63. *Chronicle of Nath*, Yergler (Lovecraft-Rimel).

A passage from this mythical work is cited in "The Tree on the Hill," a story Lovecraft revised for Duane W. Rimel. Rudolf Yergler is said to be "a German mystic and alchemist who borrowed some of his lore from Hermes Trismegistus, the ancient Egyptian sorcerer." The extract is very likely the work of Lovecraft, but the title and author may have been invented by Rimel.

64. Delrio

Cited in "The Horror at Red Hook," Martin Anton Del Rio (or Delrio) (1551–1608) was a Jesuit priest and author of *Disguisitionum Magicarum Libri Sex* [*Six Books of Disquisitions on Magic*] (1603), from which the quotation was taken. Lovecraft found it in the article on "Demonology" (by Edward Burnett Tylor) in the 9th edition of the *Encyclopaedia Britannica*.

65. *Ghorl Nigral* (Conover).

Mulder's infamous *Ghorl Nigral*" is the invention of Lovecraft's young correspondent Willis Conover, apparently one of many titles invented by

Conover ("Your catalogue of hellish and forbidden books sounds highly impressive, and the very names make me shudder"). Though the *Ghorl Nigral* figured in no published Mythos tale until Lin Carter's own "Zoth-Ommog" forty years later, Lovecraft himself, in the same August 1936 letter just quoted, spun out a miniature history concerning the blasphemous tome:

> It was many years ago in Arkham — at the library of the Miskatonic University. I was in a shadowy corner of the great reading-room, and noted a huge volume in somebody's hands across the table from me. The reader's head was completely hidden by the massive tome, but on the book itself I could descry the words "Ghorl Nigral" in an archaic Gothic lettering. What I knew of it made me shudder — and I felt vaguely alarmed when others began glancing at the silent reader and quietly edging out of the room one by one. When I saw that I was wholly alone but for the unspeaking page-turner, my feeling of disquiet became almost overpowering — and I too edged toward the door keeping my eyes resolutely away from the reader for some unknown reason or other. Then I saw that the room was growing very dark, though the afternoon was by no means spent. I stumbled over a chair, and gave vent to a wholly involuntary cry — but heard no answering sound. At this point came a horrible glare of lightning and a deafening stroke of thunder, though those outside the building observed no sign of a storm. Attendants came running in, and someone brought a candle after the lights were found out of commission. The man who had been reading was dead, and his face was not pleasant to contemplate. He had a queerly foreign look, and his hair and beard seemed to adhere in unhealthy patches. The book, from which all eyes were sedulously averted, was tightly clasped in the brown, bony hands — and the attendants seemed slow in trying to dislodge it. When at length they did so, they encountered something very singular. For the hands, instead of releasing the book, came irregularly off at the wrists amid a cloud of red dust — whilst the body, pulled forward by the attempt, collapsed suddenly to a powder, leaving only a heap of greenishly mouldering clothes in the chair. Those clothes were later identified as belonging to a man buried 30 years before — whose tomb in Christchurch Cemetery was found to be empty. Never since that day has the *Ghorl Nigral* been taken from its locked vault in the library basement.

Where Lin Carter could find no extant bibliographical data he enjoyed creating them. Here is his own sketch of the origin and character of the *Ghorl Nigral* (to which he added typographical spice with an umlaut) from his story "Zoth-Ommog":

> . . . that dread chronicle, the *Ghörl Nigral,* whose ultra-telluric origin is the secret of one of the most horrible of the dark myths locked within the dim pages of the *Book of Eibon.* There it is called

H.P. LOVECRAFT: THE BOOKS

The Book of Night, and it is told that the clawed, snouted, nonhuman wizard Zbauka, on a world called Yaddith of the Five Moons, thieved it from the monstrous Dholes. Von Junzt records of this *Ghörl Nigral* that only one copy has ever been brought down to this planet from frightful Yaddith in all the immeasurable ages of Earth's existence in this part of space. The single copy is hidden somewhere in the black depths of Asia, at a place called Yian-Ho; there the book is whispered in a thousand legends as "the hidden legacy of aeon-old Leng." . . . Gottfried Mulder [was] a scientist who accompanied von Junzt in his travels, and who contributed a foreword to the *Unaussprechlichen Kulten.* . . . This same Mulder, long after the death of von Junzt [who had managed to consult the book,] attempted a written reconstruction of what he remembered von Junzt telling him about the contents of this mysterious book using Mesmerism and . . . self-hypnosis to obtain perfect recall. His book, *The Secret Mysteries of Asia, with a Commentary on the "Ghörl Nigral,"* was published at Mulder's own expense in Leipzig in 1847; copies are exceptionally rare, for the authorities seized and burned almost the entire printing, and Mulder himself narrowly escaped hanging by fleeing to Metzengerstein, where he died in a madhouse eleven years later.

66. *Regnum Congo,* Pigafetta.

Home occupies much space discussing this work (cited in "The Picture in the House"), but much of his information is erroneous. Filippo Pigafetta (1533–1604) was an Italian explorer who published *Relatione del reame di Congo et della cironvicione contrade* (*An Account of the Realm of the Congo and of the Surrounding Regions*) in 1591; the account was derived largely from information given to Pigafetta by Eduardo Lopez. The work was translated from the Italian into Dutch in 1596, into English in 1597, into German in 1597, and into Latin (as *Regnum Congo*) in 1598. The plates depicting the Anzique cannibals, drawn by the brothers De Bry, first appeared in the German edition and were then transferred to the Latin edition the following year.

However, Lovecraft never saw the actual volume (even though a copy of it was in the John Carter Brown Library in Providence during his lifetime); all he knew of Pigafetta, the brothers De Bry, and the *Regnum Congo* comes from Thomas Henry Huxley's essay "On the Methods and Results of Ethnology," in *Man's Place in Nature and Other Anthropological Essays* (1894). Lovecraft copies information directly from Huxley, and also copies some of Huxley's errors; in particular, Lovecraft's mention that the De Bry plates depict Africans as anomalously white and Caucasoid derives not from the actual illustrations but from woodcuts inaccurately copied from the De Bry plates by W.H. Wesley for Huxley's essay. See further S.T. Joshi, "Lovecraft and the *Regnum Congo,*" *Crypt of Cthulhu* No. 28 (Yuletide 1984): 13–17.

H.P. LOVECRAFT: A BASIC READING LIST

compiled by Darrell Schweitzer

Works by Lovecraft

1. *The Dunwich Horror and Others.* Sauk City WI: Arkham House, 1984. Corrected 6th printing, with an introduction by Robert Bloch and texts edited by S.T. Joshi. The only textually reliable edition. Contains virtually all Lovecraft's major stories.

2. *At the Mountains of Madness and Other Novels.* Sauk City WI: Arkham House, 1985. Corrected 5th printing, with introduction by James Turner and texts edited by S.T. Joshi. The only reliable edition. Contains the major long works such as the title novel and *The Case of Charles Dexter Ward,* plus the Randolph Carter series.

3. *Dagon and Other Macabre Tales.* Sauk City WI: Arkham House, 1986. Corrected 5th printing, with an introduction by T.E.D. Klein and texts edited by S.T. Joshi. All the rest, with the exception of a few fragments and minor items. Also contains *Supernatural Horror in Literature,* with corrections, notes, and an index by Joshi.

4. *The Horror in the Museum and Other Revisions.* Sauk City WI: Arkham House, 1989. Edited, with an introduction by August Derleth. Corrected 3rd printing. Texts edited by S.T. Joshi. The most extensively revised of the standard Arkham Lovecraft volumes. Recent scholarship, determining authorship, has caused Joshi to drop one tale and add five. All these are tales HPL ghosted for other writers, sometimes from an existing draft, sometimes merely from notes or suggestions. They should be counted as collaborations at least, or, in the case of "The Mound" and a few others, wholly by Lovecraft.

5. *The Ancient Track: Complete Poetical Works.* Edited by S.T. Joshi. San Francisco CA: Night Shade Books, 2001.

6. *Uncollected Prose and Poetry 2.* West Warwick RI: Necronomicon Press, 1980. Edited by S.T. Joshi and Marc Michaud. Fiction consists

of two parodies, plus, "The Trap" by Henry Whitehead, which is apparently a previously unidentified Lovecraft collaboration.

7. *Uncollected Prose and Poetry 3*. West Warwick RI: Necronomicon Press, 1982. Edited by S.T. Joshi and Marc Michaud. Duplicates much material found in the Lovecraftiana volumes listed below. No significant fiction.

8. *To Quebec and the Stars*. West Kingston RI: Donald M. Grant, Publisher, 1976. Edited by L. Sprague de Camp. A major collection of essays.

9. *Selected Letters I*. Sauk City WI: Arkham House, 1965. Edited by August Derleth and Donald Wandrei.

10. *Selected Letters II*. Sauk City WI: Arkham House, 1968. Edited by August Derleth and Donald Wandrei.

11. *Selected Letters III*. Sauk City WI: Arkham House, 1971. Edited by August Derleth and Donald Wandrei.

12. *Selected Letters IV*. Sauk City WI: Arkham House, 1976. Edited by August Derleth and James Turner.

13. *Selected Letters V*. Sauk City WI: Arkham House, 1976. Edited by August Derleth and James Turner.

14. *Uncollected Letters*. West Warwick RI: Necronomicon Press, 1986. With an introduction by S.T. Joshi. Previously published letters, primarily from amateur journals, most significantly the complete text of the source for the famous "All my stories, unconnected as they may be . . ." misquotation.

15. (with Willis Connover). *Lovecraft at Last*. Arlington VA: Carrolton Clark, 1975. Correspondence with Connover, often quoted and arranged to form a dialogue; plus some material by others. Shows Lovecraft at his best and fullest development, near to the end of his life.

16. *Miscellaneous Writings*. Sauk City WI: Arkham House, 1995. Edited by S.T. Joshi. A massive, scholarly compilation of Lovecraft's major non-fiction, on literary, philosophical, and autobiographical topics, etc. Collects much otherwise scattered among assorted other Arkham House and Necronomicon Press volumes.

17. *Lord of a Visible World, An Autobiography in Letters*. Edited by S.T. Joshi and David E. Schultz. Athens OH: Ohio State University Press, 2000. Lovecraft letters, skillfully re-edited to illuminate his life, thought, and aesthetics. Contains material not in *Selected Letters*.

Lovecraftiana

Note: The following four books are often listed as works by Lovecraft, although they are in fact compilations of Lovecraftian essays, revisions, and poems, plus memoirs of Lovecraft by other writers, critical essays, bibliographies, etc. They are best described as an excellent Lovecraftian journal which happened to be published as a series of books.

17. *Marginalia*. Sauk City WI: Arkham House, 1944. Edited by August Derleth and Donald Wandrei.

18. *Something About Cats and Other Pieces*. Sauk City WI: Arkham House, 1949. Edited by August Derleth.

19. *The Shuttered Room and Other Pieces*. Sauk City WI: Arkham House, 1959. Edited by August Derleth.

20. *The Dark Brotherhood and Other Pieces*. Sauk City WI: Arkham House, 1966. Edited by August Derleth.

Books About Lovecraft

21. Beckwith, Henry L.P., Jr. *Lovecraft's Providence & Adjacent Parts*. West Kingston RI: Domald M Grant, Publisher, 1979. A Tourist's guide to Lovecraftian sites. Interesting and useful.

22. Burleson, Donald R. *H.P. Lovecraft, A Critical Study*. Westport CT: Greenwood Press, 1983. A somewhat disappointing work by a major scholar, lacking any overall thematic plan, but filled with rare nuggets of information.

23. Cannon, Peter. *H.P. Lovecraft*. Boston: Twayne Publishers, 1989. This excellent general overview is part of the Twayne Authors Series.

24. de Camp, L. Sprague. *Lovecraft: A Biography*. New York: Doubleday & Co., 1975. The first major biography. Controversial, but well worth reading.

25. Derleth, August. *HPL: A Memoir*. New York: Ben Abramson, Publisher, 1945. Long since superceded as a biography, but still an interesting source.

26. Long, Frank Belknap. *Howard Phillips Lovecraft: Dreamer on the Night Side*. Sauk City WI: Arkham House, 1975. A memoir, by one of Lovecraft's closest associates.

27. Joshi, S.T. *A Subtler Magick: The Writings and Philosophy of H.P. Lovecraft*. Starmont, 1996. Wildside Press, 2000. Enormously rewritten version of the 1982 Starmont volume, *H.P. Lovecraft,* in effect a new work. A study of Lovecraft as literary artist and philosopher.

28. _____ *H.P. Lovecraft: A Life*. West Warwick RI: Necronomicon Press, 1996. Definitive for the forseeable future. A massive and thoroughly researched biography, with an emphasis on Lovecraft as a thinker.

29. _____. *H.P. Lovecraft: An Annotated Bibliography*. Kent OH: Kent State University Press, 1981. Amazingly exhaustive, accurate, certain to remain definitive for decades to come. The most important Lovecraftian reference work ever compiled.

29. _____. *H.P. Lovecraft: Decline of the West*. Mercer Island WA: Starmont House, 1990. Wildside Press, 2001. A major study of Lovecraft as a thinker, explicating his "cosmicism" and exploring its relationship to both classical and 20th century philosophy.

30. _____, ed. *H.P. Lovecraft: Four Decades of Criticism*. Athens OH: Ohio State University Press, 1980. A major compilation. Virtually every significant Lovecraft scholar is represented.

31. Levy, Maurice. *Lovecraft, A Studyin the Fantastic*. Detroit MI: Wayne State University Press, 1988. Translated by Translated by S.T. Joshi. Important thematic and critical study, by a leading French critic.

32. Mosig, Yōzan Dirk W. *Mosig at Last: A Psychologist Looks at H.P. Lovecraft*. West Warwick RI: Necronomicon Press, 1997. The collected critical writings of a pioneering Lovecraft scholar, who paved the way for most subsequent work in the field of Lovecraft studies. Essential.

33. St. Armand, Barton Levi. *The Roots of Horror in the Fiction of H.P. Lovecraft*. Elizabethtown NY: Dragon Press, 1977. Jungian study, focussing on "The Rats in the Walls."

34. Schultz, David E. and Joshi, S.T. (ed.) *Epicure of the Terrible*. Rutherford, Madison, & Teaneck NJ. Fairleigh Dickinson University Press, 1991. Essays in honor of HPL's 100th birthday, by most of the major scholars in the field.

35. Schweitzer, Darrell. *The Dream Quest of H.P. Lovecraft*. San Bernardino CA: The Borgo Press, 1978. A reader's guide, for the beginner. To be revised.

Journals

36. *Crypt of Cthulhu*. Robert M. Price, Editor. Published by Mythos Books, 218 Hickory Meadow Lane, Poplar Bluff MO 63901–2160. $4.50 an issue. An amazingly varied, lively, often witty magazine, containing important items of Lovecraft scholarship, rare Lovecraft writings, previously-unpublished fiction by members of the Lovecraft circle, etc. Price will soon retire in favor of Joe Pulver.

37. *Lovecraft Studies*. Edited by S.T. Joshi. Published by Scott Connors, 200 Berryhill Rd, #37, Columbia NC 29210. $4.50 per issue. More formally scholarly than *Crypt of Cthulhu* but never stuffy. Both publications are indispensable to the serious student of Lovecraft.

ABOUT THE CONTRIBUTORS

Darrell Schweitzer is the author of three fantasy novels, *The White Isle, The Shattered Goddess,* and *The Mask of the Sorcerer* and about 250 short stories, many of which are collected in seven short story collections (most recently, *The Great World and the Small* from Wildside Press). His critical writings have appeared in *Lovecraft Studies, Nyctalops, The New York Review of Science Fiction* and elsewhere and include, at book-length, *The Dream Quest of H.P. Lovecraft* and *Pathways to Elfland: The Writings of Lord Dunsany.* He is presently one of the two editors of the magazine *Weird Tales* the Terminus Publishing Company incarnation of *Weird Tales,* for which he and George Scithers shared a World Fantasy Award in 1992.

Previous essay anthologies edited by Darrell Schweitzer include *Exploring Fantasy Worlds, Discovering Modern Horror Fiction* (two volumes), and *Discovering Stephen King.*

Robert Bloch (1917–1994) was a member of the original Lovecraft circle, a major contributor to *Weird Tales* in its heyday, and went on to a successful career in books, films, and television. He was one of America's finest psychological suspense writers, and is certainly one of the most important figures in the twentieth century horror field. His books include *The Opener of the Way, The Scarf, The Dead Beat, Blood Runs Cold, Pleasant Dreams, Psycho, Dragons and Nightmares, Cold Chills, Out of the Mouths of Graves, The King of Terrors, American Gothic, Psycho II, Lori, Psycho House,* and a delightful "unauthorized autobiography," *Once Around the Bloch.* His *Strange Eons* is of particular interest to Lovecraftians as attempted euthanasia on the Cthulhu Mythos — the Old Ones win at the end!

Fritz Leiber (1910–1992) was also a member of the Lovecraft circle and a contributor to *Weird Tales.* He was one of the truly major science-fiction and fantasy authors of our time, and won many Hugo Awards, a Grandmaster Nebula (for a lifetime of achievement) and the World Fantasy Award. He pioneered the modern, urban horror story with such stories as "The Hound" and "Smoke Ghost." His books include such classics as the seven-volume Fafhrd and Gray Mouser series, plus *Conjure Wife, Gather, Darkness!, The Big Time, Night's Black Agents, The Wanderer, Our Lady of Darkness,* and *The Ghost Light.*

Yōzan Dirk W. Mosig was, until he stopped writing in the field, the leading Lovecraft scholar. He is widely credited with inspiring and mentoring most of the significant Lovecraft scholars since. His surprisingly small, but very important body of critical writings has been collected in *Mosig at Last: A Psychologist Looks at H.P. Lovecraft.* He is a professor of psychology. Other interests include karate and collecting tarantulas.

R. Boerem was born in Munich, raised in Illinois, and has lived in California in recent years, where he works as a remedial-reading teacher. He writes occasional articles, enjoys music, collects books, and is a charter member of the Esoteric Order of Dagon.

By now, you know who **H.P. Lovecraft** (1890–1937) was.

Arthur Jean Cox is a specialist in Victorian literature and the author of occasional, quite distinguished short stories.

Richard L. Tierney is a poet of note, whose work has been collected by Arkham House. With David C. Smith, he has written several novels continuing series by Robert E. Howard. His first novel, solo, was *The Winds of Zarr.* His second is an adventurous Cthulhu Mythos tale, *The House of the Toad,* which appeared from the Fedogan and Bremer. His contributions to Lovecraft studies have been few, but distinguished. His "The Derleth Mythos" caused a sensation when first published, and has had a major impact on the direction the field has taken since.

George Wetzel was a pioneering Lovecraft scholar of the 1940s and '50s. He edited *The Lovecraft Collector's Library,* a series of pamphlets containing rare Lovecraft material. He wrote many articles and a few short stories. Most appear in Weirdbook Press's *A Gothic Horror.*

Ben P. Indick has been published in *Plays* magazine and won theatrical prizes. His memoirs of Hannes Bok have appeared in *And Flights of Angels* and Gerry de la Ree's *Bok.* He is the author of *The Drama of Ray Bradbury* (1977), the publisher of *Ibid* (for the Esoteric Order of Dagon), and a notable essayist, who, so far, has managed to appear in *all* Schweitzer-edited essay anthologies. His recent reader's guide to the work of George Alec Effinger was published by The Borgo Press.

Robert Weinberg is the author of *The Weird Tales Story,* the editor of many anthologies of classic pulp material, and writer of occult thrillers in the Dennis Wheatley/Dion Fortune mode, such as *The Devil's Auction* and *The Black Lodge*. His other works include *A Biographical Dictionary of Science Fiction and Fantasy Artists* (1988) and *Horror in the 20th Century* (2000).

S.T. Joshi is, incontestably, the leading Lovecraft scholar at present. His accomplishments are legion: the definitive bibliography (*H.P. Lovecraft, An Annotated Bibliography*), a fine anthology of essays, presenting Lovecraft to the academic world (*H.P. Lovecraft, Four Decades in Criticism*), a popular reader's guide (*H.P. Lovecraft*, in the Starmont series, exhaustively revised as *A Subtler Magic: The Writings and Philosophy of H.P. Lovecraft*), a penetrating study of Lovecraft's philosophy (*H.P. Lovecraft: Decline of the West*) and, most important of all, years of textual study which have resulted in Arkham House's first-ever publication of the restored, corrected texts of Lovecraft. He has also edited Lovecraft's *Miscellaneous Writings* and has written a new, definitive, and exhaustive biography, *H.P. Lovecraft: A Life*. He is the editor of *Lovecraft Studies* and has written, as he sometimes points out with chagrin, more about Lovecraft than Lovecraft himself wrote, not counting letters. Joshi has also done work on Ambrose Bierce, George Sterling, Lord Dunsany, H.L. Memcken, and other writers.

Lin Carter (1930–1988) is best remembered as editor of the breakthrough Ballantine Adult Fantasy Series of paperback books in the early 1970s. He also wrote a survey of fantasy, *Imaginary Worlds* (1973), and the dated, if still interesting *H.P. Lovecraft: A Look Behind the Cthulhu Mythos*. He produced many pastiche fantasy novels. He was once editor of a reincarnation of *Weird Tales* (for Zebra Books in the early 1980s) and, in his last years, the author of charming columns for *Crypt of Cthulhu* magazine.

Robert M. Price was for many years, by day, a mild-mannered and respectable member of the clergy, but by night the editor of the eldritch, squamous, partially rugose, and all-around wonderful Cryptic Publications, which included such titles as *Shudder Stories, Pulse-Pounding Pulp Adventures, Risque Stories,* and a variety of other works which nostalgically, but not too seriously recalled the pulp era. The final Price-edited issues of the important (and often very funny) Lovecraftian Journal, *The Crypt of Cthulhu* are now appearing from Mythos Books, after which he passes on the eldritch torch to Joe Pulver. Price has edited several books of *Crypt* material for Starmont House. His own Lovecraftian scholarship is considerable — he is the only person who ever did a textual analysis of the *Necronomicon* from the point of view of a professionally-trained theologian and Biblical scholar — and he has also published some fiction, mostly in and around the Cthulhu Mythos.

INDEX

Note: In this index, all the spurious Lovecraft-Derleth "collaborations" are listed as works by August Derleth. Lovecraft's "revisions" (which are largely ghost-written works) are listed as works by Lovecraft, rather than under the names of their alleged authors.

A

The Acolyte, 61, 96, 110
Aeschylus, 35
After Many a Summer Dies the Swan, 28
The Age of Fable (Bullfinch)
The Age of Mammals (Osborn), 139
Al Azif (see *The Necronomicon*)
Alhazred, Abdul, 80, 110, 122–123
  Necronomicon, 14, 15, 16, 45, 49, 57, 60–61, 65, 80, 107, 112, 117, 122–134, 140
"The Alchemist and the Scientist: Borellus and the Lovecraftian Imagination" (Bryant), 145
Alice in Wonderland (Carroll), 85
Amazing Stories, 98, 105
Aristophanes, 35
Aristotle, 8
Arkham House, 92, 94, 96, 98, 102, 104, 140
The Arkham Sampler, 132, 142
Ars Magna et Ultima (Lully), 110
Astounding Stories, 98, 100, 101–102, 103
Astronomicon (Manilius), 133

B

Barlow, Robert H., 92, 95, 96, 102–103, 104, 105
Benson, E.F., 2, 42
Beware the Dark! (Harré), 99
Bierce, Ambrose, 92, 133
  In the Midst of Life, 122
  "The Man and the Snake," 122
Biographie Universelie, 122, 142
Bishop, Zealia, 95
The Black Rites (Luveh-Keraphf), 110
Blackwood, Algernon, 7, 42, 79, 87
Blavatsky, Helena, 129
  The Book of Dyzan, 108, 110–111
  The Secret Doctrine, 111
Blish, James, 133
Bloch, Robert, 109, 113, 114, 115, 116, 117, 134
  "Black Bargain," 117
  "The Dark Demon," 115, 139
  "Fane of the Black Pharaoh," 131

Atlantis and Lost Lemuria (Scott-Eliot), 11
Azathoth and Other Horrors (Derby), 100, 136

Waugh, Evelyn, 104
Weird Tales, 4, 37, 43, 74, 93, 95, 96, 97, 98, 99, 100, 119, 142
Wells, H.G., 1, 8
Wetzel, George, 123, 132
Wilson, Edmund, 1, 47
  "Tales of the Marvelous and Ridiculous," 1, 47

Wormius, Olaus, 122, 130, 132, 133
Wright, Farnsworth, 43, 142

Z

Zohar, 143–144